Robert Brown

Demonology and Witchcraft

With Especial Reference to Modern Spiritualism

Robert Brown

Demonology and Witchcraft
With Especial Reference to Modern Spiritualism

ISBN/EAN: 9783337372767

Printed in Europe, USA, Canada, Australia, Japan

Cover: Foto ©Thomas Meinert / pixelio.de

More available books at **www.hansebooks.com**

DEMONOLOGY

AND

WITCHCRAFT:

WITH ESPECIAL REFERENCE TO MODERN "SPIRITUALISM," *SO-CALLED;* AND THE "DOCTRINES OF DEMONS."

By ROBERT BROWN,

AUTHOR OF

"OUTLINES OF PROPHETIC TRUTH"; "THE HIDDEN MYSTERY; OR, THE REVELATIONS OF THE WORD"; "THE PERSONALITY AND HISTORY OF SATAN"; "GLEANINGS FROM THE BOOK OF RUTH"; "BABYLONIANISM"; "JESUITISM"; &c., &c., &c.

"In the latter times some shall depart from the faith, giving heed to seducing spirits, and doctrines of Demons . . . . . . If thou put the brethren in remembrance of these things, thou shalt be a good minister of Jesus Christ."— I *Tim.* iv. 1. 6.

LONDON:

JOHN F. SHAW AND CO.,

48, Paternoster Row.

MDCCCLXXXIX.

PREFACE.

A FEW words as to the *origin* of this Work. In April, 1886, a young friend, who had been in the habit of attending my " Bible Readings," at the Y.M.C.A., in Aldersgate Street, London, asked me to see a former school-fellow of his, who had become a " Spiritualist." After an interview, which I had with this young man, in which I pointed out to him the awful sin which he was committing, in thus consulting demons; he sent me a book, entitled, " Spirit Teachings," (which is referred to in the after part of this Work,) accompanied by a letter; in which he said, he hoped that I " should be instructed and enlightened by it; as he himself had been : " for " to relapse into a belief in the doctrines of Christianity, and the scheme of redemption "—which in a subsequent letter, he scrupled not to characterize as " a gigantic imposture " — " would make him thoroughly unhappy " ! !

After having returned him the book, with a letter, in which I denounced his unscriptural dogmas, and gave him a final, pointed, and faithful warning; I purposed writing a small tractate upon the identity of the doctrines of the demons, with *so-called "modern thought:"* but being then engaged in other work, I deferred the matter until a more favourable opportunity: but when that opportunity arrived, on reflecting that several other persons had written on the subject of Spiritualism, *so-called,* I had then serious thoughts of giving up the matter altogether.

Returning home, however, from an Evangelistic tour, in the middle of January last, the matter seemed then *to be pressed home upon my conscience;* and not knowing of any work on this subject, which dealt with it, *as a whole;* and the text in James iv. 17—" to him that knoweth to do good, *and doeth it not,* to *him* it is *sin*" —having dropped in upon my spirit, more than once, as it seemed to me *reproachfully;* I began to think that the Lord Himself must be calling me to this work; and so, on the 21st of January last, I began to write. I had no sooner done so, however, than the whole subject-matter of this Work, in the order in which it is now presented to my readers, seemed to flash into my mind at once; and such a number of passages in various works and periodicals, which I had read, some so far back as forty years ago, and upwards; and so many circumstances that had taken place in years gone by, came trooping into my mind, so *appositely,* to fit into the various divisions of my subject; that I could not but call to mind Bunyan's description of the state of his mind, when he first began to write his " Pilgrim's Progress:" although of course I am not so vain as to suppose that there is *any other* likeness in the two cases than *this particular one !*

Nevertheless, as I am certain that the Lord Himself has wonderfully and most graciously helped me in the writing of the book itself—having from time to time furnished me, in so marked a manner, with the fact or illustration exactly needed, and *at the very time when needed*, and frequently *not until the time when needed;* I am bound to give, and I do most thankfully and gratefully give, Him all the glory of it. Moreover, as the book was completed on the 20th of March last, *exactly two months after I had first commenced it;* with the exception of some two or three illustrations, which occurred after the first portion had been sent to the press; and the book itself was in the printer's hands before the month was out; and I have moreover had such manifest proofs in my own soul of the Lord's gracious help in the writing of it; I am bound to believe, that He means to use it for the enlightenment at least of *some* of His dear children in Christ Jesus; as well as for the deliverance of *others*, " out of the snare of the devil," who may have been " taken captive by him at his will "—2 Tim. ii. 26. And should any of my readers feel quickened, or encouraged, by the perusal of the Work itself; I would earnestly ask them to plead with the Lord for His blessing to rest, both upon it, as well as upon its Author.

My believing readers will of course perceive, *why* I have given an Exposition of the " Gospel of the grace of God," in the latter part of the Work: which was needed, not only *as an antidote* to the false teaching, which I have thus been compelled to set forth, for the purpose of exposing ; but also *as a guide* to any poor soul, whom it may please the Lord Himself to " convict of sin," in its perusal ; that it may be led to trust in Him, Who " saveth to the uttermost " all who " come unto God by Him "—Heb. vii. 25.

Lastly, I think it only right to state, that most of the italics, small capitals, and notes of admiration, in the quotations given in the book, are *mine.*

SCARBOROUGH,
    April 15th, 1889.

CONTENTS.

—o—

DIVISION IV.

APPENDIX.

" In the latter times some shall depart from the faith, giving heed
to seducing spirits, and doctrines of Demons . . . . . It thou
put the brethren in remembrance of these things, thou shalt be a good
minister of Jesus Chsist."—1 *Tim.* iv. 1, 6.

DEMONOLOGY, &c.

Paul, the great "Apostle of the Gentiles,"[1] in one of his letters to his "son Timothy,"[2] written, as "all Scripture" was, by the inspiration of the Holy Ghost,[3] tells us, that "*in the last days* perilous times shall come," ἐνστήσονται, "shall set in :"[4] while in a former letter to him, he had said, that "the Spirit speaketh expressly," ῥητῶς, distinctly and emphatically, as if to impress it the more upon the hearts of believers—just as our blessed Lord, in the Book of "the Revelation," (which relates more particularly to these last days,) no less than seven times (the perfect number,) solemnly utters the warning words, "He that hath an ear, let him hear what the Spirit saith unto the Churches "[5]— "that *in the latter times* some shall depart from," ἀποστήσονταί, "shall apostatize from," "the faith, giving heed to seducing spirits, and doctrines of

---

[1] Rom. xi. 13.   [2] 1 Tim. i. 2.   [3] 2 Tim. iii. 16.   [4] 2 Tim. iii. 1.
[5] Rev. ii. 7, 11, 17, 29 ; iii. 6, 13, 22.

1

demons "[1] — or, in other words, not only invoking demons, and consulting them upon their conduct and affairs ; but giving themselves up to them, and following out and obeying (for this is the full import of the Greek verb, $\pi\rho\sigma\acute{\epsilon}\chi\omega$, when used, as here, with a dative), the doctrines, teachings and instructions imparted to them by them.

Some apply this last mentioned passage exclusively to the so-called Church of Rome : and it no doubt *does* apply to Rome, but *not exclusively*. Others again think that it applies only to what is called the " Spiritualism " of the last days ; which they suppose to be of *modern* origin : but this is a great mistake : as " Spiritualism," *so-called*, is nothing more nor less than *witchcraft*, which the Holy Ghost associates with *idolatry ;* declaring both of them to be " works of the flesh ";[2] and therefore, as the Scriptures elsewhere assert, *of the devil.* What this Scripture, therefore, teaches us is, not that this so-called " Spiritualism " is a *new* thing, to appear only at the close of this Dispensation ; but that, in consequence of a general apostacy from the truth, it would again largely prevail over those, who had formerly *professed* the truth ; and that, through these apostates, the demons would, on being invoked, inculcate *a code of " doctrines,"* for the guidance of those deluded persons, who would thus give themselves up to their influence ; and that when *this* took place, (as it has now done,) we were to look upon

---

[1] 1 Tim. iv. 1.   [2] Gal. v. 20.

it, as one of the many signs, that the close of the Dispensation itself was at hand.

In treating, therefore, upon this subject, I shall (1) shew what the Scriptures themselves say about Demonology and witchcraft; (2) note that these "works of the flesh" have prevailed, more or less, throughout all ages; (3) enter into some details respecting the more modern manifestations of "Spiritualism" *so-called;* (4) set forth some of the "doctrines," or teachings, "of" the "demons" themselves; (5) shew the identity of many of such doctrines with what is called "modern thought": proving that they both emanate from the same source; (6) point out from the Prophetic Word, that the final result will be, the utter rejection of Jehovah and His Christ, by all the nations inhabiting the platform of the Roman earth; and the reception, and subsequent worship, of the Antichrist of the last days: who will be indwelt of Satan himself: just as spiritualistic mediums in these days are indwelt of the demons, whom they invoke; and who now speak and act through them; and (7) lastly, conclude with some admonitions and exhortations, which naturally arise out of the subject itself.

I.—Let me then in the first place shew, what the Scriptures themselves say upon the subject of Demonology and witchcraft: and with this object in view, I shall first open out the meaning of several Hebrew and Greek words, relating to the subject; and then examine some of the more prominent passages, wherein these words occur.

Hebrew words occurring in the Old Testament.

1. אוֹב, *Ohv*, singular, אוֹבוֹת, *Ohvoth*, plural. According
to Gesenius, this word is (1) "used of wine bottles,"
i.e., skins filled with new wine, ready to burst: and he
refers to Job xxxii. 19, where Elihu says, "Behold, my
belly is as wine which hath no vent," or, as the margin
has it, "which is not opened"; "it is ready to burst like
new bottles," *Ohvoth*. (2) νεκρόμαντις, or νεκρυόμαντις,
i.e., *a soothsayer*, who evokes the *manes* of the dead by
the power of incantations and magical songs, in order
to give answers as to future or doubtful things. And
then he indicates several texts as examples in proof.
(3) "Specially, it denotes *a python*, or a soothsaying
demon, of which these men," *he* says, "were *believed*
to be possessed"; but of which *the Scriptures* say, and
which facts indubitably prove, that they *were* possessed.
"A man or woman when a python is in them"—
"whence a sorceress is called 'a woman in whom is a
soothsaying demon'"; for which he refers to texts in
proof. The passages of Scripture, where the word
occurs, are Lev. xix. 31, xx. 6, 27; Deut. xviii. 11;
1 Sam. xxviii. 3, 7, 8, 9; 2 Kings xxi. 6; xxiii. 24;
1 Chron. x. 13; 2 Chron. xxxiii. 6; Job xxxii. 19; Isa.
viii. 19; xix. 3; xxix. 4. The LXX. translate the word
in Job xxxii. 19, by the word ἀσκὸς, a skin; in 2 Kings
xxi. 6; xxiii. 24, by γνώστας—γνώστης literally meaning one who knows, or foretells the future, *i.e.*, a prog-
nosticator, or fortune teller; and in all other places by
the word εγγαστριμύθος, literally a ventriloquist—the

word being applied chiefly to the *Priestesses* of the idol temples, who delivered the oracles of the demons there worshipped, by these means. In the A. V. the word is invariably translated *familiar spirit*, except in the text in Job xxxii. 19, before cited.

2. יִדְּעֹנִי, *Yid-d'"gōh-nee*, singular, יִדְּעֹנִים, *yid-d'"goh-neem*, plural. According to Gesenius, (1) "properly knowing, wise, hence *a prophet, a wizard*, always used in a *bad* sense of *false* prophets." (2) "*A spirit of divination, a spirit of python.*" The word occurs in the following passages, Lev. xix. 31; xx. 6, 27; Deut. xviii. 11; 1 Sam. xxviii. 3, 9; 2 Kings xxi. 6; xxiii. 24; 2 Chron. xxxiii. 6; Isa. viii. 19; xix. 3. The LXX. chiefly translate the word by ἐγγαστριμύθος, once by γνώστας— words which I have before noticed, and once by ἐπαοιδούς, for ἐπῳδούς—ἐπῳδός meaning an enchanter, who uses songs and charms to heal the sick; the word literally meaning *singing over*. In the A. V. the word is invariably translated *wizard*.

3. עָנַן, "*gāh-nan'*. According to Gesenius, to act covertly; hence to use hidden arts, *i.e.*, magic, to practise sorcery: and he says many of the ancients understood by it *a particular kind* of divination—referring to the Syriac, *fascinating with the eyes;* or, in other words, to the mesmeric trance of the medium, which is produced through the fascination of the eye of the mesmerizer, acting upon him or her, through the influence of the unseen demon, who is thus invoked. The

word is used in this connexion in the following passages,. Lev. xix. 26 ; Deut. xviii. 10, 14 ; Jud. ix. 37 ; 2 Kings xxi. 6 ; 2 Chron. xxxiii. 6 ; Isa. ii. 6 ; lvii. 3 ; Jer. xxvii. 9 ; Micah v. 12. The LXX. generally render the word by *οἰωνίζομαι*, to divine from omens, and in three instances by *κληδονίζω*, to practise omens. The A. V. variously render it by enchanter, soothsayer, sorceress, or observer of times.

4. כָּשַׁף, *Kăh-shaph'*, in Piel. According to Gesenius,. to use enchantment, an enchanter, a magician ; in the plural, incantations, sorceries. The word is used in the following passages, Exod. vii. 11 ; xxii. 18 ; Deut. xviii. 10 ; 2 Kings ix. 22 ; 2 Chron. xxxiii. 8 ; Isa. xlvii. 9, 12 ; Jer. xxvii. 9 ; Dan. ii. 2 ; Mic. v. 12 ; Nahum iii. 4 ; Mat. iii. 5. It is rendered in the LXX. by *φαρμακός*, and *φαρμακεία*, words which we find in the New Testament, and which I shall presently refer to ; and in the A. V. by witch, witchcraft, sorcerer and sorceries.

5. חָבַר, *ghch'-ver*, primarily, to bind, to join together ; then, to bind, *to fascinate*, spoken, according to Gesenius, of some kind of *magic*, which was applied to *the binding of magical knots*. Greek, *καταδέω*, to bewitch by magical knots. The word is used in the above sense in the following passages, Deut. xviii. 11 ; Psa. lviii. 5 ; and Isa. xlvii. 9, 12. The first passage is translated by the LXX. *φαρμακὸς ἐπαείδων ἐπαοιδὴν*, a sorcerer employing incantation ; the 2nd, *φωνὴν ἐπαδ-*

ὄντων, φαρμάκου τε φαρμακευομένου παρὰ σοφοῦ, " the voice of charmers, nor heed the charm prepared skilfully by the wise " ; and the 3rd and 4th, by φαρμακεία. In the A. V. it is rendered by charmer, charming, enchantments.

6. קָסַם *Käh'-sam'*, to divine, to practise divination, to evoke the dead, and קֶסֶם *Keh'-sem*, divination, witchcraft ; words which occur in the following passages, Num. xxii. 7 ; xxiii. 23 ; Deut. xviii. 10, 14 ; Josh. xiii. 22 ; 1 Sam. vi. 2 ; xv. 23 ; xxviii. 8 ; 2 Kings xvii. 17 ; Prov. xvi. 10 ; Isa. iii. 2 ; xliv. 25 ; Jer. xiv. 14 ; xxvii. 9 ; xxix. 8 ; Ezek. xiii. 6, 9, 23 ; xxi. 21, 22, 23, 29 ; xxii. 28 ; Micah iii. 6, 7, 11 ; Zech. x. 2. The LXX. render the words in most passages either by μάντις, a diviner ; μαντεία, the power of divination ; μαντεῖον, an oracular response ; or μαντεύομαι, to consult an oracle, or seek divinations ; and once by οἰώνισμά, literally, divination by the flight, or cries of birds. In the A. V. the words are rendered, to divine, divination, diviner, witchcraft, soothsayer:

7. נָחַשׁ, *Näh-'ghash'*, enchantment, omen, augury ; from a root, signifying to hiss, whisper ; hence the same letters, with a change of vowel points, mean *a serpent*. The word is used in the above sense, in the following passages, Gen. xliv. 5, 15 ; Lev. xix. 26 ; Deut. xviii. 10 ; 2 Kings xvii. 17 ; xxi. 6 ; 2 Chron. xxxiii. 6. The LXX. translate the word by οἰωνίζομαι, to divine by omens, and οἰώνισμα, an omen, augury ;

while in the A. V. it is rendered by, enchanter, using enchantments, divining.

There are several other words in the Hebrew Scriptures referring to this subject, some of which I shall have occasion to notice afterwards ; but I have specially referred to these only in the first instance, because they are all mentioned in the passages in Exodus, Leviticus, and Deuteronomy ; where these practices are solemnly condemned and prohibited, under pain of death. The passages are as follow :—

" Thou shalt not suffer a witch," *Kăh-shaph'*,[1] " to live," Exodus xxii. 18.

" Regard not," or, as Young has it, " *do not turn unto,* them that have familiar spirits," or, literally, " unto *the Ohvoth*,[2] neither *seek after* wizards," *Yid-d"goh-neem*,[3] " to be defiled by them"; " I am Jehovah "— Lev. xix. 31.

" And the soul that turneth after such as have familiar spirits ;" after *the Ohvoth*,[4] " and after wizards," *Yid-d"goh-neem*,[5] " to go a whoring after them, I will set My face against that soul, and will cut him off from among his people." Lev. xx. 6.

" The man also or woman that hath a familiar spirit," literally, " when an *Ohv*[6] shall be *in them*," " or that is a wizard," *yid-d"goh-nee*,[7] " shall surely be put to death ; they shall stone him with stones : their blood shall be upon them." Lev. xx. 27.

---

[1] See page 6.   [2] See page 4.   [3] See page 5.   [4] See page 4.
    [5] See page 5.   [6] See page 4.   [7] See page 7.

" When thou art come into the land which Jehovoh thy God giveth thee, thou shalt not learn to do *after the abominations of those nations*. There shall not be found among you, anyone that maketh his son or his daughter to pass through the fire, or that useth divination," *Kăh-sam'*,[1] " or an observer of times," *"găh-nan'*,[2] " or an enchanter, *năh-'ghash*,"[3] " or a witch," *Kah-shaph*,[4] " or a charmer," *'gheh'-ver*,[5] " or a con- sulter with familiar spirits," literally, " one asking at, or of *an Ohv*,"[6] *i.e.*, a medium, or, one applying to a medium for consultation, " or a wizard," *yid-d'"goh-nee*,[7] " or a necromancer," וְדֹרֵשׁ אֶל־הַמֵּתִים correctly ren- dered by the LXX., *ἐπερωτῶν τοὺς νεκρούς*, " *one asking questions of, or interrogating the dead*." " For all that do these things are an abomination to Jehovah : and because of these abominations Jehovah thy God doth drive them out from before thee. Thou shalt be perfect with Jehovah thy God." Deut. xviii. 9-13.

Greek words occurring in the New Testament.

1. Φαρμακός, *pharmakos*, literally a poisoner : but in the New Testament, a magician, a sorcerer, an en- chanter. The LXX. employ this word for its Hebrew equivalent in Exod. vii. 11 ; ix. 11 ; xxii. 18 ; Deut. xviii. 10 ; Jer. xxxiv. 7 ; Dan. ii. 2 ; Mal. iii. 5. It only occurs once in the New Testament in Rev. xxii. 15, where it is translated " sorcerer."

---

[1] See page 7.   [2] See page 5.   [3] See page 7.   [4] See page 6.
[5] See page 6.   [6] See page 4.   [7] See page 5.

2. Φαρμακευς, *pharmakeus*, a word having pretty much the same signification as the former; denoting one who prepares the magical enchantment. It is not used by the LXX.; and is only employed once in the New Testament in Rev. xxi. 8, where it is translated " sorcerer."

3. Φαρμακεία, *pharmakeia*, from φάρμακον, *pharmakon*, a medicinal drug, in its secondary sense, used in enchantments; and hence in the New Testament, sorcery, witchcraft, pharmaceutical enchantment, magical incantation with drugs, whether animal, vegetable, or mineral. Herodotus applies the verb φαρμακεύω, *pharmakeuo* (which is employed by the LXX. for its Hebrew equivalent in 2 Chron. xxxiii. 6, and Psa. lvii. 6; but is not found in the New Testament), in the like manner, vii. 114, where, after telling us that when Xerxes, in his invasion of Greece, came to the river Strymon, the Magi sacrificed white horses to it, he adds, φαρμακεύσαντες δὲ ταῦτα ἐς τὸν ποταμὸν, " and having used these *enchantments* to the river," &c. The word is used by the LXX. for their rendering of its Hebrew equivalent in Exod. vii. 11, 22; viii. 7, 18; Isa. xlvii. 9, 12: and it is employed in the New Testament, in Gal. v. 20; Rev. ix. 21; and xviii. 23.

4. μάγος, *magos*, plural μάγοι, *magoi*, Magi, the name for priests and wise men among the Medes, Persians and Babylonians; whose learning was connected with astrology and enchantment. Hence in the

New Testament, magician, sorcerer, diviner. It is the word employed by the LXX. in Dan. i. 20 ; ii. 2, 10, 27 ; iv. 4 ; v. 7, 11 and 15 ; and is found in the following passages in the New Testament, Mat. ii. 1, 7, 16—where the word is translated " wise men "—and Acts xiii. 6, 8 ; where it is rendered " sorcerer."

5. μαγεία, *mageia*, magic, magical art, sorcery. This word is not used by the LXX. ; and is only to be found in Acts viii. 11 : where it is translated " sorceries."

6. μαγένω, *mageuō*, to practise magic, or sorcery. This word is not found in the LXX. ; and is only used once in the New Testament in Acts viii. 9 ; where it is translated " used sorcery."

7. μαντεύομαι, *manteuomai*, to utter responses as from an oracle, to divine, to foretell—occurring only in Acts xvi. 16, where it is translated " sooth-saying." The verb is evidently derived from μάντις, a sooth-sayer : which Eustathius deduced from μαίνομαι, to be mad : such persons being possessed by a demon. The LXX. employ the verb chiefly as their translation of the Hebrew words, *Kăh-sam' and Keh-sem*,[1] in the following passages in the Old Testament—Deut. xviii. 10 ; 1. Sam. xxviii. 8 ; 2 Kings xvii. 17 ; Jer. xxxiv. 7 ; Ezek. xii. 24 ; xiii. 6, 23 ; xxi. 21, 23, 29 ; xxii. 28 ; Micah iii. 11.

---

[1] See page 7.

II.—And now I come, in the second place, to shew that these " works of the flesh " have prevailed, more or less, throughout all ages.

1. Let us first notice the Scripture testimony to the fact. When the Spirit tells us that " *witchcraft* " is a " work of the flesh," and allies it essentially with " *idolatry*,"[1] He does in effect assure us that these enter into the very constitution of natural men, and are the direct result of the fall ; and that consequently they must of necessity prevail, more or less, in every man in whom there is no knowledge of the true God. And since man was lost by the belief of a lie—the devil's lie, he is of course always more prone tó believe a lie than the truth ; and inasmuch as " the whole world " outside the true Church of God, " lieth in," or, under the dominion of " the wicked one " ;[2] and " the flesh " is utterly Satanic, " the children of disobedience " necessarily mistake Satan's operations in them for the spontaneous movements of their own will. They " walk," as the Scripture says, " according to the prince of the power of the air, the spirit that now energizeth in " them ;[3] and they are not conscious of the fact ; because there is such a resemblance between the devil's character and their own, that they do not perceive any difference. Hence they become an easy prey to the adversary ; and where God interposes not, and man is not outwardly enlightened by the truth of God, there,

---

[1] Gal. v. 20.   [2] 1 John v. 19.   [3] Eph. ii. 2.

as all history testifies, " idolatry," in association with its twin-sister, " witchcraft," has invariably prevailed.

Even Abraham, " the father of the faithful," seems to have been an idolater, before Jehovah revealed Himself to him, and " took " him " from the other side of the flood " :[1] where " idolatry " and " witchcraft " reigned supreme. Rachel also had evidently been in the habit of consulting *the teraphim*, which she took away with her from her father Laban's house, when Jacob fled from his service ;[2] and there were " strange gods " in Jacob's " household " long after this, which he urged them to " put away."[3] When Joseph likewise, at a later period, after the discovery of his " silver cup " in his brother Benjamin's sack, thus addressed his brethren, " What deed is this that ye have done ? Wot ye yet not that such a man as I can certainly *divine ?* "[4] —he evidently alludes to a practice well known to his brethren, of *divining by the cup*, for the discovery of a thief: of which I shall afterwards give an instance in modern times. This does not of course prove that Joseph *himself* divined by the cup: although for a time, in order to conceal himself from his brethren, he might wish them to think so : and his meaning seems to be, " If I am a diviner by the cup for the discovery, amongst other things, of theft : how could you suppose that I should be unable to find out the thief, who had stolen the very cup by which I divine ! "

---

[1] Josh. xxiv. 2, 3.   [2] Gen. xxxi. 19, 30-37.   [3] Gen. xxxv. 1-3.
[4] Gen. xliv. 2, 12, 15.

That the whole heathen world, and especially the inhabitants of Canaan, were steeped in "idolatry" and "witchcraft," the passages I have already quoted from Exodus, Leviticus and Deuteronomy, abundantly prove. And that the Israelites themselves were naturally prone to these "works of the flesh"; and were constantly being seduced into them by the surrounding nations, their history likewise abundantly testifies. When "Balaam, the soothsayer," or diviner, *Kah-sam'*,[1] was applied to, by Balak, the King of Moab, to curse Israel, "the elders of Midian" came to him "with the rewards of divination" *Keh'-sem*,[2] "in their hands": but Jehovah forced the false prophet to declare, that "surely there is no enchantment," *nah'-'ghash*,[3] *i.e.*, any evil resulting from any omen, or augury, "against Jacob, neither is there any divination," *Keh'-sem*,[4] "against Israel,"[5] *i.e.*, as a nation before God: because, although the Lord says, He will "make a full end of all nations, whither" He has "scattered" Israel: yet He "will *not* make a full end of" them: although He will "correct" them "in measure" and will not "leave them wholly unpunished."[6]

---

[1] See page 7.   [2] See page 7.   [3] See page 7.   [4] See page 7.

[5] Num. xxii. 4-7; xxiii. 23. Archbishop Leighton, in his Theological Lectures, No. X., "On the Decrees of God," speaks of the "saying of the Hebrews, *non esse planetam Israeli*"—"There is no *planet* to Israel": by which I doubt not they meant that Astrologers may employ their horoscopes, and cast their nativities, against Israel in vain!   [6] Jer. xxx. 11.

That the Israelites themselves, however, were from time to time seduced into these practices, their history plainly proves. Nay, very shortly after this very prophecy of Balaam they were, through his devilish counsel,[1] seduced into the worship of the idols of Moab; for we are told that when "Israel abode in Shittim, the people began to commit whoredom with the daughters of Moab. And they called the people unto *the sacrifices* of their gods : and the people did eat, and bowed down to *their gods.* And Israel joined himself unto Baal-peor, and the anger of Jehovah was kindled against Israel "[2]—an event, which is thus referred to by the Psalmist, " They joined themselves unto Baal-peor, and ate the sacrifices of *the dead* : "[3] for " the things which the Gentiles sacrifice," says the Holy Ghost, " they sacrifice to *demons*, and not to God."[4]

So when Saul " put away those that had familiar spirits," *Ohvoth*,[5] " and the wizards," *yid-d'ⁿgōh-neem*,[6] " out of the land," it is clear that there must at that time have been many such in Israel ; and that he did not succeed in exterminating them all is shewn likewise from the fact, that when, in his despair of an answer from Jehovah, he asked his servants to " seek him out a woman " that was " mistress of an *Ohv*,"[7] (*i.e.*, who was possessed by a demon, whom she invoked) ; that he might " enquire of her," they could find him such an one at once. Saul's object was, as the

---

[1] Num. xxxi. 16; Rev. ii. 14.   [2] Num. xxv. 1-3.   [3] Psa. cvi. 28.
[4] 1 Cor. x. 20.   [5] See page 4.   [6] See page 5.   [7] See page 4.

narrative shews, to have converse with, and to consult *the dead*, Samuel; and he thought this woman would, through the medium of the *Ohv*,[1] have the power of bringing him up out of Sheol, in which place he of course knew that he then was. Hence in consulting her, he says, " I pray thee, *divine* unto me *by the Ohv*,[2] *and bring me him up* whom I shall name unto thee." No demon, however, ever possessed such a power as this *over the Lord's people:* but the Lord permitted it in this instance, or Himself brought up the spirit of Samuel out of Sheol, in judgment upon Saul for his sin; and to the profound astonishment and conster- nation of the woman herself.[3] Hence we are told, in a subsequent Book, " So Saul died for his transgression which he committed against Jehovah, even against the word of Jehovah, which he kept not, and also for *asking*," i.e., *counsel*, " *of an Ohv*,[4] to enquire of it. And enquired not of Jehovah : therefore He slew him, and turned the kingdom unto David the Son of Jesse."[5]

Notwithstanding this warning, however, many of the subsequent kings, both of Israel and Judah, as well as the Priests and people, fell into the like ini- quity and idolatry.[6] Thus we read, for example, that " Manasseh " " did that which was evil in the sight of Jehovah, *like unto the abominations of the heathen*, whom Jehovah had cast out before the children of

---

[1] See page 4.   [2] See page 4.
[3] 1 Sam. xxviii. See also my book of " Outlines of Prophetic Truth :" Sec. " Sheol," where this case is fully gone into.
[4] See page 4.   [5] 1 Chron. x. 13, 14.   [6] 2 Chron. xxxvi. 14.

Israel." For " he caused his children to pass through the fire in the valley of the son of Hinnom : also he observed times, and used enchantments," *nāh-'gash'*,[1] omens or auguries, " and used witchcraft," *Kāh-shaph*,[2] " and dealt with *an ohv*,[3] and with wizards," *Yid-d'"goh-neem :*[4] " he wrought much evil in the sight of Jehovah, to provoke Him to anger." " So Manasseh made Judah and the inhabitants of Jerusalem to err, *and to do worse than the heathen*, whom Jehovah had destroyed before the children of Israel."[5]

And it is with reference (prospectively as well as retrospectively) to such abominations as these, that the Psalmist says, " They did not destroy the nations, concerning whom Jehovah commanded them; but were mingled among the heathen, *and learned their works. And they served their idols :* which were a snare unto them. Yea, they sacrificed their sons and their daughters unto *demons*, and shed innocent blood, even the blood of their sons and of their daughters, whom *they sacrificed unto the idols of Canaan :* and the land was polluted with blood."[6]

In the New Testament, indeed, these demons appear very prominently : and our Saviour informs us that Satan is their " Prince ; " and that they are the chief instruments, under him, in the support of his " king-dom " among men.[7] Their numbers are very great : for to accomplish a certain purpose, Satan could spare

---

[1] See page 7.   [2] See page 6.   [3] See page 4.   [4] See page 5.
[5] 2 Chron. xxxiii. 1, 2, 6, 9.   [6] Psa. cvi. 34-38.
[7] Mat. xii. 22, 24-30.

2

a legion of them—about 3,000—to enter and possess one man.[1] They are subtle, cruel, and unclean ;[2] and so powerful that they are able to impart superhuman strength to those whom they possess. We read of one so possessed, whom it was impossible to bind, even " with fetters and chains : " for " the chains had been plucked asunder by him, and the fetters broken in pieces."[3] We read of another, who fell upon " *seven* " evil men, who came to cast out the demon that was in him, and so completely " overcame them, and prevailed against them, that they fled out of that house naked and wounded."[4]

They all knew that Christ was the Son of God ; and trembled at His presence : but He would not suffer them on any account to confess Him : for His kingdom is diametrically opposed to the kingdom of Satan ; whose works He " came to destroy."[5] A subtle demon attempted to make men believe that this was *not* so in the time of the Apostle Paul, (as we shall see that the demons seek to do this in *these* days). For we are told, that " a certain damsel possessed with a spirit of Python," (*i.e.*, one of the demons, who spoke through the medium acted on, at the Temple of Apollo, at Delphi,) " met " the Apostle, " which brought her masters much gain by soothsaying," *manteuomenee ;*[6]

---

[1] Mark v. 1-13 ; Luke viii. 27-33.
[2] Mat. xvii. 14-18 ; Mark vii. 25 ; Luke iv. 33, 35 ; ix. 42.
[3] Mark v. 4.   [4] Acts xix. 13-16.
[5] Mark i. 34 ; Luke iv. 33-35, 41 ; Mat. viii. 29 ; James ii. 19 ; Mat. xii. 22-32 ; 1 John iii. 8.   [6] See page 11.

and " following Paul and " his company " many days,"
she " cried, saying, These men are the servants of the
most High God, which show unto us the way of
salvation." Whereupon, " Paul, being grieved " at the
dishonour thus done to the Lord Jesus, " turned and
said to the spirit," who possessed her, " I command
thee in the name of Jesus Christ to come out of her.
And he came out the same hour ; " and her occupation
of course was at an end.[1]

That these practices were very general in the heathen world is shown likewise from what took place at
Ephesus ; where " many that believed came and confessed, and shewed their deeds. Many of them also
which used curious arts," τa $\pi\epsilon\rho\iota\epsilon\rho\gamma a$, meaning here,
the magic arts, (or in other words, who practised sor-
cery,) " brought their books together, and burned them
before all men : and they counted the price of them,
and found it fifty thousand pieces of silver. So
mightily grew the word of God and prevailed."[2]

And the very thought of association with persons,
who were guilty of such wickedness, is condemned in
the New Testament in the most emphatic terms, " I
would not that ye should have *fellowship* with *demons*.
Ye *cannot* drink of the cup of the Lord, and the cup of
demons : ye *cannot* be partaker of the Lord's table and
the table of *demons*. Do we provoke the Lord to
jealousy? are we stronger than He ? "[3]

" Idolatry " and " witchcraft " being then " works

---

[1] Acts xvi. 16-18.   [2] Acts xix. 18-20.   [3] 1 Cor. x. 20-22.

of the flesh," they necessarily have their germs in all hearts by nature. Nevertheless there must have been a time, when they were first overtly manifested in the world, and the Scriptures teach us, as I have shewn in my "Outlines of Prophetic Truth," that this took place in the days of Nimrod: while they also reveal to us that they attained their ignoble perfection in ancient Babylon. For thus it is written, "Babylon hath been a golden cup in Jehovah's hand, that made *all* the earth *drunken :* the nations have drunken of her wine ; therefore the nations are *mad :* "[1] and she consequently called herself, "the lady of Kingdoms."[2] While her sister Nineveh, which rivalled her in her iniquities and idolatries, was called by the Holy Ghost "the well-favoured harlot, the mistress of witchcrafts," *Kah'-shäh-pheem,*[3] "that selleth *nations* through her whoredoms, and families through her witchcrafts," *Kah'-shäh-pheem.*[4] Hence we read in Daniel of "the magicians," '*ghar-toom-meem*,' Priests skilled in the interpretation of the hieroglyphics, (whether Babylonian, or Egyptian)[5] "and the astrologers," *ash-shäh-pheem*', " and the sorcerers," *Kah'-shäh-pheem*',[6] " and the Chaldeans,"[7] meaning here the Chaldean Priests, who were skilled in magical arts : who were the persons who ruled the spiritual destinies of the nation, and to whom all doubtful

---

[1] Jer. li. 7.　　　　[2] Isa. xlvii. 5.　　　　[3] See page 6.
[4] Nahum iii. 4.　See page 6.
[5] Gen. xli. 8, 24 : Exod. vii. 11, 22; viii. 7, 18, 19; ix. 11.
[6] See page 6.　　　　[7] Dan. ii. 2.

matters were always referred.[1] These men were undoubtedly possessed, and ruled, by *demons ;* as were also their Egyptian namesakes : for none but those, who were aided by supernatural power, could possibly have performed such miracles, as did "Jannes and Jambres," when they "withstood Moses," in the presence of Pharaoh, King of Egypt.[2]

And just as " idolatry " and " witchcraft " were first openly practised, and afterwards fully developed, " in the plain of Shinar," where was situate Babylon of old : so the Holy Ghost assures us will they there again attain an awful prominence, and be headed up in the personal individual Antichrist, at the close of this Dispensation. But there also will they be judged, and stamped out, and come to an end. For " as Babylon hath caused the slain of Israel to fall, so *at Babylon* shall fall the slain of *all* the earth."[3] For " by thy sorceries," *pharmakeia*,[4] " were *all* nations deceived. And in her was found the blood of prophets, and of saints, and of *all* that were slain on the earth."[5]

---

[1] It is *in this sense* that the name is here used. Hence the term " *Chaldean* " came ultimately to be associated exclusively with *astrology*, and the practice of occult science as professed by astrologers : for this body of men were the only persons who retained the knowledge and use of the ancient Cushite language of the Kaldi, whence their name. See Walter's " Genuineness of the Book of Daniel," p. 63 ; where in a note he refers in proof of this to Juvenal, Sat. vi. 533, x. 94 ; and Cic. de Div. 2, 47.

[2] Tim. iii. 8 ; Exod. vii. 11, &c.   [3] Jer. li. 49.   [4] See page 10.
[5] Rev. xviii. 23, 24.

Hence we read of the re-establishment of "this wickedness" in the symbol of "a woman," whose "*house*" is to be again "*built*" "*in the land of Shinar :*" where she is to " be *established*, and *set there upon her own base*,"[1] a prophecy which has certainly not yet been fulfilled. The Book of the Revelation reveals this system to us in the 17th Chapter: while the 18th Chapter portrays the city of Babylon wherein it is to rule and reign, (having previously been rebuilt,) as destroyed, just before the second coming of the Lord— and as the parallel passages shew, when Antichrist will be then coming with his whole strength, as he supposes, to sweep away Israel from off the face of the earth ; but only then to be himself destroyed, with his whole host, "in the valley of Jehoshaphat," outside the walls of Jerusalem.[2] For Babylon is to be cast down, like a huge "stone," " cast into the midst of Euphrates," "*in a moment, in one day* "[3]—which clearly shews that *the whole* of the prophecies, both in Isaiah and Jeremiah, have not yet been fulfilled : for when " Jehovah " " will " *thus* " punish the king of Babylon and his land "—which is moreover to *become* " burning pitch "[4]—"in *those days*, and in *that time*, saith Jehovah, the iniquity of Israel shall be sought for, and *there shall be none ;* and *the sins of Judah*, and *they shall not be found :* for I will pardon them whom I reserve."[5]

---

[1] Zech. v. 5-11.

[2] Isa. x. 24-34 ; xiii. 25 ; Dan. xi. 40-45 ; xii. 1-3 ; Joel iii. 9-21 ; Zech. xiv. 1-9. [3] Jer. li. 63, 64 ; Rev. xviii. 8, 10, 17, 21.

[4] Compare Isa. xxxiv. 9, 10, with xiii. 19, &c. [5] Jer. l. 18-20.

" For Jehovah will have mercy on Jacob, and will yet choose Israel, and set them in their own land." "And it shall come to pass *in the day* that Jehovah *shall give thee rest* from thy sorrow, and from thy fear, and from the hard bondage wherein thou wast made to serve, that thou shalt take up this proverb," margin, " taunting speech," " against *the king of Bábylon*, and say, How hath the oppressor *ceased!* The golden city *ceased!*"[1]

Yes, and Jehovah Himself will take up " a taunting proverb" against the "idolaters" and dealers in " witchcraft" in those days;[2] and will say unto the consulters of them, " Stand now with thine enchantments," *gheh 'vereech*,[3] and with the multitude of thy sorceries, " *Kah-Shapheem*,"[4] wherein thou hast laboured from thy youth; if so be thou shalt be able to profit, if so be thou mayest prevail. Thou art wearied in the multitude of thy counsels. Let now the astrologers," *ashapheem*, " the stargazers," magicians who divided the heavens, for the purpose of taking horoscopes, with a view of foretelling future events, " the monthly prognosticators," (like Zadkiel,) " stand up, and save thee from these things that shall come upon thee. Behold, they shall be as stubble; the fire shall burn them; they shall not deliver themselves from the power of the flame" :—Rev. xviii. 8, 15, tells us that the city " shall be utterly *burned with fire*," and that " *the merchants*,"

---

[1] Isa. xiii. 1, 3, 4.   [2] Rev. ix. 20, 21; xviii. 23; xxii. 15.
[3] See page 6.   [4] See page 6.

" which were made rich by her, shall stand afar off *for
the fear of her torment*"—" there shall not be a coal
to warm at, nor fire to sit before it. Thus shall they
be unto thee with whom thou hast laboured, even
thy merchants, from thy youth: they shall wander
every one to his quarter; *none shall save thee.*"[1]

2. To trace the progress of " idolatry " from Babylon
over the whole earth, would not only be a needless
digression, but would also occupy more space than
I have at command. Nevertheless, with a view of
completing the subject, as well as of shewing that
" witchcraft," in all ages, and in whatever part of the
world it may be manifested, is derived from one source,
and has had but one origin; I shall, in this connexion,
give several instances of it, taken from various parts of
the world, and at different periods of its history, but
chiefly within the last 200 or 300 years.

The so-called " fathers," who lived when heathen-
ism was in the height of its evil pre-eminence, and
when " witchcraft " had full sway in the Roman world,
knew it well, and give us many instances of its evil
influence. Justin Martyr speaks of the disembodied
spirits of wicked men, *appearing as demons under
various forms*, for the purpose of deceiving men.
Pliny mentions one Apion, in his time, who told him
that *he had invoked departed spirits*, to enquire of
Homer, of what country he was born. Tertullian,

---

[1] Isa. xlvii. 12-15.

in his "Apology," says, "*Magicians produce apparitions, and bring into evil repute the spirits of men now dead.*" And again, addressing the heathen, he says, "Do not your magicians *perform amazing feats?* Call departed souls from the shades? And all this *by the assistance of demons, by which they can make stools and tables prophecy*"—a practice, which has erroneously been supposed to be of modern origin. So Augustine in his Civ. Dei, i. 18, tells us of one, who went to a celebrated philosopher, in the daytime, for the resolution of some intricate question, but could get no answer from him ; but that in the night the philosopher came to him, and resolved all his doubts. On calling upon the philosopher afterwards, and enquiring of him, why he could not answer him in the day time, as well as in the night, the philosopher told him that he had never been to him in the night at all ; but that he had dreamed in his sleep, that he had had such a conversation with him. He also states that two persons, named Paulus and Palladius, had both assured him that one *in his shape, whom they supposed to be himself*, had at various times, and in several places, *appeared to both of them.*

Such instances might be greatly multiplied, and brought down from that time to the present : and although there was undoubtedly much delusion, and some deception, in the cases of "witchcraft," which occurred in "New England," as recorded by Cotton and Increase Mather in 1692 : yet unquestionably there were also many cases of *real* possession likewise : for it would have been impossible for several of the possessed persons to have accomplished what they did, apart from superhuman agency. And it is instructive to note, what Cotton Mather says about charms, and spells and omens; which are relics of " witchcraft," and which, abounding in heathen and Popish countries, are but too prevalent in so-called Protestant ones also. " So 'tis to be feared " he says, " the children of New England have *secretly* done many things that have been *pleasing to the devil*. They say, that in some towns it has been an usual thing for people to cure hurts with *spells*, or to use detestable conjurations, with *sieves*, *keys*, and *pease*, and *nails*, and *horse-shoes*, and I know not what other implements, to learn the things for which they have a forbidden, and an impious curiosity. 'Tis *in the devil's name*, that such things are done ; and *in God's name* I do this day charge them as vile impieties. By these courses 'tis, that people play upon *the hole of the asp*, till that cruelly venomous *Asp* has pulled many of them into the deep *hole* of *witchcraft* itself. It has been acknowledged by some who have sunk the deepest into this *horrible pit*, that they *began* at these little *witch-crafts*."

Touching such incantations as these, the late Rev. James Knight, who was for some years the Incumbent of a Church in Sheffield, told me several years ago, that his father, who was the Vicar of Halifax, in Yorkshire, once broke the neck of a superstition of this nature, while he was staying at a large farmhouse in the country. Going into the kitchen on one occasion for some purpose or other, he observed one of the servants, who was preparing to churn, take up a handful of salt and go towards the fire. On making enquiries of her what she was going to do, she told him that she was going to make an offering : for unless she did this, the butter would never come. He at once forbade her doing anything of the kind ; and reasoned with her upon the sinfulness of her conduct, in following out so heathenish a custom. She complied with his request ; but told him she was certain that they would get no butter. Butter or no butter, he was determined that nothing of the sort should be done, while he was in the house : and my informant told me that on that occasion they had to churn away until two o'clock in the morning, until the butter came : but as the practice was thenceforth abandoned, on all subsequent occasions the butter came in the ordinary way.

The Rev. David Brainerd, who was a celebrated Missionary amongst the North American Indians, gives an account, in his diary, in the year 1746, of the conversion of an aged *Powaw*, or *conjuror*, who had been a very wicked man, and a murderer ; and who had attended on his preaching, while he still " followed his old charms and juggling tricks ; *giving out that he was some great one ; and to him they gave heed*, supposing him to be possessed of a great power : so that," he said, " when I have instructed them respecting the miracles wrought by Christ, in healing the sick, &c., and mentioned them as evidences of His divine mission and the truth of His doctrines, *they have quickly observed the wonders of that kind which this man had performed by his magic charms :* whence they had a high opinion of him and his superstitious notions, *which seemed to be a fatal obstruction to some of them, in the way of their receiving the Gospel."* But after his conversion, when the demon was cast out of him by the Spirit of the living God, " on his '*feeling the word of God in his heart,*' as he expressed it," he said, " *his spirit of conjuration left him entirely ;* and that he had no more of that nature since, than any other man living : and declares, *that he does not now so much as* KNOW HOW HE USED TO CHARM AND CONJURE ; and that he *could not* do anything of that nature, if he was never so desirous of it."[1]

A lady, who was at one time a Missionary amongst the North American Indians, lately gave me a remarkable account of the conversion of *a Medicine woman,* upwards of twenty years ago, on the borders of Lake Manitoba ; where she was then labouring. This woman had been *a sorceress,* and a very wicked woman ; and had done much evil among the Indians in the neighbourhood ; and was indeed so much dreaded by them, on account of her magic arts, that they tried to poison her, and nearly succeeded in doing so. She was, however, after a time, brought under deep conviction of sin, through hearing the Gospel preached by the Missionary Clergyman, stationed in that District :

---

[1] The Life of David Brainerd, pp. 284, 285. This case is likewise mentioned by Mr. B. W. Newton, in his pamphlet on " Spiritualism."

and then an awful struggle took place within her ; the devil doing his utmost, both internally, and externally through the heathen around her, to retain possession of her, and to prevent her from becoming a Christian. Her conflicts were so dreadful, that she completely lost her reason, and went raving mad. The Indians then succeeded in getting possession of her, and were making arrangements to kill her ; as they usually do those among them, who become insane : although they still seemed to be in mortal dread of her. At this juncture the little Missionary band earnestly pleaded with the Lord, that He would rescue the poor woman out of their hands, restore her to reason, and truly convert her to Himself.

Early the next morning, the Missionary Clergyman, therefore, called at the tent, where the woman was kept in confinement, and asked for her to be delivered up to him ; but met with a decided refusal. He called again at noon, with a like result. The Missionary band then redoubled their prayers ; and the Missionary himself once more called in the evening, and told the chiefs that he had now come for the woman, and insisted on their giving her up to him. He was only just in time : for an Indian was stealing up behind the woman, with his tomahawk uplifted in his hand, with the evident intention of despatching her. Astonished at the Missionary's boldness, in coming unarmed amidst so many warriors, and at the peremptory nature of his demand, they seemed quite taken aback, and gave her up to him at once—he undertaking to take the entire charge of her, and that she should do them no harm. As, however, she was still perfectly mad, the Missionary seemed at first perplexed what to do with her; but laying the matter again before the Lord, a young converted Indian came forward, and undertook, in conjunction with some others, to keep watch over her, in his mother's tent, during the night. They then all knelt down, and again pleaded earnestly with the Lord, that He would put the woman into a sound sleep, and that she might wake up in her right mind. This prayer was fully answered: for shortly after she was removed into the tent, she fell into a sound sleep; and actually awoke in the morning, not only " in " her " right mind," but also a believing Christian woman—the demon having been cast out of her by the Spirit of the living God. And she afterwards gave the clearest evidence, of having been truly converted to God, by her consistent Christian life and conduct; indeed her faith in Christ was so child-like and simple, that she received the most remarkable answers to her prayers.

This case is indeed very similar to the one recorded by Brainerd; and it shews likewise, as we see indeed in the accounts of demoniacal possessions recorded in the Gospels, that the Evil One will not give up possession of those who have yielded up themselves to him, without a struggle.[1] And it is not to be wondered at, that he can find means also of punishing them for disobeying him—aye, and of predicting evil against them,

---

[1] Mark i. 26; ix. 20; Luke ix. 42.

which he takes care that some of his many instruments shall ultimately bring upon them. Hence, we see in God's Word, that although Satan had to ask permission of Jehovah to touch His servant *Job ;* yet he asked no such permission, when he stirred up the Sabeans and Chaldeans to kill his servants. [1]

The following instance, which is, I believe, admitted to be an historical fact, fully illustrates this point ; and shews likewise the Evil One's intense subtlety as well : for the fulfilment of the prediction, would also serve to confirm the heathen in their belief of the religion thus assailed.

Colonel Meadows Taylor, in his " Story of My Life," speaking of Beejanugger, says :—" After breakfast I ordered my palanqueen, and wandered over the western portions of the city. I saw the barriers of rock extended to the south, forming a strong line of defence, the only aperture being a pass between them and the spurs of the Rama Mully mountain. This was the pass by which a Bahmany King, Mujahid Shah, entered the line of defence in 1378, and endeavoured to take the city ; but owing to the neglect of one of his Generals, who had been directed to occupy an eminence to the west of the city, which was the real key to the pass, and who failed in his duty, the King could only penetrate the first line of defence, *where a huge image of Hanooman, the monkey-god, stands alone, carved out of a great granite boulder.*

---

[1] Job. i. 11.

"The King, on seeing it surrounded by Brahmins, charged and dispersed them; then dismounting, *he struck the image with his steel mace, breaking off a portion of the right leg.*

" ' *For this act,*' cried a dying Brahmin, ' *thou shalt die before thou reach the city !* ' a prophecy strictly fulfilled; for *King Mujahid was assassinated on his march to Gulburgah.*"[1]

I have already referred to the Satanic miracles performed by the Egyptian Magicians in the days of Moses; and such Magicians still exist in Egypt, and in other parts of Africa at the present day. I remember reading, now upwards of forty years ago, an account of some extraordinary performances by an Egyptian enchanter, before some naval officers several years before. Among other things, he told them that he could bring before them any person living, or dead, whom they chose to name. The method was to pour an inky fluid into the palm of the hand, and to shew them the person called for depicted therein. Looking into the fluid, which if I remember rightly he poured into the two closed palms of the hands of a boy, they first saw a besom sweeping the ground violently, without any person holding it. Then on their calling for Lord Nelson, whom the Magician had never even heard of, to their profound astonishment, he instantly appeared—an effect which could on no possible ground have been produced, except by the instrumentality of demons.[2]

---

[1] " Story of my Life," Vol. II. pp. 312, 313.
[2] See Div. iii. Sec. 2, Subsec. 1, on the Magic Crystal.

As an instance likewise of the identity of all idolatry, and of its original transmission from Babylon to the ends of the earth, I might here mention the case of the emancipated African slave, recorded in the Preface to my " Outlines of Prophetic Truth," who had been originally kidnapped from one of the central tribes in Africa, and who was subsequently converted in the only (then I believe) Church in Sierra Leone, through having heard the 44th Chapter of the Book of the Prophet Isaiah read as one of the lessons for the day. He was amazingly struck with what he had heard ; and afterwards conversing with the Missionary, who had conducted the service on that occasion, he told him, that " the book he had read *must* be *God's* book : *because* none but *God* could possibly have *known*, and so truly have *described* the practices of the *Gree Gree* men " (or *conjurors*) " in his country : " who, it appeared from his testimony, not only planted two trees ; but, when they were sufficiently grown, made one of them into an idol, and burnt the other in the manner there described ; actually clapping their hands over it, and uttering the very words of the text, " Aha, I am warm, I have seen the fire ! " while certain portions of the " ashes " were afterwards gathered up, and, after having been immersed in water, were swallowed by the worshippers.[1]

Those who have read the extraordinary career of *Obi* Jack, once a kidnapped slave from Africa, in Jamaica,

---

[1] " Outlines," Preface, p. xviii.

3

in the latter part of the last century, if they knew anything of " Spiritualism," could be under no doubt as to his having been *possessed by a demon*—the very name *Obi*, which prevails among the African tribes, and is applied by them to their magicians, not only suggesting, but proving *its* original with, the Hebrew word *Ohv*, a soothsaying demon ! And that there are still representatives of these *Obi* men in Africa, the following extract from the late Dr. Livingstone's Journal, quoted by Mr. B. W. Newton, in the appendix to his pamphlet on " Spiritualism " abundantly proves.

" Suleiman-ben-Juma lived on the mainland, Mosessamé, opposite Zanzibar. *It is impossible to deny his power of foresight*, except by rejecting all evidence, for he frequently foretold the deaths of great men among the Arabs, and he was pre-eminently a good man, upright and sincere—none like him now for goodness and skill. *He said that two middle-sized white men, with straight noses and flowing hair down to the girdle behind, came at times and told him things to come.* He died twelve years ago, and left no successor ; he foretold his own decease, three days beforehand, by cholera."

As the East, however, was *the cradle* of " idolatry " and " witchcraft : " so it is still *in the East*, where these abominations have ever been more peculiarly manifested, and where they even now most extensively prevail. It is here again where Satan seems to be putting forth all his power ; for it is *from the East* that these iniquities are again coming in upon us like a mighty flood. Who could have supposed that Buddhism, with its new and formidable ally of Theosophy, would ever again have assumed an *aggressive* attitude; or that learned and educated men in these so-called Protestant countries, would have succumbed to its evil influence? but so it is. And can any godly Christian doubt for a moment, that God has righteously permitted these things, as an awful judgment upon the people of these kingdoms, in consequence of our national support of idolatry, and the exclusion of the Word of God from our public schools, both here and in the Colonies? And is it to be wondered at, that tons of blasphemous and infidel literature are being sent into India, which is eagerly read by the educated natives, and is rapidly supplanting the Word of the living God? Had we ears to hear, we might surely hear the Lord saying of us, "A wonderful and horrible thing is committed in the land!" "Shall I not *visit* for these things?" "And shall not my soul be *avenged* on such a nation as this?"[1] But this, for the present, by the way.

The Indian jugglers have ever been famous for their conjuring tricks all the world over; as almost every officer who has been in India can testify: and many of their *seeming* miracles are undoubtedly performed by them in a natural way, through long practice, by mere dexterity and sleight of hand: but *some* of them are

---

[1] Jer. v. 29, 30.

far beyond what any mere unassisted human being could possibly accomplish ; and must of necessity have been wrought by demoniacal power. Take the following as illustrations in point.

In an article on the " Autobiography of the Emperor Jehangueir," which appeared about 40 years ago in a number of "The Quarterly Review," the following account is given of some of the wonders, which were performed by several Bengal jugglers before that Emperor. Among many other things, they "in a moment covered a pond with ice sufficiently strong to bear an elephant." " They caused two tents to be set up, the one at the distance of a bow shot from the other, the doors or entrances being placed exactly opposite; they raised the tent-walls all around, and desired that it might be particularly observed that they were entirely empty. Then, fixing the tent walls to the ground, two of the seven men entered, one into each tent, none of the other men entering into either of the tents. Thus prepared, they said they would undertake to bring out of the tents any animal we chose to mention, whether bird or beast, and set them in conflict with each other. Khaun-e-Jahaun, with a smile of incredulity, required them to show us a battle between two ostriches. In a few minutes two ostriches of the largest size issued, one from either tent, and attacked each other with such fury that the blood was seen streaming from their heads ; they were at the same time so equally matched, that neither could get the better of the other, and they were therefore separated by the men, and conveyed within the tent. In short, they continued to produce from either tent whatever animal we chose to name, and before our eyes set them to fight in the manner I have attempted to describe ; and although," says the writer, " I have exerted my utmost invention to discover the secret of the contrivance, it has been entirely without success."

Continuing his narrative, he says, "they were furnished with a bow and about fifty steel-pointed arrows. One of the seven men took the bow in hand, and shooting an arrow into the air, the shaft stood fixed at a considerable height ; he shot a second arrow, which flew straight to the first, to which it became attached, and so with every one of the remaining arrows, to the last of all, which striking the sheaf suspended in the air, the whole immediately broke asunder, and came at once to the earth. They produced a chain of fifty cubits in length "—I suppose about seventy-five feet—" and in my presence threw one end of it towards the sky, where it remained, as if fastened to something in the air. A dog was then brought forward, and being placed at the lower end of the chain, instantly ran up, and reaching the other end, immediately disappeared in the air. In the same manner a hog, a panther, a lion, and a tiger, were alternately sent up the chain, and all equally disappeared at the upper end of the chain. At last they took down the chain, and put it into a bag, no one ever discovering in what way the different animals were made to vanish into the air in the mysterious manner above described. This I may venture to affirm," says the narrator, " was beyond measure strange and surprising ; " as indeed it was.

This power of fixing things in the air, seemingly without support, we shall see frequently possessed, and exercised, by Spiritualistic mediums : and indeed some marvellous instances of this kind have been exhibited in public, from time to time, by so-called professors of mesmerism. A lady told me that about six or seven years ago, she witnessed in a large town in the North of England a sight which very greatly astonished her. A professor of mesmerism was operating upon a young girl of between sixteen and seventeen years of age. She was called " The beautiful Astarte "—Astarte being the name of the Assyrian Venus ! She was a lovely girl, with a very beautiful figure, which was shewn to perfection ; as she was dressed in flesh-colored silk tights, with a short tunic only round her waist, which reached no more than one-third of the way down her thighs. Among other things, the mesmerizer put her into the mesmeric sleep, whilst she was standing upright ; when she remained in that position perfectly rigid. He then placed a thick wand under one of her arms, and gently lifting up the lower part of the arm, he reclined her head gracefully upon her hand. Then retiring from her to a short distance, he waived the other arm in a horizontal position away from her body ; in which position it remained perfectly motionless. He then in a similar manner, waived up one of her legs, which remained suspended horizontally, level with the arm. After which he waived up her whole body into the same horizontal position : when she actually remained thus rigidly fixed in the air, as if suspended upon nothing : while her head still rested upon the hand of her other arm, which remained leaning upon the wand : the wand itself still continuing to stand in an upright position, and perfectly motionless, as if it had not been in the least degree subjected to any strain whatever ! My informant told me that the people present seemed awe-struck ; and that they all retired from the building in silence, as if they had (as she herself felt that she had), seen something weird and supernatural : as no doubt they had.

Take another instance. Several sects in Persia and Hindostan regard the art of apparent death as part of their religious ritual, and practise it with the assiduity of devotees. In the ancient books of the Hindoos it is called " stopping the breath." The writer of an article in Scribner's Monthly for December, 1880, quotes the following facts from Sir Claude M. Wade, political resident at Ludianah, and agent to the British Government at the Court of Runjeet Singh. A fakir, he says, was buried for forty days, then disentombed and resuscitated. Sir Claude says, that although he arrived at the spot a few hours after the fakir was interred, he had the testimony of Runjeet Singh himself, and the most credible witnesses at his Court, as to the truth of the fakir having been so buried before them ; and having been present himself when he was disinterred and restored to vitality, in a position so close to him as to render deception impossible. Sir Claude firmly believes that there was no collusion in producing the extraordinary fact which he relates. When the forty days were ended, Sir Claude accompanied the Rajah and suite to the spot where the fakir was interred. The building was first examined. It contained four doors, three of which had been hermetically sealed, and the fourth fastened by a strong door, plastered with mud up to the padlock and sealed with the Rajah's private seal, in his own presence, at the date when the fakir was entombed. The walls and door-ways bore no marks of having been disturbed. Runjeet Singh, himself a little sceptical, identified the impression of the seal. Besides these precautions, the Rajah had kept two companies of his personal escort stationed near the building, from which four sentinels were furnished and relieved every two hours, night and day, to protect the fakir from intrusion. One of his principal officers also regularly visited the spot, and reported to the Minister of State; whilst the Rajah himself kept the key of the padlock.

On the door being opened, Runjeet Singh and Sir Claude entered the dark room, accompanied by the servant of the fakir. In a cell three feet below the surface of the square apartment was a wooden box containing the body of the experimentalist. This box was locked and sealed in the same way as the outer door. The cell was so small that, on trying to sit down, their hands and knees came in contact with the body of the fakir. The body was enclosed in a bag, upon which the servant commenced pouring warm water, but Sir Claude objected, and caused the bag to be torn open that they might view the body. This was easily accomplished, as the bag proved to be mildewed. The legs and arms of the fakir were shrivelled and stiffened, but the face was full of life. He was then, at the request of the narrator, examined by a medical gentleman, but he could discover no pulsation in the heart, temples, or wrist. There was, however, a heat about the coronal region of the brain. The body was then bathed in warm water, Runjeet Singh himself assisting. A hot wheaten cake was then placed on the head of the apparently lifeless body—a process repeated twice or thrice before success was accomplished. The servant then removed from the nostrils and ears of his master the wax and cotton plugs with which they had been sealed, then opened the rigid jaws by inserting the point of a knife between the teeth and prising them apart, holding the jaws open with his left hand, whilst he drew the tongue forward with the forefinger of his right hand; that usually flexible member flying back to its curved position, so that its tip closed the gullet repeatedly during the process. He then rubbed the fakir's eyes with clarified butter for some seconds, until he succeeded in opening them. The eye-ball was glazed and motionless. The wheaten cake was then renewed, and the body heaved convulsively, the nostrils became inflated, respiration was resumed, and life was restored. In a few minutes the experimentalist commenced to articulate, in scarcely audible tones, inquiring if the Rajah was now convinced. The period that elapsed between opening the box and restoring the voice was about half an hour. Sir Claude remarks, in concluding his narrative, that he took some pains to investigate the manner in which this result was effected, and was informed that the *rationale* of the process rested on the view of Hindoo physiologists that heat constitutes the self-existent principle of life, and that even if the functions be so far interrupted as to leave this one only in perfect purity, life can be continued for long periods without air, food, or other means of sustenance. My enlightened readers, however, will probably be of opinion that something more than this was needed, to produce the result achieved in this instance, after such an ordeal.

Most of my readers will no doubt remember the forty days' fast of Dr. Tanner several years ago; as well as that of the Italian (by name Succhi, I believe), who professed that he possessed a liquid, which not only would keep him alive during his fast, but keep him in his usual normal state of vigour, both of body and mind. Since then other proposals have been made, and hints thrown out, that persons can be made to possess the power, not only of putting themselves into trances, and awaking at periods which they choose to name beforehand; but likewise of suffering themselves to be entombed, and rising again, after the manner of the fakir, whose case I have given above: and as a sequal to this history, I might here mention a remarkable case, which occurred in the house of a very dear friend of the Rev. Foster Rogers; who was for upwards of twenty years Chaplain in the Gaol at Winchester, and was afterwards Rector of Barrow, near Chester; who communicated it to me some six or eight years ago. And I doubt not, as we near the end of this Dispensation, such cases as these, and others far more astonishing, will take place, under the influence of demoniacal agency, to prepare the unconverted and unwary to receive the Antichrist, when he at length makes his appearance on the scene —"whose coming," the Scriptures assure us, "is *after the working of Satan with all power and signs and lying wonders, and with all deceivableness of un-righteousness in them that perish;* because they received not the love of the truth, that they might be saved. And for this cause God shall send them strong delusion, that they should believe a lie : that they all might be damned who believed not the truth, but had pleasure in righteousness "[1]—a passage, which has been *exclusively* applied to Rome; and to which it *does* no doubt in a measure apply, but certainly *not* exclusively, as I shall hereafter shew. For in those days, as our Lord assures us, " there shall arise false Christs and false prophets, and *shall shew great signs and wonders;* insomuch that, if it were possible, they shall deceive the very elect."[2]

The case I allude to is as follows. The Rev. Foster Rogers, who was then Rector of Barrow, and at whose

---

[1] 2 Thes. ii. 9-12.　　[2] Mat. xxiv. 24.　See also Rev. xiii. 13.

house I was staying in the month of November, 1878, told me, that the sons of his friend before referred to were in the habit of going out with the sons of a neighbouring gentleman to course; and that they occasionally took their butler with them to carry their game: he being passionately fond of the sport. On one occasion, when they were preparing to go out, the butler was told that he could not accompany them; for as there were friends in the house, his services would be required at home. He seemed put out, and observed in a somewhat rude and pettish manner, "Well I'll see '*the run*' at all events!"

In the afternoon on the return of the sportsmen, and while they were narrating the events of the day; giving the particulars of where they had *found* the hares, and where the dogs had *killed* them, &c.; the butler, who was listening to their recital with great interest, broke in upon their statement, and told them that they had made one or two mistakes in it, which he corrected. The young people were greatly surprised at the accuracy of the correction; and asked him how he could tell the details of the chase so correctly, without having been present on the occasion. He did not then afford them any satisfactory solution of the difficulty; and some of the young people hinted that he must have had dealings with the Evil One. This circumstance led to enquiry; and some of the other servants confirmed the fact of the possession by the butler of some wonderful power; for they stated that on two or three occasions they had found him, either in his room, or in the hay-

loft, in what at first was mistaken by them for a fainting fit : but the coldness and rigidity of his body, and
the extreme difficulty of removing it into the house,
subsequently caused them to think that he was actually
dead. When consciousness returned, however, he told
them that *he possessed the power of " disembodying*
himself ; " and that he exercised this power in order
that he might see things that took place at a distance !

This revelation so affected both his master and mistress, who were pious people, that they could not bear
to have such a man in their house ; and they at once
gave him the usual notice to leave their service.

Since then I have heard of several other modern
cases of a like character ; and one in particular, where
a man so possessed exceeded his powers, and never
again recovered consciousness, but actually died under
the experiment. Such cases as these, however, are not
of *modern origin*, but might, I dare say, if the secrets
of the past could all be brought to light, be shewn to
have occurred, more or less, during all ages. When
Richard Baxter was writing his " Certainty of the
World of Spirits," which was published in 1691, the
Rev. Thomas Tilson, the minister of Aylesford, near
Maidstone, having heard that he was " writing about
witchcraft and apparitions," sent him a detailed
account of a similar case, with proof of its authen-
ticity, &c.

He says : — " Mary, the wife of John Goffe, of
Rochester, being afflicted with a long illness, removed
to her father's house at West Malling, which is about

nine miles distant from her own. There she died, June the 4th, this present year, 1691. The day before her departure she grew very impatiently desirous to see her two children, whom she had left at home to the care of a nurse. She prayed her husband to hire a horse, for she must go home and die with the children." As she was " not fit to be taken out of her bed," her request was refused. This grieved her much : and " between one and two o'clock in the morning *she fell into a trance.* One Widow Turner, who watched with her that night, says that *her eyes were open and fixed, and her jaw fallen.* She put her hand upon her mouth and nostrils, but could perceive no breath. She thought her to be in a fit, and doubted whether she were dead or alive. The next morning this dying woman told her mother that *she had been at home with her children.* 'That is impossible,' said the mother; 'for you have been in bed all the while.' 'Yes,' replied the other, 'but I was with them last night when I was asleep.'

" The nurse at Rochester, Widow Alexander by name, affirms, and says she will take her oath on't, before a magistrate, and receive the sacrament upon it, that a little before two o'clock that morning she saw the likeness of the said Mary Goffe, come out of the next chamber (where the elder child lay in a bed by itself), the door being left open, and stood by her bedside for about a quarter of an hour; the younger child was then lying by her. Her eyes moved and her mouth went; but she said nothing. The nurse, moreover, says that she was perfectly awake; it was then daylight, being one of the longest days in the year. She sate up in her bed, and looked stedfastly upon the apparition. In that time she heard the bridge-clock strike two, and a while after said, ' In the name of the Father, Son, and Holy Ghost, what art thou?' Thereupon the appearance removed and went away; she slipped on her cloaths and followed, but what became on't she cannot tell. Then, and not before, she began to be grievously affrighted, and went out of doors and walked upon the wharf (the house is just on the river side) for some hours, only going in now and then to look to the children. At five-a-clock she went to a neighbour's house, and knocked at the door; but they would not rise. At six she went again; then they rose, and let her in. She related to them all that had passed; they would persuade her she was mistaken or dreamt. But she confidently affirmed, ' If ever I saw her in all my life, I saw her this night.' "[1]

---

[1] This brings to my remembrance a singular circumstance, which was narrated to me by the late J. G. Teed, Esq., then judge of the County Court of Lincolnshire. He said that a friend of his, one of the old masters in Chancery, I believe, once fell into a trance, and was supposed to be dead. In this state he continued for several weeks; but afterwards regained his consciousness. The Judge asked him, if he *remembered* anything during that period; when he told him that the only thing that he could remember was that " *his soul seemed to have left his body*, and was fluttering like a bird against the window to get out; but could not, because it was closed!" This reminded me of the old saying of the Lincolnshire women, who laid out the dead when I was a boy, " Mind, and open the window, to let the soul out!"

The Scriptures speak, as we have seen, in contempt of " the astrologers, the star-gazers," and " the monthly prognosticators," as *unable to " save "* their victims from the judgments that the Lord will bring upon them ;[1] although they had been *able*, under Satanic influence, *to predict* some events, which had actually come to pass. And as instances of their skill in this respect, I will here recount, out of many others that might have been adduced, two only—one of which occurred in India, and the other in Great Britain.

The one which occurred in India is given by Col. Meadows Taylor in his " Story of my Life." He was at that time " an Officer of the Nizam," for the administration of the Shorapoor State, during the minority of the Rajah Enketappa Naik ; his mother, the Ranee, being a woman of much energy, but dissolute to a degree. The Ranee becoming very ill, and thinking she was going to die, sent for Col. Taylor ; and in his presence, told the priest of the family, one of the professors, as it were, in the Brahmin Sanscrit College, to bring a certain box, which contained the secret papers of the house, and bade him open it. The man demurred.

" ' These papers have never been seen by any one but my lord the Rajah, who is gone to heaven, yourself and me. No one else knows of them,' he cried ; ' why should you show them to Taylor Sahib ? '

---

[1] Isa. xlvii. 13.

" The Ranee sat up straight in her bed, and glared at him. I had never seen such a look on any human face before.

" 'Do as you are told,' she cried, savagely ; 'what is it to you what I do ?'

" The *Shastree* trembled all over, and without speaking, he unlocked the padlock and opened the lid. The first thing I saw was a roll tied with red silk.

" 'Tell him first about that,' said the Ranee, and fell back again.

" 'It is not fit that you should hear it,' said the *Shastree*, who spoke both Mahratta and Hindoostanee fluently.

" '*It is the Rajah's horoscope that I wrote.* The moment he was born I noted the time, and the conjunction of planets, *and the result was bad.*'

" 'Yes, it is bad !' cried the Ranee, seizing my arm, as I was sitting on the ground by her bedside—' it is bad ! All that concerns that base-born boy is bad ! . . . . . Yes! *he is fated to die in his twentyfourth year*, and I shall not see it. . . . . Is it not so, *Shastree ?* Did we not spend a lakh of rupees over this, and it availed nothing ?' and she stopped for want of breath, her eyes flashing with excitement. 'Is it not so ? Tell the truth !'

" 'You speak truth, lady,' said the *Shastree*, who was sobbing. 'It is only the truth, Taylor Sahib ; I have tested all the calculations and find them exactly conforming to the truth according to the planets. The Rajah is safe till then ; but when

4

that time comes, how, I know not, but he will surely die. *He will never complete his twenty-fourth year! never! never!'*

" 'No!' cried the Ranee, interrupting him—'he will not live; he is the last of his race. He will lose his country, and all the lands, and all the honour that the Sumnothan has gained for 500 years.' "[1]

This took place in the year 1847.

When the Rajah attained his majority, Colonel Taylor's connection with Shorapoor came to an end. This was in the year 1853. Then came the Indian mutiny, which the Rajah of Shorapoor was, under evil advice, induced to join; but when the mutiny was quelled, the Rajah was captured; and taken as a prisoner to Secunderabad, to be tried for his life by a military commission. Colonel Taylor having then occasion to go again to Shorapoor, a few hours after his arrival there, "the old Brahmin priest came to him privately.

" 'Do you remember, Sahib,' he asked, 'what I once told you, and what the Ranee said when we were with her at her bedside?'

" 'Perfectly,' I answered; 'you said the Rajah would not live to complete his twenty-fourth year, and that he would lose his country.'

" 'Yes, Sahib,' he went on, 'part of the prediction is already fulfilled, and the rest will surely follow—it is quite inevitable.'

---

[1] "Story," &c., Vol. II., pp. 10-13.

" ' Do you think the Rajah knew of the prediction ? ' I inquired. ' If he did, it may have made him reckless.'

" ' I do not think he knew it,' replied the old priest ; ' for the last time I saw the box it was in the treasury, with the seals unbroken, as you left it.'

" ' We cannot say,' I continued, ' what may yet happen ; the proceedings are not over, and the Resident and I are both determined to save the Rajah's life if we can.'

" ' It's no use, Sahib,' returned the Shastree, shaking his head mournfully ; ' your intentions are merciful, but you are helpless before his fate. He will die—how we may not see ; but he must die—he cannot live. You, Sahib, and I, are the only two living that possess this secret, and you must be so good as to tell me directly you know his sentence. I cannot believe that the Government will spare him. I firmly expect that he will be blown away from a gun.' "[1]

" At last the news came.

" The Rajah of Shorapoor had been sentenced to death ; but the Resident had commuted his sentence to transportation for life, which was the most his power admitted of.

" I sent off at once for the Shastree.

" ' Listen,' said I, ' to the gracious and merciful determination of the Governor-General. The Rajah's life is safe. . . . What becomes now of the prophecy ? This letter proves it is false.'

" ' I wish I could think so, Sahib,' he sighed, ' and

---

[1] "Story," &c., Vol. II., pp. 282, 283.

that my poor young master were really safe ; but, alas ! he is in the greatest danger.'

" A few days after, a runner entered the palace court, and his packet was soon in my hands. It contained a few lines only, from the Resident :—

" ' *The Rajah of Shorapoor shot himself this morning dead*, as he arrived at his first encampment. I will write particulars when I know them.'

" My countenance naturally changed ; and the old Shastree, who was beside me, and had been reading over the Sanscrit deeds and grants to me, caught hold of my arm, and peering into my face, cried, almost with a shriek—

" ' He's dead ! he's dead ! I know it by your face— it tells me, Sahib, he's dead ! '

" ' Yes,' I said sorrowfully. ' Yes, he is dead ; he shot himself at the first stage out of Secunderabad, and died instantly.'

" ' Ah ! ' said the old priest, as soon as he could speak, ' he could not escape his fate, and the prophecy is fulfilled.'

" It was indeed a strange accomplishment of the prediction. *In a few days more the Rajah would have completed his twenty-fourth year ; and now he had died by his own hand !* "[1]

Colonel Taylor adds, that it never could be ascertained, whether it was " accidental or intentional ! "[2]

---

[1] " Story," &c., Vol. II., pp. 285-288.

[2] A correspondent in " The Standard," of Jan. 30th, 1889, speaking of the obstacles to the " extension of the Tien-Tsin Railway

The second instance is one, the particulars of which have been kindly furnished to me by Mrs. Meredith, the head of "The Prison Mission," and the foundress of "The Princess Mary Homes," at Atherstone, in Surrey. She says, "I will tell you a fact that you may publish, with my name: as authentication is all-important in such cases.

"My mother, Mrs. Lloyd, had a friend, who gave much attention to the study of *Astrology*, under the instruction of the late Zadkiel (Lieut. Morrison, R.N.). One of the exercises of the astrological course is the construction of the arc of the heavens, at a certain date, and the calculations of the influence of the stars then above the horizon. The deduction from this conclusion is that certain events will occur to persons, or in places, under the ruling of the stars in their relations to the localities, or the people denoted! In order to connect items such as spots of the earth's surface, or individuals of any race, animal or human, with the astral effects, it is necessary to fix on an incident in the history of the subject, and ascertain the exact time of its occurrence, erect for the same precise moment an arc of the heavens, and then proceed to combine the

---

to Tung-Chow," says :—"The great fire which destroyed part of the Imperial Palace in Pekin on the 17th of this month, caused much disturbance in the minds of the old-fashioned and superstitious, who are still strong in the capital. In consequence, the Emperor and his mother *consulted the Imperial Astrologers*, who, after much deliberation, declared that the fire was an evil omen, and *was intended as a warning against permitting the approach of the ' Western invention ' to the sacred city!*"

relations between the courses of the stars and the life of the subject !

" These intricate and difficult problems are worked out with intense application by those who desire to trace the career of persons from their birth to their death. When they wish to test their powers, *they* take a future date, and *address to the heavenly bodies* A ' HORARY QUESTION ! ' So calculating forward to the day and hour specified, they ascertain "—undoubtedly through the demon, whom they thus, *sometimes*, it may be, *un-knowingly* address—" what will happen to a person or a place at that time "—should the demon be able to predict it, and bring it about !

" My mother lived at a seaport, and in the reach before her house, ships anchored to refit for sea. As she sat in her room and sewed, she watched the vessels come and go ; and was in some degree interested in their changes and movements. Her friend, the Astrologer, came to visit her, and, in course of conversation, she said, ' I recommend you not to go out on such a day : for on *that* day you will see a death.'

" ' Of what, or of whom ? ' enquired my mother.

" ' Oh, I really can't tell you,' said the Astrologer : ' but it would be best to encounter any painful event in your own home.'

" My mother had had some experience of the fore-telling powers of her friend ; and though she strongly objected to their application, she had a certain sense of their accuracy, and a shrinking from their exercise. She on this occasion determined not to let them in-fluence her movements, and she replied :

" ' I will not be directed by your prophecies ; and I will go out as usual on that day, as well as other days.'

' " The morning of the day of date opened with very severe weather ; and as the day went on, it became imprudent for my mother to expose herself to it. She sat down to her work in her window seat, and watched the ships as they proceeded with their repairs, notwithstanding adverse weather. Men went on the yards, mended sails, altered ropes, and generally dealt with the great combination, that prepares a vessel for her voyage.

" Among other matters, men hung down a scaffold, and began to paint the sides of one of the ships. My mother watched this operation with special attention ; *and afterwards recalled having felt a sort of fascination for it !* The painters, as they worked, often stepped back to observe the effects of their painting ; and, as she kept looking at them, *an awful shock seized her*—a man fell into the water, *as she expected*, from the way in which they were moving on the platform ! As she described the event :—' I could not take my gaze off them, from the moment they began to work ; for I was impressed with the fear, that one of them would be drowned : though no memory, nor idea, at the moment connected them with the prediction that I was to witness a death on *that* day !'

" *This fact was made great use of*, IN THE CAUSE OF ASTROLOGY, *by our friend, the pupil of Zadkiel !*"

Mrs. Meredith adds :—" There were many other similar occurrences, that attested her skill in foretelling events. *This one* I can tell *on my own authority* : for I was in the house, and heard the prediction ; and was present when the man fell overboard. The current was strong, and the body was not reached until life was extinct."

One can easily imagine how such occult sciences, in ancient times, led to " the *worship* of the host of heaven " :[1] but no enlightened person could ever suppose that the planets, or the stars, could *of themselves* rule, or influence, the destinies of men ; and the only reason why educated persons in these days, fall into such " snares of the devil," and are thus " taken captive by him at his will,"[2] is because they have rejected " the Scriptures of truth " : which tell us that " all things pertaining to life and godliness " are by the " Divine power " " given " unto the people of the Lord, " through the knowledge of Him that hath called " them " to glory and virtue : whereby are given unto " them " exceeding great and precious promises : that by these " they " might be partakers of a Divine nature " ; *and thus " escape* the corruption that is in the world through lust."[3] And it need surprise no one that Satan is able to predict *some* future events : because the Lord Himself has expressly told us that such will be the case ; and that He will permit it, to test the faith, and to try the obedience of His people. " If there arise among you,"

---

[1] Deut. iv. 19 ; 2 Kings, xvii. 16 ; Jer. viii. 1, 2 ; Zeph. i. 4, 5 ; Acts vii. 41-43.　　　　　[2] 2 Tim. ii. 26.　　　　　[3] 2 Pet. i. 3, 4.

says He, "a prophet, or a dreamer of dreams, and *giveth thee a sign or a wonder, and the sign or the wonder* COMETH TO PASS, whereof he spake unto thee, saying, Let us go after other gods, which thou hast not known, and let us serve them; thou shalt not hearken unto the words of that prophet, or that dreamer of dreams: for *Jehovah your God* PROVETH YOU, to know whether ye love Jehovah your God with all your heart and with all your soul."[1] And again, "The prophet, which shall presume to speak a word in My name, which I have not commanded him to speak, or that shall speak in the name of other gods, even that prophet shall die. And if thou say in thine heart, How shall we know the word which Jehovah hath not spoken? When a prophet speaketh *in the name of Jehovah*, if the thing *follow not*, nor come to pass, that is the thing which Jehovah hath *not* spoken, but the prophet hath spoken it presumptuously: thou shalt not be afraid of him."[2] These two directions, then, will *alone* enable any enlightened person, to test the pretensions of *any* false prophet whatsoever.

I have spoken in a former part of this work, of divining by the cup;[3] and I will here give a case of this kind, which took place in India, some few years since. A nephew-in-law of mine, who was then a merchant in Calcutta, and the Danish Consul there, told me that a merchant friend of his lost a considerable sum of money

---

[1] Deut. xiii. 1-3.   [2] Deut. xviii. 20-22.   [3] See page 13.

in rupees ; which he suspected had been stolen by one of his Hindoo clerks ; but he was unable to trace the theft home to any one of them. A merchant friend of his advised him to consult a Brahmin diviner, who would soon discover who the thief was; and, acting upon his suggestion, he employed him. When the diviner came, he requested the merchant to summon all his clerks into one of his large warehouses; and, disposing them in a circle, he placed himself in the centre of the circle, and setting down a small vase, or divining cup, before him, he performed over it some magical incantations; shortly after which it began to move. Its movements were first in small circles, which gradually increased, until they nearly approached the outer circle of the several clerks ; when it suddenly darted towards one of them, whom the Brahmin at once declared to be the thief. The man, struck with terror, confessed that it was true, and restored the money which he had stolen.

And is it not a " sign of the times " that " divining " is now coming up again in this, and other countries? Only as late as October, 1888, the " Hull and North Lincolnshire Times " devoted several columns to the successful operations of a diviner by the rod, for the discovery not only of water, but of metals likewise. The " Standard " newspaper had an article also upon the subject in its issue of the 25th of December, in the same year. This was followed by no less than 21 letters from various writers in the same paper, most of whom spoke of its virtues ; and one of them actually *advocated its use for the discovery of murderers and other criminals!* ignoring the solemn statement of the Divine Word, that Jehovah hath threatened to " frustrate the tokens of the liars, and " to " *make diviners mad.*"[1] " For these nations, which thou shalt possess," said He, addressing the Israelites, who were about to enter Canaan, " hearkened unto observers of times " Astrologers—" and unto *diviners : but as for thee, Jehovah thy God hath not suffered thee so to do.*"[2]

The late Bishop Smith, in his work on China, speaking upon Buddhism, which was undoubtedly of Babylonian origin, says : — " An honest Romanist priest must often be stumbled at the similarity between the religious forms of Popery and those of Buddhism. The existence of monasteries and nunneries, the celibacy, the tonsure, the flowing robes, and the peculiar caps of the priesthood (of Buddha) ; the burning of incense, the tinkling of bells, the rosaries of beads, the sacred candles on the altar tables ; the intonation of services, the prayers in an unknown tongue, purgatory, and the offerings for the dead in their temples ; and above all, the titles of their principal goddess, the ' Queen of Heaven,' and ' Holy Mother,' represented by the image of a woman with her child in her arms, present features of resemblance which must strike every candid mind. Such a remarkable similarity of details, although it may facilitate a transition from Buddhism to Popery, must occasionally

---

[1] Isa. xliv. 25.   [2] Deut. xviii. 14.

give rise to perplexing comparisons. A former Popish missionary declared," the Bishop says, " in the distress of his mind, that Buddhism must have been the rival system and master-plot of Satan, to hinder the progress of the Christian (*i.e.*, Romish) faith." Poor man ! he little knew that his own religion was, like the Buddhists, derived from the same Babylonian source ; both being undoubtedly of Satanic origin, and expressly designed by the author of them in direct antagonism to the truth.[1]

And if it be true, as some writers, well versed in this subject have affirmed—and I have myself not the least doubt of the fact—that when the Talé-Lama in Thibet dies, and his child successor is elected, and Buddh is said to come down and possess the one, who is to manifest him in future to the faithful, a child of not more than three or four years old is made to assume the countenance of a wise and solemn legislator, and to utter discourses that none but the most highly cultivated intellect could possibly have delivered ; we have in this case the clearest and most unmistakable evidence of demoniacal possession ; and that Buddhism itself was invented by Satan, and is still upheld by spirit mediums and demoniacal power.[2] That Satan

---

[1] See the Writer's " Babylonianism ; or, the Devil's Travesty of the Kingdom of the Son," advertised at the end of this volume.

[2] Messrs. Huc and Gabet, in their Travels in Tartary, Thibet and China, speak of the then Talé-Lama, as " a child of nine years old," and state that he had *then* " for six years occupied the palace of the Buddha-La " : so that he could have been only *three years old*, when he was elected ! Vol. ii., p. 197.

is now energizing with mighty power in that subtle system of iniquity; and that its worshippers are awfully deluded thereby, and are intensely earnest and sincere in their belief of its being of Divine origin, is shewn by the recent self-sacrifice of a Phoongyee, who was the inheritor of the monastery of the late Thinka-raja, the most revered priest of Akyab; and who lately immolated himself before certain relics of Buddha, by first wrapping himself with a cloth saturated with kerosine oil, and then tying himself over a pot full of oil; when he set the whole on fire, and thus destroyed himself. The full account is given in "The Graphic," of the 12th January, 1889, where some illustrations are appended of the pan over which he sat, of some remains of his body, and of the temple built to receive his ashes. As it appears he was only thirty-two when he died; and he had been Phoongyee for nearly twenty years, he must have been very young, when the so-called "spirit of Buddh" entered into him!

One can easily understand, under such circumstances, that many of the miracles performed to attest such false doctrines, may have been genuine ones, *i.e.*, performed by a power more than human—but most assuredly that power must have been demoniacal. And I have not the slightest doubt myself, that *several* of the miracles recorded by Romish writers have been *real* ones: only as they have been performed to attest *false* doctrines, we can most unhesitatingly pronounce them, under the authority of Deut. xiii. 1-3, and other passages, to have been *performed through Satanic or demoniacal agency.* The Romish Church has exorcisms for the casting out of devils; and Liguori in his Chap. X., Sec. 5, upon "The Adjuration of Devils," speaks against "holding *useless* conversations with the possessing devil;" and cautions the exorciser to "beware lest he should *joke with the devil:*" but as Bishop Taylor truly says, when speaking of the Romish adjuration :— "This is the manner of their devotion, described for the use of their exorcists; in which is such a heap of folly, madness, superstition, blasphemy, and ridiculous guises and *playings with the devil*, that if any man amongst us should use such things, he would be in danger of being tried at the next Assizes for *a witch* or a conjuror; however, certain it is, whatever the devil loses [?] by pretending to obey the exorcist, he gains more by this horrible debauchery of Christianity"! It is certain, however, that *the devil loses nothing by it;* for *he* cannot *thus* be cast out : because our Lord Himself has expressly told us that "If Satan cast out Satan, he is divided against himself; how shall then his Kingdom stand?"[1]

III.—And this leads me to the third division of my subject : in which I propose to enter into some details, respecting the more modern manifestations of "Spiritualism," *so-called.*

Mesmerism, which is essentially allied with Spiritualism, has been supposed to have originated with

----

[1] Mat. xii. 26.

Fried. Anton. Mesmer, who was born at Meersburg, on the 25th of May, 1733; and whose system was brought into notice about 1776: but this is a great mistake; as the paintings on the Egyptian temples shew that it was practised by the Egyptian priests thousands of years before his time. " Spiritualism " has also been supposed to have *originated* with the Fox family at Hydesville, in the State of New York, in the year 1848: but this is as great a mistake as the other; for Spiritualism, *as such*, originated in ancient Babylon, even if it be not as old as the days of Nimrod.

But to come down at once to modern times.

The celebrated Daniel De Foe, who was the author of " Robinson Crusoe," and who wrote the History of the Plague, in the reign of Charles the 2nd, published a book, under the name of Andrew Moreton, Esq., entitled, " The Secrets of the Invisible World disclosed," (a third edition of which was published, after his death, in 1738); in which he gave an account of many remarkable " apparitions, both antient and modern." But, so far as I can ascertain, I believe it was the Rev. Joseph Glanvil, who was Chaplain-in-ordinary to Charles the 2nd himself, and a Fellow of the Royal Society, who first published a record of any attempt of the demons *to communicate with men;* and thereby to induce men *to communicate with them.*

His work is entitled, " Sadducismus Triumphatus; or, Full and Plain Evidence concerning Witches and

Apparitions;" the third edition of which was published in 1689. In this book, he gives a remarkable account of the persecution of a Mr. John Mompesson, of Tedworth, in the county of Wilts, by a demon, or demons: which commenced in 1661, and lasted nearly two years. —he himself having witnessed some of the occurrences which he records. It appears that in the month of March, in that year, Mr. Mompesson, as a county Magistrate, had ordered the arrest of a vagrant drummer: who had been greatly annoying people by begging and drumming about the country; and had taken his drum away from him. About the middle of April following, Mr. Mompesson and his family began to be disturbed by " strange noises and hollow sounds," and " thumping and drumming "; not only in different parts of his house, but " on the top of it; " until " by degrees that went off into the air." " For an hour together it would beat ' Round-Heads and Cuckolds,' the ' Tattoo,' and several other points of war, as any drummer. After this, they would hear a scratching under the children's bed, as if by something that had iron talons." Mr. Cragg, a minister, was called in to investigate the matter; and " he went to prayers with them, kneeling at the children's bedside; where it was then very troublesome and loud. During prayer time it withdrew into the cock-loft; but returned as soon as prayers were done: and then, in sight of the company, the chairs walked about the room of themselves, the children's shoes were hurled over their heads, and every loose thing moved about the chamber." He afterwards remarked, "that *it would exactly answer* in drumming anything that was beaten, or *called for*."

Mr. Mompesson and his friends, believing that the vagrant drummer must have been in league with the devil, who was at the bottom of the whole affair; on one occasion, "during the time of the knocking when many were present, a gentleman of the company said, 'Satan, if the drummer set thee to work, give three knocks and no more'; which it did very distinctly, and stopt. Then the gentleman knockt *to see if it would answer him as it was wont;* but it did not. For further trial, he bid it, for confirmation, if it were the drummer, to give five knocks and no more that night, which it did; and left the house quiet all the night after. This was done in the presence of Sir Thomas Chamberlain, of Oxford, and divers others."

The drummer was consequently apprehended again; this time for felony under James I., chap. 12, and indicted for witchcraft; but although there was abundant evidence on oath in proof of the *disturbances*, there was not the least evidence adduced of *the drummer having caused*, or been connected with, *them :* and so he was discharged—the *demon's evidence not being admitted !*

These things created an immense sensation at the time in the country; but what followed, or whether this was or was not, the *first* time, in a Protestant country, when the demons sought to induce men to communicate with them, I know not: but they certainly made another, and a bolder attempt, to do so in

5

the time of the Wesleys; and through the Wesley family. Dr. Adam Clarke, in his " Memoirs of the Wesley Family," says, " Mr. John Wesley believed that it was a messenger of Satan sent to buffet his father for his rash promise of leaving his family, and very improper conduct to his wife, in consequence of her scruple to pray for the Prince of Orange as King of England."

It would seem from the narrative of Mr. John Wesley, who then came to see his father, the Rev. Samuel Wesley, at the Parsonage at Epworth, in the Isle of Axholme, Lincolnshire, that the disturbances commenced on the 2nd of December, 1716. Knockings at the doors, " a hand mill whirled about very swiftly," without anybody to turn it, " the gobbling of a turkey cock close to the bed side," and the " sound of one stumbling over boots and shoes," when nobody was there, were the first manifestations to two of the servants, a man and a woman: who afterwards related these things to the other maid; who called them " a couple of fools," and " defied anything to frighten her" ! However, on the evening of the next day, she was so frightened herself at what she heard, that she threw down a tray, with all its contents, which she was then carrying, " and ran away for life."

The demon then turned its attentions to the children: for " the next evening," says Mr. John Wesley, " between five and six o'clock, my sister Molly, then about 20 years of age, sitting in the dining-room reading, heard as if it were the door that led into the hall open, and a person walking in that seemed to have on a silk night-gown, rustling and trailing along. It seemed to walk round her, then to the door, then round again; but she could see nothing. She thought, 'It signifies nothing to run away; for, whatever it is, it can run faster than me.' So she rose, put her book under her arm, and walked slowly away." After supper, she told " what had happened " to her " sister Sukey (about a year older than her) in one of the chambers:" who " made quite light of it, telling her, 'I wonder you are so easily frighted: I would fain see what would frighten me.' Presently a knocking began under the table. She took the candle and looked, but could find nothing. Then the iron casement began to clatter, and the lid of a warming-pan. Next the latch of the door moved up and down without ceasing. She started up, leaped into the bed without undressing, pulled the bed-clothes over her head, and never ventured to look up until next morning. A night or two after, my sister Hetty (a year younger than my sister Molly) " . . . " heard one coming down the garret stairs, walking slowly by her, then going down the best stairs, then up the back stairs, and up the garret stairs; and at every step it seemed the house shook from top to bottom.

" In the morning she told this to my eldest sister, who told her, ' you know I believe none of these things : pray let me take the candle to-night [*i.e.* to their father] and I will find out the trick.'" The next night, however, she heard the knockings herself, and opened the door, and found no one there; and " when she went to shut the door it was violently thrust against her; but she set her knee and her shoulder to the door, forced it to, and turned the key. Then the knocking began again; but she let it go on, and went up to bed. However, from that time she was thoroughly convinced that there was no imposture in the affair.

"The next morning, my sister telling my mother what had happened, she said, 'If I hear anything myself, I shall know how to judge.' Soon after she begged her to come into the nursery. She did, and heard, in the corner of the room, as it were the violent rocking of a cradle; but no cradle had been there for some years. She was convinced it was preternatural, and earnestly prayed it might not disturb her in her own chamber at the hours of retirement; *and it never did!* She now thought proper to tell my father. But he was extremely angry, and said, ' Sukey, I am ashamed of you. These boys and girls frighten one another; but you are a woman of sense, and should know better. Let me hear of it no more.'

"At six in the evening he had family prayers as usual. When he began the prayer for the king, a knocking began all round the room, and a thundering knock attended the *Amen!*" On this Mr. John Wesley remarks, " The year before King William died, my father observed my mother did not say amen to the prayer for the king. She said she could not, for she did not believe the Prince of Orange was king. He vowed he would never cohabit with her until she did. He then took his horse and rode away; nor did she hear anything of him for a twelvemonth. He then came back and lived with her as before. But I fear his vow was not forgotten before God."

Mr. John Wesley then " walked over " to Haxey, to see " Mr. Hoole, the vicar of Haxey (an eminently pious and sensible man)," on the subject ; and he came back with him, as it would seem, at the request of his father, the Rev. Samuel Wesley himself, to investigate the matter. Mr. Hoole, in narrating what then took place, says, " We went up-stairs ; he [*i.e.*, the Rev. Samuel Wesley] with much hope, and I (to say the truth) with much fear. When we came into the nursery, it was knocking in the next room ; when we went there, it was knocking in the nursery. And there it continued to knock, though we came in, particularly at the head of the bed (which was of wood), in which Miss Hetty and two of her younger sisters lay. Mr. Wesley, observing that they were much affected—though asleep, sweating, and trembling exceedingly—was very angry, and, pulling out a pistol, was going to fire at the place from whence the sound came. But I snatched him by the arm, and said, ' Sir, you are convinced this is something præter-natural. If so, you cannot hurt it ; but give it power to hurt you.' He then went close to the place, and said, sternly, ' Thou deaf and dumb devil ! why dost thou fright these children, that cannot answer for them-selves ? Come to me, in my study, that am a man !' *Instantly it knocked his knock* (the particular knock which he always used at the gate) as if it would shiver the board to pieces ; and we heard nothing more that night."

" Till this time," says Mr. John Wesley, " my father had never heard the least disturbance in his study. But the next evening, as he attempted to go into his study, (of which none had the key but himself,) when he opened the door, it was thrust back with such violence as had like to have thrown him down. However, he thrust the door open and went in. Presently there was a knocking, first on one side, then on the other, and after a time in the next room, wherein my sister Nancy was. He went into that room, and, the noise continuing, adjured it to speak, but in vain."

That these disturbances were produced by demons, there seems to me to be no question whatever : for the Rev. Samuel Wesley himself said, " I have been thrice *pushed by an invisible power*, once against the corner of my desk in the study, a second time against the door of the matted chamber, a third time against the right side of the frame of my study door, as I was going in." Mr. John Wesley also said, that " when it was in any room, let them make what noise they would, as they sometimes did on purpose, *its dead, hollow note would be clearly heard above them all !* The sound very often seemed in the air in the middle of a room ; *nor could they ever make any such themselves, by any contrivance !*" Moreover, " our large mastiff dog," said he, when the disturbances first began, " used to bark and leap, and snap on one side and the other " : but " after two or three days *he used to tremble, and creep away before the noise began.* And by this the family knew it was at hand ; nor did the observation ever fail."

It is perfectly clear also to me, from a perusal of the whole narrative, that the demon, or demons engaged in this business, *sought to induce some of the members of the family at least to communicate with them;* and thus to put themselves in their power : for when Mrs. Wesley, in the first instance, " believed it to be rats, and sent for a horn to blow them away," Emily Wesley said, " from that time it was so outrageous, there was no quiet for us after ten at night;" and *it was always " more loud and fierce if anyone said it was rats, or anything natural !"* But she said afterwards, " it would *answer my mother* if she stamped on the floor and *bid it !* It would knock when I was putting the children to bed, just under me, where I sat. One time *little Kezzy*, pretending to scare Polly, as I was undressing them, *stamped with her foot on the floor ; and immediately it answered with three knocks, just in the same place !"*

And the effect of all this is seen, in what Mr. John Wesley himself afterwards says about it :—" *By this time all* my sisters were so *accustomed* to these noises that they *gave them little disturbance.* A GENTLE TAPPING at their bed-head usually began between nine and ten at night. Then they commonly said to each other ' Jeffrey is coming : it is time to go to sleep.' And if they heard a noise in the day, and said to my *youngest sister*, ' Hark, Kezzy, Jeffrey is knocking above,' she would run up-stairs and pursue it from room to room, saying *she desired no better diversion* " *!* Indeed one of the daughters, Emily Wesley, afterwards Mrs. Harper, seems to have been troubled by the spirit for years after : for writing to her brother John, on the 16th of February, 1750, (*i.e.*, 34 years afterwards,) she says, "You won't laugh at me for being superstitious if I tell you how certainly that *something* calls on me against any extraordinary new affliction ; but so little is known of the invisible world that I, at last, *am not able to judge whether it be a* FRIENDLY *or an* EVIL SPIRIT " !¹

"Several gentlemen and clergymen," says Mr. John Wesley, " advised my father to quit the house. But he constantly answered, 'No : let the devil flee from

---

¹ Since the above was written, I have met with the following, which is extracted from *Cassell's Old and New London* for April :— "Towards the end of February, 1772, the Rev. John Wesley was in conclave with some of his preachers, when a Latin note was put into his hand. It caused him evident astonishment, for the substance of it was as follows :—

"' Great Bath-street, Coldbath Fields, 1772.

"' Sir,—*I have been informed in the world of spirits* that you have a desire to converse with me. I shall be happy to see you if you will favour me with a visit.

"' I am, Sir, your humble servant,

"' E. Swedenborg."

" Wesley frankly acknowledged that he had been strongly impressed with a desire to see him, but that *he had not mentioned that desire to anyone.* He wrote an answer that he was then preparing for a six-months journey, but he would wait upon Swedenborg on his return to London. Swedenborg wrote in reply that *he should go into the world of spirits on the 29th of the next month,* NEVER MORE TO RETURN ! The consequence was that these two remarkable persons never met." For " *Swedenborg died on the day he had predicted to Wesley,* at 26, Great Bath-street, Coldbath Fields ! " See also page 34.

me ; I will never flee from the devil ' : " and so acting upon the Scriptural admonition, " Resist the devil, and he will flee from you ; "[1] he was at length, (*i.e.,* after about two months of it,) entirely delivered from any further molestation on his part.

And here I would only remark, that *if* the demons, *by these means, then* sought to induce men generally to communicate with them, they were certainly on *that* occasion, baffled in their attempt to do so : possibly, because their hour had not then come.[2]

It was different, however, in the year 1848 : for *then* the demons found a people ready to be deceived by them ; and since then " Spiritualism," *so-called*, has made fearful progress in the world : and it ought to be specially noted that *the means* which the demons *then* adopted for making their presence known, and thus inducing men to communicate with them, were *precisely the same*, as those which they adopted in the time of Charles the 2nd, as well as in the days of the Wesleys ! These last manifestations, as is now well

---

[1] James iv. 7.

[2] Although the demons were unsuccessful in their attempt to induce *the Wesley family* to communicate with them : yet it is quite possible, nay even probable, that they induced *some others* at that time to do so : for the writer of " Spirit-workers in the Home Circle," whose book I shall hereafter have occasion to refer to, heads one of his chapters, with a quotation from a work, entitled, " *Justice and Reason, Faithful Guides to Truth*," by Charlotte McCarthy, dedicated to King George the Third, published by subscription, 1767, in which she speaks of a spirit-voice, and of a spirit lighting her fire, &c.—several instances of which the writer himself of " Spirit-workers " also gives from his own experience.

known, commenced in a house, situate in the village of Hydesville, not far from Newark, in the County of Wayne and State of New York, U.S.A.—the house having been taken by a Mr. John D. Fox, during the erection of another dwelling-house by him in the County. Mr. and Mrs. Fox had 6 children; the two youngest only of whom, Margaret, then 12 years old, and Kate, then 9, removing with them into the house in question, on the 11th of December, 1847.

The manifestations commenced, almost as soon as they entered; various noises and knockings occurring in different parts of the house, which they could not account for; and which they at first *attributed to rats!*[1] *Then the knockings became louder, and more frequent;* and noises were heard, as of people walking about in different parts of the house. On the family trying to persuade themselves, that there must be some *natural* cause for the disturbances, the bedclothes began to be *pulled by an invisible hand;* the youngest child felt as if a cold hand had been put over her face; and the chairs were moved from their places, &c., yet, notwithstanding, all this, they still imagined that there must be some *natural* explanation of the disturbances, which they had not yet fathomed; and this hope they clung to until the 31st of March, 1848; when wearied out by restless nights, and vain attempts to solve the mystery, they retired that evening very early to rest. The parents had removed the children's beds into their

---

[1] See also page 71.

own bedroom ; but scarcely had the children been put to bed by their mother, before they cried out, "Here they are again!" Then the noises became much louder than usual, and more startling in their character. The night being stormy, the father was called in, and examined the window-sashes, to see if any of them were loose ; but could discover nothing to account for the noise ; only it was remarked with astonishment, that when he shook one of the sashes, *the noise seemed to reply to him in precisely the same way !* Whereupon Kate, the youngest child, who was then sitting up in bed, (and like the youngest child of the Rev. Samuel Wesley, seemed to have got accustomed to the rappings,) snapped her fingers towards the place from whence the noise proceeded ; and, I doubt not, at the secret suggestion of one of the demons themselves, called out, "Here, old Splitfoot, *do as I do!" when the knocking at once responded at her bidding !* Then she mentally sought for a response by bringing her thumb and forefinger together ; and was *answered at once by the spirit knocking in reply !* Calling her mother's attention to it, "Only look, mother;" and repeating the movement in her sight, the mother now for the first time began to suspect that there must be something supernatural about the whole affair : as it was evident that the intelligent being directing these movements, could both *see,* as well as *hear,* what was going on !

Whereupon *she at once addressed the spirit herself ;* and put various questions to it, *all of which it replied*

to in an intelligent manner, which greatly astonished
her. Then she asked, "Are you *a man?*" to which
question, she received no reply. "Are you *a spirit?*"
when it instantly rapped out, to indicate that it was!
"*May my neighbours hear if I call them?*" she said:
*when it again rapped out a cordial assent to the
proposal!* Thereupon she called in a neighbour, a
Mrs. Redfield, who came in laughing; but who was
afterwards immensely astonished to find, on questioning the spirit, that it gave answers which thoroughly
convinced her that it must have been an intelligent
being, who had replied to them! Then the neighbours, attracted by the rumour, crowded in one after
another, many of whom put questions to the spirit,
and received pertinent replies; until at length the
whole neighbourhood was aroused; and in an incredibly short space of time "Spiritualism" began to spread
over the face of the whole country. And thus the
demons at length succeeded, not only in communicating
generally with men, *but in inducing professing Christians to "apostatize from the faith," by also communicating with them!* And the Editor of "Psychic
Notes," a publication to which I shall hereafter have
occasion more particularly to refer, writing on the 2nd
of January, 1882, (only 34 years after!) *then* estimated
the number of "Spiritualists" *in America alone* at
about 20 millions! And in a number of "Word and
Work," for April 7th, 1887, the Editor refers to an
American writer of some note, whom, however, he
does not name, who thus, he says, "graphically de-

lineates in a few lines one aspect of Boston life"—
Boston, which used to be considered *the most religious
city* in the whole of the United States :—"There is one
singular aspect of the intellectual life of Boston. It is
that presented, not by its sturdy scepticism, but by its
popular credulity. There is probably no city in the
world that is more sceptical and more superstitious
and more credulous than Boston. *Everywhere* are
to be seen the sign and advent of the seer, the
prophet, *the soothsayer*, THE PYTHONESS, *the turner of
tables*, THE MEDIUM OF SPIRITS, *the reader of stars*, and
the measurer of souls. Walking the streets, *one is
carried back to the times of Elymas the sorcerer, and of
Simon Magus ;* to the world of Appolonius of Tyana,
and of Alexander of Abonotichus! Yet at the same
time is the modern Athens the citadel of New England
Puritanism, and the headquarters of open-eyed Uni-
tarianism ; while perhaps the apex of absurdity and
contradiction is the curious fact that the Irish have
captured the city, and run the political machine" !

"Spiritualism," as is well known, was introduced
into *this* country from America, about the year 1852 ;
and alas! *the demons found a people also willing to be
deceived by them even here ;* and now they number
many hundreds of thousands ; and their numbers seem
to be increasing every year. Even in the year 1858,
only 6 years afterwards, the "Westminster Review"
for January in that year, thus spoke of the movement :
—"We should be in much error if we supposed that
table-turning, or that group of asserted phenomena

which in this country is embodied under that name,
and which in America assumes the loftier name of
Spiritualism, in ceasing to occupy the attention of the
public generally, has also ceased to occupy the attention of every part of it. *The fact is very much otherwise.* Our readers would be astonished were we to lay
before them the names of several of those who are
unflinching believers in it, or who are devoting themselves to the study or reproduction of its marvels. Not
only does it survive, but survives *with all the charm
and all the stimulating attractiveness of a secret science,*
until the public mind in England shall be prepared to
receive it, or until the evidence shall be put in a shape
to enforce general conviction, *the present policy is to
nurse it in quiet, and enlarge the circle of its influence
by a system of noiseless extension !* Whether this
policy will be successful remains to be seen ; but there
can be no doubt that, should ever the time arrive for
the revival of this movement, the persons at its head
would be men and women *whose intellectual qualifications are known to the public, and who possess its confidence and esteem* " !

Since then Spiritualism has vastly increased in extent
and influence ; and no longer seeks to hide itself, but
lyingly and unblushingly vaunts itself as a heaven-sent
messenger from the God of Truth Himself, as the after
pages of this book will abundantly prove. The Editor
of " Psychic Notes," writing in January, 1882, amongst
other learned and able men, claims for spiritualists, the
Earl of Dunraven ; the late Lord Lytton ; the late Mr.

Sergeant Cox, President of the Psychological Society of Great Britain; the late William Howitt, the brilliant writer; the late George Thompson; Gerald Massey; S. C. Hall, F.S.A.; the late Hon. R. Dale Owen, some time Minister of U.S.A. at the Court of Naples; the Hon. J. L. O'Sullivan, some time Minister of the U.S.A. at the Court of Lisbon; the Hon. J. W. Edmunds, some time Chief Justice of the Supreme Court of New York; the late Professor Maples, the eminent chemist, U.S.A.; the late Dr. Robert Hare, Professor of Chemistry at the Medical University of Pennsylvania, U.S.A.; Bishop Clarke (Episcopalian) of Rhode Island, U.S.A.; Darius Lyman, of the Treasury Department, Washington; William Crookes, Editor of the "Quarterly Journal of Science," Gold Medallist, and Member of the Council of the Royal Society; A. R. Wallace, F.R.G.S., the eminent naturalist, some time President of the Biological Section of the British Association for the Advancement of Science; Captain R. F. Burton, the celebrated traveller; and a host of others, of equal celebrity.

A mere catalogue even of the permanent literature of Spiritualism and cognate subjects would fill many pages of this book:[1] but the following must suffice as samples

---

[1] Mr. H. D. Jeneken, Barrister-at-law, M.R.I., in a paper read by him before a Committee appointed by the "London Dialectical Society," on the 13th of April, 1869, stated that there were then "upwards of 500 works which had been published by different authors upon Spiritualism and its phenomena; and that periodicals on the subject were being published in all known languages."

—" The Report on Spiritualism of the Committee of the London Dialectical Society "—" Researches on the Phenomena of Spiritualism," by William Crookes, F.R.S. — " Transcendental Physics," by Professor Friedrich Zöllner, of Leipzig—" Miracles and Modern Spiritualism," by Alfred Russel Wallace—" Psychography," by M. A. Oxon—" Spirit Identity," and " The Highest Aspects of Spiritualism," by the same author— " The Debateable Land," and " Footfalls on the boundary of another World," by Robert Dale Owen— Howitt's " History of the Supernatural," &c., &c., &c.

Their organs also are very numerous, and are ably edited ; among which might be mentioned, " Light," " The Spiritualist," " The Theosophist," " The Banner of Light," " The Phrenological Journal and Science of Health," " The Religio-Philosophical Journal," " The Harbinger of Light," &c., &c.

And when we consider that it is only about 36 years since " Spiritualism " first began to put forth its energies in *this* country, its progress in these kingdoms has been truly marvellous. In opening out this part of my subject, therefore, I shall (1) give details of various cases, which have been communicated to me by persons upon whose testimony I can implicitly rely ; and (2) give extracts from various printed documents, detailing circumstances, that have taken place in the presence of other persons unknown to me ; but whose veracity I have no reason whatever to question.

While a Mr. Hockley, to whose testimony before the Committee I shall hereafter have occasion to refer, said that he had " nearly 1,000 volumes on occult sciences " *himself!*

1. Accounts which have been communicated to me by persons upon whose testimony I can implicitly rely.

When Mesmerism came more particularly into notice in this country, now upwards of 40 years ago, many Physicians and Clergymen adopted it, with a view of practising upon, and curing, persons afflicted with such diseases as epilepsy and paralysis, &c. ; and it certainly is a sign of the times, that " Medical Mesmerism " is now so rapidly coming to the front, and is finding much favour amongst a class, which once branded it as charlatanism. The " Standard," in an article on this subject, on the 12th of January, 1889, quoting from an enthusiastic paper by a medical man in the " Nineteenth Century," observes that " it is now seriously contended that there is a scientific basis for *a revival of the old use of mesmeric trances* in the way of curing such chronic diseases and morbid habits as ordinarily come under the notice of the Physician ;" and he refers, amongst others, to a " Mesmeric Hospital " at Calcutta, to the Hospital Clinique at Nancy, and to the famous old Salpetrière Hospital in Paris, which " has been of late years the scene of numberless trials of ' hypnotism ' and ' suggestion,' under the general countenance of Professor Charcot, but really by that Physician's assistants, and on their individual responsibility." He also states " that it is now practised extensively among the upper and middle classes at Amsterdam ;" and that " the movement, both scientific and practical, has so far progressed as to support a *Revue d'Hypnotisme*, published at Paris once a month."

6

I remember about the time I have named, having
the curiosity to attend a Lecture, which was adver-
tized to take place in the Temperance Hall, in Barton-
upon-Humber, professedly upon "Phrenology;" but
which really turned out to be a Lecture upon "Mesmerism." Among other things, the operator, after
having put his medium, a slim lad of about 16 years
of age, into the mesmeric trance, and done various
things with him, suddenly de-mesmerised him; and
then told 6 of the strongest men in the room to hold
back his arms, which the mesmerizer had stiffened
horizontally to his body; the lad at the time standing
upright. Six powerful men from the brick yards immediately came forward, and held fast hold of his
arms; 3 on each side. The mesmeriser then threw
intense energy into his countenance, his eyes starting
almost out of his head, and made the passes with great
force and rapidity; when the lad swept his arms in
front of him, towards the operator, with the greatest
ease imaginable; pulling the 6 men forward with him
with great violence, notwithstanding their intense
efforts to resist the impulse, and to their utter and
profound astonishment; while the lad himself remained
otherwise perfectly motionless, as if this had been no
effort on his part whatever! Can there be any doubt,
that the power that was communicated to this youth,
on this occasion, was of the same character, as that
which was imparted to the man possessed of the
demons, recorded in Mark v. 1-7, and Luke viii. 26-29,
to which I have before referred ?[1]

---

[1] See page 18.

An elderly lady some short time since told me that several years ago, she was paying a visit to a physician, who practised mesmerism, with a view of curing diseases; who had at that time under his care, a lady, who had been addicted to opium eating. Having of course, as a medical man, to keep the drug, he hid it behind some bottles on the top shelf of his surgery; where he thought it was impossible for her to reach it, as there were no steps in the room. To his profound astonishment, however, it disappeared; and he could not find out how, or who had taken it: as the lady herself denied all knowledge of the fact. Then he bethought him of putting her into the mesmeric trance; and touching the organ of conscientiousness, while she was under the influence, and again questioning her on the subject, she told him that she *had* taken it; and that she had succeeded in procuring it, by piling up pieces of the furniture one upon the other, until they had reached the top shelf; when she had mounted up upon them and abstracted it.

A lady friend of mine, the late Mrs. Carter of Epsom, who resided for some years in that town, told me several years ago, that the then vicar of the parish, used to practise mesmerism, with the object of curing diseases; and on one occasion, he took her to see one of his epileptic patients. Among other things, to shew her his complete power over her, he told my friend that he would draw an imaginary line upon the table in the room, and then bid his patient pass her hand over it, which she would be unable to accomplish, until he had removed the hindrance he had interposed. This he did: and then asked the poor woman, to pass her hand over the table. This she was able to do, until she came to the imaginary line; when, strive as she could, she seemed utterly powerless to advance any further; and then, with a look at my friend, he removed the obstruction; and asking the woman to make another attempt, she at once passed her hand freely over whatever part of the table she chose.

There can be no doubt that the so-called " Thought Reading" movement likewise, which is now making such a stir among a certain class of sight-seers, is very much allied to mesmerism; and a physician, who attended at a "so-called 'Thought-reading,'" at the Literary and Scientific Institution at Croydon, in September, or October, 1888, writing to the Editor of the " Croydon Chronicle," says, " The operator seemed to be in a state of nervous excitability, *suggesting the recorded condition of* THE DELPHIC PYTHA, *when inhaling the natural gas which gave her prophetic power!*" But this is of course a mistake: as *no gas could ever give any such power:* and the Scriptures themselves assure us (as we have seen),[1] that it was *a demon,* who inspired *the Delphic Pytha* to utter the oracular responses, which were given forth from that Temple.[2]

Some time since I happened to overhear a portion of a conversation between a Doctor and a young minister; who were evidently discussing some such subject as this. The Doctor observed,

---

[1] See pages 18 & 19.   [2] Acts xvi. 16-19.

" Have you done anything *yourself* lately in that line ?"

" No ; " replied the young minister, " I haven't : *it takes it out of one so !* "

" This testimony is true ; " and we shall see it abundantly confirmed later on : but does this not form the strongest possible objection to such practices ; as well as the clearest proof even *in itself*, of its not being of God ? For " where the Spirit of the Lord is, there is *liberty*."[1] But where Satan rules, there is, and ever must be, *bondage ?*[2] " And as he was yet a-coming," *i.e.*, to Jesus, " *the demon threw him down, and tare him. And Jesus* rebuked the unclean spirit, and *healed* the child.' '[3] " Will he plead against me," says Job, " with His great power ? No ; but *He* would *put strength in me.*"[4] " Surely, shall one say, *In Jehovah* have I righteousness and *strength :* even to *Him* shall men come ; and all that are incensed against Him shall be ashamed.' '[5] Therefore, " I will go *in the strength* of the Lord Jehovah : I will make mention of Thy righteousness, even of Thine only.' '[6]

With reference to table-turning, I remember many years ago, some young children of a clergyman, near Halifax, in Yorkshire, whom I well knew, through the evil example of some companions, I believe, trying their hands at this sort of thing ; and after *ordering a table* to perform all sorts of antics, which *it obeyed* ;

---

[1] 2 Cor. iii. 17.　　[2] John viii. 34 ; 2 Tim. ii. 26.　　[3] Luke ix. 42.
[4] Job xxiii. 6.　　[5] Isa. xlv. 24.　　[6] Psa. lxxi. 16.

they at length succeeded in actually getting it *to follow them*, without any intervention on their part—indeed they could not possibly of themselves have accomplished it—*up a pair of stairs*, to their profound amusement and delight: little imagining, poor things, by whose power such a result had been attained!

A very intelligent old lady, who is moreover an excellent Hebrew and Greek scholar, and whose husband several years ago kept a School in Derbyshire, for the education of children of the upper classes, related to me the following extraordinary circumstances, which she strictly vouched for, as being perfectly true.

She said that she first heard of " Spiritualism," so-called, in the year 1851, from a lady, who had sent her son to be educated with her husband, who is since dead. This lady, in the course of conversation, said to her,

" Don't you find it difficult to find amusement for your pupils in the evening? Why don't you introduce table-turning among them? "

Not having heard of it before, and in consequence of what this lady said, she thought she would investigate the matter. About the same time also, her husband, who took in the " Morning Advertiser," a paper then edited by the late Mr. James Grant, pointed out to her therein an account of a séance by Mr. Home, in the house of a clergyman at Ealing. This awakened her curiosity; and when a clergyman from a neighbouring village, who it appeared had had frequent séances at his own house, called upon them some short time afterwards, and had some conversation with her on the subject, at his request, she consented to have a séance in her husband's school-room: the Clergyman and his sons undertaking to conduct it. In this room there was a long heavy school-room table, upon the four corners of which the boys put their hands. This table had four heavy legs; and under the manipulation of these boys, *and at their request*, it performed many wonderful things; amongst others, turning gently over; *seemingly* of its own unaided power, and settled upside down, with its four legs in the air. The Clergyman then got into it, as into a boat, the four boys placing their fingers on the bottom part of each of the upturned legs of the table: when some one present called out, "Turn him out:" upon which the table immediately sprang up, and with a violent jerk, to the astonishment of all present, threw the clergyman out with great force upon the floor! This took place about the year 1856.

On the same occasion, this same table, *without any direction or suggestion from anyone*, pushed a relation of my informants, into a corner of the window: while those present tried in vain to hold it back. The husband of the lady becoming alarmed fled to the door, to get out of the room; *when the table immediately followed him*, and would evidently have gone out after him, had it not been stopped by a projection near the door, which further barred its progress! This séance was quite sufficient for the lady in question: who then began to suspect that some evil supernatural power must have been at the bottom of the whole business.

The mother of these boys had, it appeared, some time before, introduced table-turning into her own house; by requesting her eldest son, who was subject to epileptic fits, to put his hands on the table, while she was playing the piano: which he at once did, when he immediately exclaimed, " Oh, mother, all the badness is going out of my head down my arms, into the table ! "

This lady used frequently to play upon the piano, during a séance; and if she played " a jiggy sort of tune," the table, which was so heavy, that it took two men to lift it, would come up to her, and nudge her gently on the elbow, as if to tell her to desist; but if she played a lively tune, or a better class of music, the table would move about, almost gracefully, as if in unison with the music. This, and other things which took place, induced the clergyman to believe that some supernatural intelligent being must necessarily have directed the movements of the table; and at a séance not long after the above occurrence, he wrote upon a slate, " If you are *an intelligent being, directing this table*, do three things that you have never done before:" when the table at once complied, and did them. My informant now, however, only remembers one of them; which was that the table should advance towards the bell, lift up one of its legs, and ring it: which it perfectly accomplished! All these things took place in Derbyshire, in which county my informant still resides.

In another Rectory, in that County, a Curate, who

had been in the habit of attending the séances held at the house of the Clergyman above mentioned, prevailed on his Rector to have a séance at his Rectory. At this séance the Rector, his wife, and the Curate, sat for about half an hour with their hands upon a small round table, without any result. The table then began to move round with great rapidity, so fast indeed that the old Rector could not keep pace with it, and ran out of the room; upon which the table *broke away from his two companions and pursued him;* actually following him for some distance down the stairs, when it fell down.

About the year 1858, another lady in Derbyshire told my informant, that while she was narrating to a cousin of hers some of the marvels of " Spiritualism," which, however, she herself did not believe; her cousin, who was a large powerful man, remarked to her, while pointing to a large round heavy table in the room,

" Do you mean to say, that if I placed my hand on the centre of that table, and bid it to rise, it would do so; if I were endued with spiritual power? "

She replied, " That is what they *say.*"

Whereupon he strode up to the table, and placing his hand upon the centre of it, in a determined tone, commanded it to rise; but no movement followed. Again he repeated the command, in a louder and more imperious tone: but with a like result. A third time, in a still louder tone, and with a dreadful oath, he commanded it to rise; when the heavy table instantly sprang up, and before he could get out of its way, it

knocked him over with great violence; and so injured
him, that he was ill from the blow he then received for
several weeks! Does not this at once call to mind,
the case of the evil spirit, and the seven sons of Sceva,
recorded in the Acts of the Apostles,[1] and which I
have before referred to in the earlier part of this
book?[2]

My informant told me, that the lady, who first
mentioned the subject of "table-turning" to her,
became insane, and died a raving maniac. The Clergyman and his wife, whose sons conducted the séance
in her husband's schoolroom, are likewise both dead;
and their whole family have gone to ruin! Indeed she
assured me, that in an experience of upwards of 35
years, she never knew any person (and she has known
many,) who had been deeply engaged in "Spiritualism,"
who had not either become cripples, had died suddenly,
or had come to some terrible, or untimely end!

Since then I have met with the widow of a Primitive
Methodist Minister, a very intelligent person, who has
furnished me with the following particulars of some
other cases of a much more recent date.

She said that she was in Bradford some few years
since, and heard an American lady, who professed to
be a "Spiritualist," and who said that *she was possessed by the spirit of an eminent lawyer,* who had died
some time before in the United States, deliver in public
a most remarkable lecture, upon a subject which was

---

[1] Acts xix. 13-16.   [2] See page 18.

chosen for her by the audience, out of five other subjects, that had been named by persons present in the room at the time. At that time she utterly disbelieved in the reality of Spiritualism herself; supposing the whole thing to be imposture—the effects produced being due to conjuring tricks of some kind or other; and she attributed the power and eloquence displayed by the lecturer on this occasion to her marvellous talent and her wonderful intellectual attainments: but afterwards conversing with the lecturer herself on the subject, and being asked by her to come to a séance to be held by her, at which she promised her that she should have an interview with her dead husband, (which she positively refused to do,) she began to think that there must be something weird and unnatural about it.

Her suspicions were more than confirmed some time afterwards: for going to reside in Liverpool in 1886, she stayed for a time in a so-called " Faith-healing " Establishment ; where she was put into a room, which struck her at once as being somewhat *uncanny :* although she is naturally a person of strong nerves, and not to be put out with a trifle. In this room she was disturbed night after night by the most mysterious cracks and noises, which she could not account for. She bore it bravely for some time ; endeavouring by every means in her power to ascertain the cause of the phenomena : but without success. She then complained about it to the keeper of the Establishment, and asked to be put into another room. Her request was complied with : but this room turned out worse than the other ; for the noises were louder, more mysterious, and more continuous. She remained about 3 weeks altogether in these two rooms; until she could stand it no longer, when she left the Establishment altogether. She was afterwards informed by a fellow-lodger, that a Clergyman, *who had been a " Spiritualist,"* had been brought in ill into the *first* room, and had *died in the second!*

While there, another circumstance occurred, which was of a very remarkable character. A most fearful looking object was brought in on one occasion, and committed to the care of a black man, who was a Christian. About one or two o'clock the next morning my informant told me, that she was suddenly awakened by the most hideous howlings and awful groanings, that she had ever heard in her life. They seemed utterly unearthly, and they struck a real terror into her spirit. At first she thought that they proceeded from some persons in the street: but she soon perceived that they emanated from some one in the house. These unearthly noises were succeeded by a loud quacking as of ducks, and then as if a parrot were talking loudly: and this again was succeeded by a loud roaring as of a lion. She was perfectly horrified, and jumping out of bed, and rapidly putting on some clothing, she rushed out upon the landing. There she found a number of the other lodgers all huddled together, in a state of the wildest terror. They soon perceived that the sounds proceeded from the room occupied by the wretched creature, who had been brought in the night before; but no one durst venture into the room itself. At length some of the men in the house joined the trembling group on the landing ; and bolder than the rest, thrust open the door of the room, and entered it ; she herself peeping in cautiously after them. The sight, she said, was truly awful. There sat the wretched creature bolt upright in bed, with his eyes literally starting out of his head, his hands held up and his fingers bent like bird's claws, and with a face like a demon ; shrieking, and cursing, and blaspheming in the most awful manner possible : while the black man was vainly endeavouring to calm him ! The sight was so horrible, she said, that she could not bear to look upon him ; and she involuntarily hid her face in her hands. But being a good woman, and a bold one, she proposed that they should all enter the chamber, and unitedly pray for him ; which eleven of them did, crouching in a corner of the room, as far from the wretched object as they could ; and at the same time averting their eyes from him, and pleading with the Lord that He would have mercy upon him, and deliver him out of the power of the adversary. But the more they prayed, the louder he blasphemed and cursed ; until at length, as my informant told me, she felt that she had got a hold on God ; and *in the name of Jesus*, she implored Him to cast the demon out of the man : when in an instant, he became calm, his countenance assumed a totally different aspect ; and he praised God for his deliverance, thanked them from the bottom of his heart, for their goodness to him, and implored them to forgive him for his awful curses and blasphemies against them ;

which he said he could not help, having felt absolutely impelled to utter them !

This case thoroughly convinced my informant, that there *are* such things as demoniacal possessions in these days : and she has since been informed by the keeper of the house in question, that the man referred to became a true Christian, and is now working for the Lord. She likewise at the same time told her something of the history of the Clergyman before mentioned. From her account, it seemed that, although he knew it to be wrong, he had attended Spiritualistic meetings in London for some time, until at length he became perfectly infatuated with them : but subsequently desiring to free himself from the fatal influence, he found that *he was quite unable to do so;* as he *then* discovered to his horror and dismay, that *he was possessed by evil spirits;* WHO TORE HIM IN A MOST DREADFUL MANNER :[1] so that he could get no rest, either day or night ! At his urgent request, the keeper of the house in question went to see him ; and he was ultimately brought to her Establishment ; and *she* assured my informant, that he was at length delivered, and died in peace.

2. And now I shall give extracts from various printed documents, detailing circumstances, that have taken place in the presence of other persons unknown to me ; but whose veracity I have no reason whatever to question. And in treating upon this portion of my

---

[1] See pages 18 & 85. See also Mark ix. 20; Luke ix. 42.

subject, I shall (1) quote from the "Report on Spiritualism, of the Committee of the London Dialectical Society; together with the evidence, oral and written, and a selection from the Correspondence," published in 1871; (2) select instances, culled from "Psychic Notes—a Record of spiritual and occult Research, and of the séances held in Calcutta by Mr. Eglinton, during November 1881 to March 1882," published in Calcutta, in 1882; and (3) give several extracts from a work entitled, "Spirit workers in the Home Circle, an Autobiographic Narrative of Psychic Phenomena in family daily life extending over a period of 20 years," by Morell Theobald, F.C.A., published in London in 1887.

(1). Quotations from the "Report on Spiritualism," &c. In presenting their Report, the Committee stated that they had held 15 meetings, at which they received evidence from 33 persons, "who described phenomena which, they stated, had occurred within their own personal experience." They "received written statements relating to the phenomena from 31 persons." They "invited the attendance and requested the co-operation and advice of scientific men who had publicly expressed opinions, favourable or adverse, to the genuineness of the phenomena;" and they "also specially invited the attendance of persons who had publicly ascribed the phenomena to imposture or delusion." They stated, that "while successful in procuring the evidence of believers in the phenomena

and in their supernatural origin," they " almost wholly
failed to obtain evidence from those who attributed
them to fraud or delusion." " As it appeared to " the
Committee " to be of the greatest importance that
they should investigate the phenomena in question
by personal experiment and test, they resolved themselves into " six " Sub-Committees as the best means
of doing so." " All of these " " sent in reports, from
which it appears that a large majority of the members "
—36 in number, consisting amongst others, of Doctors
in Divinity, Physicians, Surgeons, Barristers-at-Law,
Fellows of the Royal Geographical Society, Civil
Engineers, &c.—were " actual witnesses to several
phases of the phenomena without the aid or presence
of any professional medium, although the greater part
of them commenced their investigations in an avowedly
sceptical spirit."

" These Reports," the Committee said, " substantially
corroborated each other, and would appear to establish
the following propositions :—

" 1.—That sounds of a very varied character, apparently proceeding from articles of furniture, the
floor and walls of the room—the vibrations accompanying which sounds are often distinctly
perceptible to the touch—occur, without being
produced by muscular action or mechanical contrivance.

" 2.—That movements of heavy bodies take place
without mechanical contrivance of any kind or
adequate exertion of muscular force by the

persons present, and frequently without contact or connection with any person.

" 3.—That these sounds and movements often occur *at the.times and in the manner asked for by persons present*, and, by means of a simple code of signals, answer questions and spell out coherent communications.

" 4.—That the answers and communications thus obtained are, for the most part, of a common-place character; *but facts are sometimes correctly given which are only known to one of the persons present.*"

They also stated that "the oral and written evidence received by them," "not only testified to phenomena of the same nature as those witnessed by the Sub-Committees, but to others of a more varied and extra-ordinary character"—evidence which they say "may be briefly summarised as follows :—

" 1.—Thirteen witnesses state that they have seen heavy bodies—in some instances men—*rise slowly in the air and remain there for some time without visible or tangible support.*

" 2.—Fourteen witnesses testify to having seen *hands or figures, not appertaining to any human being, but life-like in appearance and mobility, which they have sometimes touched or even grasped*, and which they are therefore convinced were not the result of imposture or illusion.

" 3.—Five witnesses state that they have been touched, by some invisible agency, on various parts of

7

the body, *and often where requested*, when the hands of all present were visible.

" 4.—Thirteen witnesses declare that they have heard musical pieces well played upon instruments not manipulated by any ascertainable agency.

" 5.—Five witnesses state that they have seen red-hot coals applied to the hands or heads of several persons *without producing pain or scorching;* and three witnesses state that they have had *the same experiment made upon themselves with the like immunity.*

" 6.—Eight witnesses state that they have received precise information through rappings, writings, and other ways, *the accuracy of which was un-known at the time to themselves or to any persons present, and which, on subsequent enquiry, was found to be correct.*

" 7.—One witness declares that he has received *a precise and detailed statement which, neverthe-less,* PROVED TO BE ENTIRELY ERRONEOUS!

" 8.—Three witnesses state that they have been present when drawings, both in pencil and colours, *were produced in so short a time, and under such con-ditions, as to render human agency impossible.*

" 9.—Six witnesses declare that they have received *information of future events,* and that in some cases *the hour and minute of their occurrence have been accurately foretold, days and even weeks before.*"

" In addition to the above," the Committee stated, that " evidence had been given " to them " of trance-speaking, of healing, of automatic writing, *of the introduction of flowers and fruits into closed rooms, of voices in the air, of visions in crystals and glasses,* and of the elongation of the human body." They also stated, that "many of the witnesses had given their views as to the sources of these phenomena"—"*some attributing them to the agency of disembodied human beings, some to Satanic influence,* some to psychological causes, and others to imposture or delusion."

Such then in brief is the Report of the Committee appointed by "The London Dialectical Society," "to investigate the phenomena alleged to be Spiritual Manifestations;" the accuracy of which I have no reason whatever to question: as it perfectly agrees with other evidence, which has been culled on this subject from many various independent sources elsewhere. And as samples of the evidence adduced before the Committee, I append the following—

At a sitting of the Committee, held on the 27th of April, 1869, Mr. Benjamin Coleman, of Upper Norwood, appeared before them; and, among other things, said, "I was staying at Malvern with my wife and daughter. We had apartments at the house of Mr. Willmore, who had a wife and daughter likewise in the house; the daughter, a young woman about 23 years of age. There were also in the house two visitors, Miss Lee, of Worcester, and Mr. Moore, of Halifax. . . . *Willmore, who had been a Bath man with Dr. Gully, asked me if I would be good enough to let him see something of Spiritualism before the mediums left the town.* I accordingly requested the Marshalls to spend an hour or two on the following day (*Sunday*) with Willmore's family, who invited some of their neighbours to form a circle. I and my family spent the day out, and returned home between 10 and 11 o'clock at night ; when my wife and daughter retired to bed and left me in our sitting-room. Shortly afterwards, Willmore, in great excitement came to me, and begged that I would come down stairs immediately for he did not know what to do ; *he said his wife, his daughter and Miss Lee were all in hysterics.* I followed him at once, and upon entering the room, *a small three-legged table met me at the door,* NO ONE TOUCHING IT, and *made me a graceful bow as if to say,* '*How do you do ?*' One of the females was on the sofa screaming, and the others in different parts of the room throwing themselves about in a state of great distress. I went up to the other end of the room to Miss Lee, *the table following me and standing by my side,* whilst I endeavoured to calm her. I had nearly succeeded in doing so, *when the table made a jump at her,* and threw her again into violent hysterics ; her screams were responded to by the other females. Matters looked so serious that I felt it necessary to take a decided part with the table, and seizing it with both hands, I lifted it into the centre of the room and said, '*Now spirits you have done quite enough,* I command you to leave this place in God's name.' *They appeared to obey my injunctions, for nothing further took place!*"

Communicating these facts the next morning to Dr. Gully, Mr. Coleman, at the doctor's request, invited the Willmores to his rooms in the evening ; when he stated that they "had some very remarkable messages through the table!" And he adds, "I believe I am right in saying that this was the first direct evidence Dr. Gully had ever had of *spirit communion* [!] *He is now, as is well known, a firm believer*, which he boldly and undisguisedly avows. Dr. Wilson, of Malvern, also investigated the phenomena about the same period, *and became a convert in consequence* [!] Both were previously *avowed materialists*."

My intelligent readers will no doubt perceive the subtlety of the demon, who acted upon, and spoke through this table ; and will note the similarity of this case with others that have been before recorded.

A Mr. Burns stated at the same sitting, that "on two occasions, when my wife has been ill, the spirits have rapped out remedies *which cured her as soon as they were applied*."

At another sitting of the Committee on the 8th of June, 1869, a Mr. Thomas Shorter said, "I have repeatedly seen a table incline forward to an angle of 45 degrees, or more ; the candle, lamp, water-bottle, ink-stand, pencils, &c., remaining on the table as if they were a part of it. At other times I have seen the table rise *perpendicularly* from the floor, our hands all resting on the top of the table. . . . I have repeatedly seen *mental questions answered by the table*. . . . We had been holding a séance in the drawing-room of

Dr. Dixon, 25, Bedford Row, and had thought the
séance was ended ; after a little conversation the doctor
began playing his concertina. *On the first note being
played the table rose from the floor, and kept up a
rhythmical motion as the tune went on* CORRESPOND-
ING TO THE MUSIC, *and which continued as long as
the air was played !* "

Compare with this, the case referred to at page 88.

At the same sitting a Mr. Hockley said, " *I have
been a spiritualist for 45 years, and have had considerable experience.* This is a crystal encircled with a silver ring. . . I knew a lady who was an admirable
seeress, *and obtained some splendid answers by means
of crystals.* The person who has the power of seeing,
notices first a kind of mist in the centre of the crystal,
and then the message or answer appears in a kind of
printed character. There was no hesitation, and she
spoke it all off as though she was reading a book ; and
as soon as she had uttered the words she saw, they
melted away, and fresh ones took their place. I have
30 volumes, containing upwards of 12,000 answers
received in this way. . . . *A crystal,* IF PROPERLY
USED, SHOULD BE DEDICATED TO A SPIRIT. [!!] Some
time ago I was introduced to Lieutenant Burton by
Earl Stanhope, and he wished me *to get him a crystal,*
WITH A SPIRIT ATTACHED. [!!] I also gave him *a
black mirror*[1] as well, *and he used that in the same
manner as you would a crystal. You invoke the per-*

---

[1] See the case of the Egyptian Sorcerer, recorded at page 32.

son whom you wish to appear, and the seer looks in, and describes all; *and puts questions and receives answers!* Lieutenant Burton was greatly pleased, and went away. One day *my seeress called him into the mirror.* She plainly recognised him, although dressed as an Arab and sunburnt, and described what he was doing. He was quarrelling with a party of Bedouins in Arabia, and speaking energetically to them in Arabic. An old man at last pulled out his dagger, and the Lieutenant his revolver; when up rode a horseman, and separated them. A long time afterwards, Lieutenant Burton came to me; and I told him what she had seen, and read the particulars. *He assured me it was correct in every particular, and attached his name to the account I had written down at the time, to certify that it was true*" [!!]

At another sitting of the Committee, held on the 22nd June, 1869, Mr. D. D. Home, the Spiritualist, was asked by a Mr. Bennett, "What are your sensations when in a trance?" when he replied,

"I feel for two or three minutes in a dreamy state, then I become quite dizzy, and then I lose all consciousness. *When I awake I find my feet and limbs quite cold, and it is difficult to restore the circulation.* When told of what has taken place during the trance, *it is quite unpleasant to me;* and I ask those present not to tell me at once when I awake."

In reply to another question from a Mr. Atkinson, as to "the difference between manifestation in and out of a trance," Mr. Home replied,

" In a trance I see spirits connected with persons present. *These spirits take possession of me ;* MY VOICE IS LIKE THEIRS. I have a particularly mobile face, as you may see, *and I sometimes take a sort of identity with the spirits who are in communication through me.* I attribute the mobility of my face, which is not natural, to the spirits. . . . . I may say *I am exceedingly sick after elongations.* While in Paris I saw the figure of my brother, then in the North Sea. I saw his fingers and toes fall off. Six months afterwards tidings came of his having been found dead on the ice, his fingers and toes having fallen off through the effects of scurvy."

Compare again with this the conversation recorded at page 85, and the statement of the widow of the Primitive Methodist Minister at page 94.

In reply to some questions put by Mr. Coleman, Mr. Home said, " Once I was elongated 8 inches. A man was standing holding my feet. In one case I was laid on the floor, and Lord Adare had hold of my head, and the Master of Lindsay of my feet. The elongations were not confined to my legs, for I seemed to grow very much from the waist. I have seen a table lifted into the air with 8 men standing on it, when there were only 2 or 3 other persons in the room. . . . . In the house of Mr. and Mrs. S. C. Hall, a table went up so high in the air, that we could not touch it. I have seen a pencil lifted by a hand to a paper and write, in the presence of the Emperor Napoleon. We were in a large room—the Salon Louis Quinze. The Empress sat here, the Emperor there. The table was moved to an angle of more than 45 degrees. Then a hand was seen to come. It was a very beautifully formed hand. There were pencils on the table. It lifted, not the one next it, but one on the far side. We heard the sound of writing, and saw it writing on note paper. The hand passed before me, and went to the Emperor, and he kissed the hand. It went to the Empress; she withdrew from its touch, and the hand followed her. The Emperor said, 'Do not be frightened, kiss it;' and she then kissed it. It was disappearing. I said I would like to kiss it. The hand seemed to be like that of a person thinking, and as if it were saying, 'Shall I?' It came back to me, and I kissed it. The sensation of touch and pressure was that of a natural hand. *It was as much a material hand seemingly as my hand is now.* The writing was an autograph of the Emperor Napoleon I. The hand was his hand, small and beautiful as it is known to have been."

Mrs. Cox, of Jermyn Street, the next witness, " stated that she had seen levitations. She saw Mr. Home rise gradually in the air, and make a cross on the ceiling with a pencil. . . . *She had felt the spirit form of her baby, and could believe she was still nursing it in the flesh!* She corroborated Mr. Home as to the existence of spirit hands and forms. . . . She was cured by a spirit touch. . . . *There was a very elevated tone in the instruction of the spirits,* AND SHE BELIEVED SHE WAS A BETTER PERSON UNDER THEIR INFLUENCE [!!].

At the same sitting, Signor G. Damiani said, "Whilst in Sicily, quite recently, a most telling poem, 200 lines long, in the Sicilian dialect, besides communications in German, French, Latin, and English, have been received in my presence, the medium in this case being a singularly illiterate person of the artisan class! I have met in Clifton with a boy medium, between 10 and 11 years of age, who would write long essays on spiritual philosophy; the matter and manner of these essays being such as would have been accepted from any accomplished writer of mature age, who was conversant with the subject. I took the well-known Alessandro Gavazzi to a *séance* with this youthful medium. The acute polemist put various abstruse metaphysical and theological questions to the medium, *or rather to the medium's controlling spirit*, and received replies so deep and learned, as to convince him that it was no mere case of ' clever boy!' This young medium—whose writings now extant would fill a dozen volumes—*exhibited a different handwriting for every controlling spirit, by whom he was directed;* and wrote occasionally in several of the dead languages!"

Compare with this also the case mentioned at page 60. See also Div. IV. Sec. 3 ; Div. VII. Sec. 5.

He then related having attended at several "voice séances," "with different mediums, and in the presence of numerous investigators;" where, he said, "I have for hours together conversed with voices, which could not on either of these occasions have proceeded from any living person in the room wherein, for the time being, we were assembled." And amongst other reasons, for his being certain that they were not produced by ventriloquism, he stated, that "these voices have conversed with me upon matters known to me alone;" and "have often foretold events about to happen, which events have invariably come to pass!"

On being asked by a Mr. Meyers, "Are there any *wicked* spirits?"

"*Yes*," said Signor Damiati, "and *lying* spirits." And then he gave a remarkable instance in point, where a spirit, at a séance at Mrs. Marshall's, had professed to be the spirit of Dr. Livingstone, and had given a minute account of how he had been killed by the natives in Africa, and afterwards boiled and eaten: which was of course a tissue of lies from beginning to end!!

He was then asked by the Chairman, Dr. Edmunds, "How can you distinguish between a *medium* who is an *impostor* and a *spirit* that is a *liar?*" to which he was obliged to confess,

"*You cannot distinguish*, but in that case *it was the spirit that was lying* [!] Mrs. Marshall would have had no object in telling me an absurd story about Livingstone being killed and boiled and eaten. *And the explanation* THE SPIRITS GAVE *was this*—'You came here,' they said, 'out of curiosity, *and you found an impertinent spirit, who amused himself at your expense.*' It was simply the trick of *a ragamuffin spirit*" [!!!]

A "Mr. Glover then described various phenomena which he had witnessed in the presence of Mr. Home. . . . . He had made a study of the time of the coming of the Lord, and *he was informed that the Lord would* come in August [!] *The spirits also pointed to texts in the Bible* [!] He made a cross in a circle, and asked, in the name of the Father, Son, and Holy Ghost, *if the communications were* OF GOD, *and the answer was* 'No!' He then asked *if they were* OF THE DEVIL, *and the answer was,* 'YES!' *He believed Satan did it all to deceive men* "!!

Upon this Mr. Coleman (a Spiritualist) asked him " If Spiritualism brings sceptics to believe in *a hereafter*, would you still think it to be *demoniacal?* " to which he at once replied,

" *Yes. For the object of the devil is to get you to deny the Atonement.* THE TEACHING IS CONTRARY TO THE GOSPEL, AND THEREFORE IT MUST BE OF SATAN! "

At a subsequent sitting of the Committee held on the 20th July, 1869, a " Mr. Chevalier, who was the first witness called, stated that he had had 17 years' experience of Spiritualism; but it was not till 1866 that he commenced experimenting on tables. He obtained the usual phenomena, such as raps and tiltings, and answers to questions. On one occasion, the answer which was given being *obviously untrue*, the witness peremptorily inquired why a correct answer had not been given, and *the spirit in reply said,* 'BECAUSE I AM BEELZEBUB' [!!] Mr. Chevalier, in continuation said. . . . At my meals, I constantly rested my hand on a small table, and *it seemed to join in the conversation.* One day the table turned at right angles, and went into the corner of the room. I asked, ' Are you my child?' but obtained no answer. [He had previously supposed that he had been talking to his dead child, through the medium of the table.] I then said, 'Are you from God?' but the table was still silent. I then said, 'In the name of the Father, Son, and Holy Spirit, I command you to answer, are you from God?' One loud rap, *a negative* was then given. 'Do you believe,' said I, 'that Christ died to save us from sin?' The answer was 'No!' 'Accursed spirit,' said I, 'leave the room.' The table then walked across the room, entered the adjoining one, and quickened its steps. It was a small tripod table. It walked with a sidelong walk. *It went to the door, shook the handle*, and I opened it. The table then walked into the passage, and I repeated the adjuration, receiving the same answer. *Fully convinced that I was dealing with an accursed spirit*, I opened the street door, and the table was immediately silent; no movement or rap was heard. I returned alone to the drawing-room, and asked if there were any spirits present. Immediately I heard steps like those of a little child outside the door. I opened it, and the small table went into the corner as before; just as my child did when I reproved it for a fault."

"Reflecting on these singular facts," he afterwards adds, "I determined to inquire farther and really satisfy myself that the manifestations were what I suspected them to be. I went to Mrs. Marshall's and took with me 3 clever men, who were not at all likely to be deceived. I was quite unknown; we sat at a table, and had a *séance; Mrs. Marshall told me the name of my child.* I asked the spirit some questions, *and then pronounced the adjuration.* We all heard steps, which sounded as if some one was mounting the wall; in a few seconds the sounds ceased, and although Mrs. Marshall challenged again and again, the spirits did not answer, and she said she could not account for the phenomenon. *In this case I pronounced the adjuration mentally; no person knew what I had done.* At a *séance*, held at the house of a friend of mine, at which I was present, manifestations were obtained, and as I was known to be hostile, I was entreated not to interfere. I sat for two hours a passive spectator. I then asked the name of the spirit, and it gave me that of my child. 'In the name of the Father, Son, and Holy Ghost,' said I, 'are you the spirit of my child?' It answered '*No!*' and the word '*Devil*' was spelled out."

And in conclusion, he justly remarks, " My opinion of these phenomena is that *the intelligence* which is put in communication with us *is a fallen one. It is of the devil, the prince of the power of the air.* I believe *we commit* THE CRIME OF NECROMANCY, *when we take part in these spiritual séances!* "

Mr. Hain Friswell said, " I may say that I can corroborate all that has been said by the witness relative to the power of the adjuration to stop the manifestations."

" The Countess de Powar in reference to the opinion of Mr. Chevalier that *a spirit which did not believe in*

Christ must be bad, said that *it was hard to suppose that good Mahometans or persons of other* NON-CHRISTIAN FAITHS *should not have* GOOD SPIRITS." [!]

" Miss Anna Blackwell then spoke. Her sister, she said, was very incredulous, and would not believe in Spiritualism in the least. Nevertheless, she herself became what is called a writing medium. The spirit would use her hand to write what communication had to be made. *The spirits wrote what was good and bad.* ONE WANTED TO SIGN HIMSELF SATAN AND BEELZE-BUB. But, continued Miss Blackwell, my sister did not believe in the least in the existence of such a spirit, and she said, ' No; if you are permitted to come to me it is not to tell such outrageous lies ! If you persist in trying to impose on me you sha'n't write.' I have been present at many of these little fights. She would resist the spirit, and when she saw the capital S of the Satan being written, she would resist and twist her hand about to prevent the name being written. *The spirit has then written,* ' I HATE YOU BECAUSE I CANNOT DECEIVE YOU!' I have on some occasions heard beautiful raps in my drawing-room—in the air, on the wall, in the ground —no one being near the furniture. *We never begin without prayer* [!] *We say to the spirits that wish to deceive us,* ' Dear spirits, we are all imperfect; *we will endeavour to benefit you by* OUR LIGHTS [!!] *in so far as they are superior to yours* ' [!] Sometimes they would overturn and break the table. *Yet they were rendered better* [!!] *by our kindness* [!!] We would never dream of addressing one as an 'Accursed spirit.' *From one who was very violent, and by whom I have been myself struck*, we have received progressive messages, *showing how he has* BECOME BETTER [!!] They have often sent us messages, saying, '*We are going up higher now; we have* THROUGH YOUR HELP, *broken the chains of earth;* and we leave you!' When my sister found the S being written, or the great B for Beelzebub, she would say, *with kindness but firmness* [!!], 'Dear spirit, *you must not deceive;* it is not for such tricks,. but *for a good end* [!] that you are permitted to come.'" [!!]

Mr. Hain Friswell said, "I will be brief in the statement which I have to make, and I will preface it by a remark which shall be still more brief. I am a loose hanger-on of the Church of England, sceptical as to spiritual tricks, and with an inclination to Mr. Chevalier's theory. Well, I was once employed by a celebrated Journal to get certain facts ; I spent ten pounds, twenty pounds, without getting them. While I was going along by Mrs. Marshall's, I thought I would look in, and I entered. The table was so crowded that I could not get a place at it, of which I was very glad, for I wanted to be a spectator only, and I sat by the fire. *The table moved tremendously and came to me!* There was a paper written underneath it; the words were, 'Let the scribe come to the table'! I sat at the table. *There was a sort of cataleptic seizure of those present,* which principally affected the ladies! *They foamed at the mouth and shook each other!* They then began to talk nonsense and to prophesy. I, wishing to put a stop to this, and *feeling that it was what the Apostles might have witnessed*, WHAT WAS DESCRIBED BY TERTULLIAN AND OTHERS, put my hand on the table and said, '*Are you the spirit who imposed on Ananias, the sorcerer?*' The answer was, '*Yes.*' I said, 'In the name of God depart—go away!' He went away, and so did the scribe" !

Mr. D. H. Dyte put the question to the witness, "You put your hand on the table when you willed that it should all cease?" to which he replied,

"Yes, I put my hand gently on the table and rose, repeating mentally the adjuration."

"Had the adjuration anything to do with it?" again asked Mr. Dyte.

"As a Christian I believe so," rejoined the witness. "*The governess of my children, one of my daughters, and another young lady*, have sat at a table and had raps, answers to foolish questions, &c. *I put a stop to it all by the use of the adjuration.*"

In addition to the *vivâ voce* evidence taken before the Committee, a great many written communications were sent to them likewise; to three only of which, however, I shall refer. Two of these relate to houses, which seem to have been haunted by spirits—one being a detailed account, thoroughly established by independent testimony, respecting a house at Port Glasgow, in Scotland, in 1864; and the other, being an account transmitted to the Committee by a Mrs. Lætitia Lewis, on the 20th Nov., 1870, from Erchless

8

Castle, Beanly, Inverness-shire, respecting her house in
South Wales, during the spring of that year: upon
"the wonderful spiritual manifestations" in which,
(which she said had "occurred *spontaneously* to" herself and her "daughter,") she had previously consulted
"a near relative who is a Clergyman in the Church of
England"—cases which tally in many respects with
the one related by the widow of the Primitive Methodist Minister, recorded at pages 91, 92.

The third communication is one from Mr. W. M.
Wilkinson, of 44, Lincolns Inn Fields, on the 12th of
May, 1869, enclosing "a piece of written evidence,
which," he says, "I attest the truth of." The evidence
enclosed is an extract from an article in, or a communication to the Editor of, the "Spiritual Magazine," for
April, 1860, by J. Lockhart Robertson, M.D., of Hay-
ward's Heath, near Brighton; in which, after enumer-
ating many of the usual manifestations of the spirits on
such occasions, he says, "At the writers' request, this
table"—"a heavy circular table, made of birch and
strongly constructed," which had previously been "lifted
a somersault in the air and thrown on the bed"—"*was
afterwards smashed and broken*, and one fragment
thrown across the room." "*This occurred in half a
minute!* The writer has since vainly endeavoured,
with all his strength, to break one of the remaining legs.
The noise of the table thrown and knocked about *by
unseen agency* on the floor. . . . *was really awful
and mysterious!*"

And he wisely concludes his paper thus:—"The
writer cannot accept as emanations from the Spirit

revelations of a spiritual nature inconsistent with his intuitive conception of the nature and attributes of God. He cannot trace the dignity of the divine power in breaking cedar pencils and tables, or ringing bells, nor its wisdom in the mild communications of the medium writings. He believes that *if God meant to reveal to him that this Spiritualism was the work of His Holy Spirit, He would not have given His will in the very heathenish oracular manner here recorded!* He fails to see anything like divine wisdom or divine power in these unreasoning medium writings and grotesque physical phenomena. . . . His own impression is, that *the power is similar to that manifested* AT THE DELPHIC ORACLE, *and by* THE ANCIENT SORCERERS AND MAGICIANS, *and he believes that* THE SPIRIT OF PYTHON, *silenced by the incarnation*, HAS REVIVED WITH SOME OF ITS ANCIENT POWER!!" And this is, of course, the real truth of the matter.

2. And now I have to furnish select instances of Spiritualistic phenomena, culled from "Psychic Notes; A Record of Spiritual and Occult Research:" the first number of which was published in Calcutta, on the 2nd Jan., 1882, and the last on the 27th of April, in the same year. And if Spiritualism has made rapid advances in these Kingdoms of late years; of which the foregoing pages have furnished ample proof; it is as nothing to its progress in India: where, in conjunction with a so-called Esoteric Buddhism and Theosophy, it is advancing with gigantic strides indeed!

Speaking of the *Theosophical Society*, the Editor says, " The rapid growth of the Society, since its foundation in 1875, is almost entirely due to the indefatigable exertions of Madame Blavatsky and Col. Olcott, both of whom work the year round, and one might say, night and day, with an energy that nothing can tire! Col. Olcott left Bombay on the 17th of February, on a tour of inspection among the Society's Branches, visiting Jaipur, Delhi, Meerut, Bareilly, Lucknow, Cawnpore, Allahabad and Berampore, on the way to Calcutta—a journey of over 2,300 miles." He then states, that after his return to Bombay, he was to " take steamer to Ceylon, where he is engaged to deliver 71 lectures on *Buddhism*, in the Southern Province ; " and " a strong desire is expressed to hear him discourse upon *Theosophy* at Calcutta." While in a subsequent number of his " notes," published on the 27th April, 1882, writing, as it would seem, *after* Col. Olcott's visit to Calcutta, he says :—" There has been a good deal of interest excited, *in the native community especially*, by the recent visit to Calcutta, of Col. Olcott and Madame Blavatsky, the Founders of the Theosophical Society. With respect to them and their work, opinions are, of course, divided, but no one will deny that if notoriety were their object they have had it to the full. .   .   .   No other Society that we know of has more untiring indefatigable and enthusiastic officers, and, as we remarked in a former number, the exceptional growth of this one is due to their exertions!"

And quoting, approvingly in a former number, from
a paper published in "Light;" in which the writer
said, "that *Theosophy* is not antagonistic to *Spiritualism*, but rather a broadening out of the latter; and
that Spiritualism, or communion with human spirits is
only *one phase of Theosophy!*"—he now adds:—
"Deep thinkers, or rather *clear* [!] thinkers, are inclined to believe that *the necessary outcome of Modern
Spiritualism is Theosophy;* after passing through the
stage of phenomenalism *that of philosophy must be
entered,* or the investigator will have wasted his time!
. . . . Is there any such noble study in nature as
this quest after the psychic powers? We think not;
and as *this quest is Theosophy,* the world owes a debt of
gratitude [?] to the founders of this Society, who have
taken materialistic science by the beard, so to say, and
forced it to look in the glass of ancient history and
discover its imperfections. . . . Our *duty* [!] is
done in calling attention to it, and *in affirming as the
result of personal experience, that* ESOTERIC THEO-
SOPHY *is a branch of research full of* SPIRITUAL CON-
SOLATION, *and* INTELLECTUAL REFRESHMENT!!"
The Madame Blavatsky here spoken of, is a Russian
lady, who was born in 1831, at Ekaterinoslav, her
maiden name being Hahn. She was ushered into the
world, according to her biographer, " amid coffins and
desolation," and was " quickened by several deaths in
the house." As the infant was but half alive, she was
at once baptised into the Greek Church; and when
"the sponsors were just in the act of renouncing the

Evil One and his deeds, a renunciation emphasised in the Greek Church by thrice spitting upon the invisible enemy, . . . the little lady, toying with her lighted taper at the feet of the crowd, inadvertently set fire to the long flowing robes of the priest, no one remarking the accident till it was too late. The result was an immediate conflagration, during which several persons—chiefly the old priest—were severely burnt." This was felt to be an ominous beginning; and her nurses seemed to have encouraged her in the belief that she was born to have dealings with the spiritual world: for they called her "Sedmitchka, an untranslatable term, meaning one connected with number seven;" and "she was carried about in her nurse's arms," when she was a mere infant, "around the house, stables and cow-pen, and made personally to sprinkle the four corners with water, the nurse repeating all the while some mystic sentences!"

When about fourteen, "amidst the strange double life she led from her earliest recollections, she would sometimes have *visions of a mature protector*, whose imposing appearance dominated her imagination from a very early period!" She married at 16 a man, whom she did not love; and she left him a year after: and then, as "Madame Blavatsky," she "abandoned her country at 17, and passed 10 long years in strange and out-of-the-way places, in Central Asia, India, South America, Africa, and Eastern Europe!" She seems first to have been *instructed in occult lore* by "an old Copt at Cairo *of great reputation as a magician!*"

Later on she made friends with *the Red Indians,* on the Fenimore Cooper basis. At New Orleans, she *learned magic from the negro Voodoos!* Afterwards she engaged the companionship of *a Hindoo " chela," or witch,* and an Englishman *in search of magic knowledge;* and she sailed with them to India; and *here* she found what she had been long seeking for! She then herself seems to have been *endued with demoniacal and superhuman power:* and was enabled to perform similar miracles to those of the Indian fakirs; such as fixing tables to the floor, so that no person could move them; breaking glasses in the hands of persons who held them; while she herself stood at a distance, with her eyes intently fixed upon the object itself, &c., &c.

Later on, in describing her own condition of advancement, she says:—" I am solely occupied, not with writing 'Isis,'[1] *but with Isis herself!* I live in a kind of permanent enchantment, *a life of visions and sights with open eyes,* and no trance whatever to deceive my senses! *I sit and watch* THE FAIR GODDESS *constantly!!* And as *she displays before me the secret meaning* of her long-lost secrets, and the veil, becoming with every hour thinner and more transparent, gradually falls off before my eyes, I hold my breath and can hardly trust to my senses! . . For several years, in order not to forget what I have learned elsewhere, I have been made to have permanently before

---

[1] She was, I suppose, then writing her book, which she has since published, entitled, " Isis unveiled "!

my eyes *all that I need to see!* Thus, night and day, the images of the past are ever marshalled before my inner eye. Slowly, and gliding silently, like images in an enchanted panorama, centuries after centuries appear before me!" . . [*"And the devil . . . shewed unto Him"*—Jesus—*" all the kingdoms of the world in a moment of time!"* Luke iv. 5.] " And I am made to connect these epochs with certain historical events, and I know there can be no mistake! Races and na- tions, countries and cities, emerge during some former century, then fade out and disappear during some other one, the precise date of which I am told by. . . ! Hoary antiquity gives room to historical periods ; *myths are explained by real events and personages who have really existed;* and every important and unim- portant event, every revolution, a new leaf turned in the book of life of nations—with its incipient course and subsequent natural results—*remains photographed in my mind!"*[1]

Such, in brief, is the history of *one of the founders of the so-called Esoteric Theosophy!!* And now for the selected instances of Spiritualistic phenomena from " Psychic Notes," to which I have before referred.

In this Fortnightly Serial, a writer stated that in a séance held at Calcutta, in the house of a Mr. Mengen, on the 29th of November, 1881, two blank cards, por- tions of which had been torn off the corners for iden-

---

[1] Extracted from " Incidents in the life of Madame Blavatsky," compiled and edited by **A. P. Sinnett.**

tification, were placed with "a morsel of pencil," "within the leaves" of two separate books, in full light. "After a very short time the first book was opened, and the following words were found distinctly written on the card :—

"'*Spiritualism* fully understood must be *the means whereby you shall derive true comfort and a thorough knowledge of the divine will!!* Since I have been in spirit life I fully perceive *the errors* one is likely to make *by a refusal to seek into new truth.* Truth which is "always strange—stranger than fiction." And I praise God that in my ascended—'

"Here the first card ended, and the conclusion of the message was found on the other card, as follows :—

"'State, *my knowledge of a glorious immortality* HAS BEEN PROVEN!! *Then hasten ye who scoff, and enter and find true solace and freedom from doubt,* which an uncertain future has for you! Your Friend, John Williams.'

"From the time of placing the first card in the book to the end of the manifestation," the writer added, "all was in full light, and when the jagged end was tried upon the card it fitted perfectly."

The Indian Mirror, of January 7th, 1882, stated, that at "the last séance, held with Mr. Eglinton at the house of Baba Denonath Mullick, *a spirit lady,* the mother of two of the gentlemen present, *fondled and caressed her sons*—tears of joy welling forth from one of them when he felt beyond a shadow of a doubt that his revered mother was still living!! A strange voice, *recognized as that of the late Mr. Benjamin Coleman*,[1] a prominent Spiritualist in London, addressed all the sitters *in a most impressive manner, and exhorted them to* GOOD DEEDS AND ACTIONS [!!] when in the midst of their communion with their friends!"

The Editor, referring to what he calls "those wonderful 'materializations' *in the light*," refers to one which had then "recently taken place at New York, through the mediumship of the Rev. T. W. Monck, D.D. Judge Daly in giving his endorsement to the manifestations, says—in the 'Banner of Light'—'A few nights ago, while at a séance the medium passed under the control of his friend and guide "Samuel." *I beheld a mist-like appearance issuing from the Doctor's side'* [a statement, which I would have my readers particularly to note] which gradually condensed, and *assumed the form and features of my little daughter in ethereal beauty and perfection!* From *this* a voice came, saying in a pretty childish way: "Papa, I am so happy." [!] This wonderful manifestation lasted a few minutes, when the form again resumed the cloud-like appearance and *returned, seemingly absorbed by the Doctor'*" !!

And he remarks, "We will reiterate a few of the facts we *know* to be true. Take the one of matter passing through matter, *i.e.*, articles coming through closed

---

[1] See Mr. Coleman's testimony to the Committee of the London Dialectical Society at pages 99—101.

doors during séances [which I wish my readers especially to note]. This is as much certainty to one who has long investigated Spiritualism, as is the fact of water becoming ice under suitable conditions. . . . Now let us put another astounding fact before our readers, as certainly verified as the former, *viz.*, the formation of *tangible* hands, faces, figures, which can be dissolved and re-made instantaneously! This seems even more startlingly impossible than the passage of matter through matter, *yet we know it is true.*" And with respect to *both* of these phenomena, his pages bear abundant evidence of many witnesses having testified that such things had actually taken place in their presence! And in an article upon "the difficulties of proselytising," he dares to say, "we have been doing so for 3 years and a half [an ominous number!], and a question is arising in our mind whether it is worth while troubling oneself so much about one's neighbours. When it is forced on one to see that *they ' love darkness rather than light'* [!!], that they prefer *their ignorance* [!] to any *knowledge* which can be gained, one is sorely tempted to go on in one's own path, *learning* [!], rather than attempting to teach! But for the encouragement one finds in the few who *listen with ' an honest and good heart'* [!!], and *' bring forth fruit with patience'* [!!], one would give up in despair, and obey the injunction uttered of old, *' Cast not* PEARLS,' &c."!!

How horrible a perversion, and misapplication, of the Divine Word, and that from one who does not

even believe in it himself!   No : the appropriate words
for such false and delusive teaching are *these* :—" Woe
unto them that call evil good, and good evil ; that put
darkness for light, and light for darkness ; that put
bitter for sweet, and sweet for bitter !   Woe unto them
that are wise in their own eyes and prudent in their
own sight "![1]   " How do ye say, We are wise, and the
law of Jehovah is with us ?   Lo, certainly in vain
made he it ; the pen of the scribes is in vain.   The
wise men are ashamed, they are dismayed and taken :
lo, they have rejected the Word of Jehovah ; and
what wisdom is in them ? "[2]   " At that time Jesus
answered and said, I thank Thee, O Father, Lord of
heaven and earth, because Thou hast hid these things
from the wise and prudent, and hast revealed them
unto babes.   Even so, Father ; for so it seemeth good
in Thy sight.   All things are delivered unto Me of My
Father : and no one, ὀυδεὶς, knoweth the Son, but the
Father ; neither knoweth any one, τὶς, the Father,
save the Son, and he to whomsoever the Son will
reveal Him."[3]

But not to weary my readers with many other
instances of demoniacal power, I will conclude this
division of my subject with two more only—which I
have selected from the periodical in question, not only
because they are of a most extraordinary character in
themselves ; but also because they exhibit Spiritualism
in its true naked, hellish deformity and falsehood.

---

[1] Isa. v. 20, 21.   [2] Jer. viii. 8, 9.   [3] Mat. xi. 25-27.

The first is extracted from the " Experiences of M. Louis Jacolliot, President of the Tribunal of Chandernagore," in the year 1867—a Frenchman, who stated that he was " quite incredulous as to the pretended action and interference of spirits ; " and " only stated the facts, as well as his own reflections on them, without any other commentary or remarks."   As I have not the whole account before me, I am unable to state how he first became acquainted with Govindaswasmi, the *Sadhu*, whose marvellous performances so astonished him : but it would seem from the account which I possess, that he must have known him as a *fakir* before ; and have invited him to his house for the purpose of finding out, if possible, *how* the *seeming* miracles, as he thought, were performed.

My account commences with the third visit of the *Sadhu :* when, at the Frenchman's request, he came " to show him the phenomena of levitation."

On this occasion, he states, the *Sadhu*, " taking an ebony cane, which I had brought with me from Ceylon, put the palm of his right hand on its knob, fixed his eyes steadfastly on the ground, and commenced to recite the necessary *Mantras* for the occasion, and to perform other mummeries, which he had probably forgotten to regale me with the preceding days. I judged from these preparations, that I was once more going to witness what I had always regarded as a mere gymnastic feat of strength ; as my reason refused to designate, or account for it, otherwise. Supported by only one hand placed lightly on the cane, the

Sadhu gradually rose ten feet from the floor, his legs continuing crossed in the eastern fashion. He remained motionless in this position, and resembled those bronze images of Buddha, which every [traveller by mail steamer brings from the East. . . . For more than 20 minutes, during which the levitation lasted, I endeavoured to comprehend *how* the *Sadhu* could thus break through the laws of gravitation and equilibrium. It was impossible to fathom the mystery." But the greater number of my readers will, I doubt not, be able to fathom it—*i.e.*, that it was produced by the very same demoniacal power, that suspended " the beautiful Astarte" in mid air, in the town in the North of England, referred to at page 38 of this book!

As "contrary to the ordinary practice of Europeans," he "allowed Govindaswasmi access to" him "at all hours, without being announced, and to do as he liked in" his "apartments: this, as well as" his "knowledge of his mother-tongue, had secured" him "his friendship;" and in consequence the *Sadhu* laid himself out to please him, by exhibiting before him all that the spirits invoked by him could accomplish; some few more examples of which I shall now give.

On another occasion, after some conversation between the two, the Sadhu remarked,

"You have spoken to me in the language of my beloved country. I have nothing to refuse you! I will do anything to please you."

The Frenchman then "taking a small round table of teakwood, which" he "could lift up with" his

" index " (*i.e.*, forefinger) " and thumb put it down on the middle of the terrace, and asked the *Sadhu* whether he had the power to fix it where it was in such a manner as to make it impossible for anyone to remove it from its place.

" The Malabari approached the small table, and placing his hand on the top, remained in this position, motionless, for nearly 15 minutes, after which he smiled and said to me,

" ' *The spirits have come and no one can now remove the table without their wishing it !* '

" I drew near the piece of furniture with a certain degree of incredulity, and laying hold of it with both hands, endeavoured to lift it up. It remained immoveable as if it had been fastened to the floor! I redoubled my efforts and wrenched up the fragile top slab, but the article itself I could in no wise move! I then furiously tugged at the legs and frame-work, which still stood upright, the legs joined by two cross pieces in the form of a cross, but it was in vain!

" Among the objects in the room there was a harmoni-flute. With a cord I suspended it from one of the iron bars of the terrace about 2 feet from the floor, and requested the *Sadhu* to be good enough to draw sounds from the instrument without touching it. He at once lightly held the cord by which the flute was suspended between his thumb and finger, and then seemed to concentrate his thoughts, remaining quite motionless. Presently the instrument began to sway gently, the bellows retracted and swelled out by themselves, *as if worked by invisible hands*, and gave out long-drawn sounds, which, however, had no harmony or unison in them, though the different notes could be distinctly marked.

" ' Can you not give us an air ? ' said I.

" ' *I shall evoke the spirits of an old musician* OF OUR PAGODA ' [!] he said, with the utmost coolness.

" I waited gravely, though I was very much tempted to smile at the reply of the *Sadhu*.

" After a somewhat long silence, the instrument, which had stopped playing while I was putting the above query to the *Sadhu*, recommenced swaying again from side to side. The sounds produced appeared to me to be the prelude of a song, to which succeeded one of those sweet airs so popular on the Malabar coast :—

> " ' Bring hither thy jewelled ornaments,
> O ! lovely virgin of Aronné.'

" During the whole time this air was being executed, the *Sadhu* remained motionless, keeping his fingers, however, on the cord by which the harmoni-flute was suspended. I knelt down near it, in order to observe more closely its movements, and I can confidently declare, unless my senses deceived me, that I saw the keys of the instrument rising and falling according to the requirements of the piece played. I again repeat that *I merely state facts* without drawing any conclusions from them."

On a subsequent occasion, on the Frenchman putting several questions to the *Sadhu* about his past life, he replied,

" ' All that I can communicate without infringing on my oath is at your service.'

" ' To what oath do you allude ? '

" ' When we leave the temple where we have been brought up, we have to swear never to reveal to any one *the mysteries* and profound secrets which have been imparted to us ! '

" ' I understand that you are forbidden to reveal *the magic formulæ, the incantations and the evocations* which you have been taught : but cannot you inform me *how one of your initiated is able to fall into a sort of catalepsy and to remain several months without any sustenance whatever ?* '

" ' *It is by the interventions of the spirits of the Pitris !* '[1]

" ' Listen,' said he, ' *I am going to invoke the Pitris :* when you observe the penholder you have given to me stand vertically, keeping its contact by one of its extremities with the ground, you can trace on the paper before you any sign or figures you choose, and you will see that sign or those figures reproduced on the surface of the sand.'

" He then stretched his two hands horizontally before him, *and began to mutter the prescribed formulæ of invocation.*

" After a few moments, the wooden penholder raised itself up little by little, as the *Sadhu* had said, and at the same time I commenced to trace with my pencil

---

[1] See pp. 39-42.

9

on the paper before me, the most strange and complicated figures, and I saw to my astonishment the penholder faithfully copy on the sand all the motions of my pencil and produce the strange, arabesque figures which I had drawn on the paper!

"The *Sadhu*, after having again smoothed the surface of the sand thoroughly, said :

"'Think of a word in the language of the gods'— (Sanskrit).

"'Why specially in that language?' I enquired.

"'*Because the spirits can more easily use that immortal language, which is interdicted to the impure*'!

"I had the tact, as well as the habit, of never discussing the religious opinions of the *Sadhu*, and I appeared to be satisfied with his reply. He then extended his hands as he had done previously. The magic penholder commenced to stir itself, rose up gradually, and without hesitation, wrote (in Sanskrit)—

"'The heavenly creator.'

"It was indeed the word I had thought in my mind.

"'Think of an entire sentence,' continued the magician.

"'It is done,' I replied.

"And the penholder traced on the sand in the Sanskrit characters,

"'Vishnu sleeps in Baikuntha.'

"At last, as a final test, I asked, placing my hand on a small closed book, which contained extracts of certain hymns of the Rig Veda, what was the first word in the 5th line of the 21st page of the book. On the sand immediately appeared the Sanskrit word 'Devadatta' (given by God). On verification, I found that the exact word had been given!

" ' Would you like to ask a question *mentally ?* ' suggested the *Sadhu*.

" I simply nodded my head in acquiescence. Immediately the word ' Vasundha ' (the earth) was inscribed on the sand. *I had mentally asked who is our common mother*" ! !

Mons. Jacolliot gives an account of various other spiritualistic manifestations, quite as wonderful as, and some even more so than, those already described—such as planting a seed selected and marked by the narrator, in a pot of earth furnished by himself, and the *Sadhu* causing it to grow into a young plant 8 inches in height in about 2 hours—producing phosphorescent clouds in the room, from out of which came at one time no less than 16 hands, some of which, at his request, detached themselves from the group, and coming floating forward, pressed his own outstretched hand ; or scattered round the room a shower of flowers ; or wrote in the air in characters of fire—the doors of the rooms being locked ; and the narrator himself having the keys in his pocket ! But all these were evidently intended by the demon, or demons, who performed them, to lead up to the crowning manifestation of all : which I shall give in the narrator's own words.

" A moment after the disappearance of the hands, the *Sadhu* having resumed his avocations, a cloud like the one seen before, but of brighter colour and greater opacity, was seen to hover over the little chafing dish, which, at the *Sadhu's* request, I had constantly kept supplied with live coals. *Gradually it assumed a human form*, and I saw the spectre or the phantasmagoria—I do not know what to call it—of an old Brahmin sacrificer (*Agiothri*) kneeling before the little brazier! *The sacred sign of Vishnu was upon his forehead*, and round his body the triple cord, symbol among the priest-caste of those initiated!

" He joined his hands above his head, *as when performing the sacrificial ceremony, and his lips moved as by the utterance of prayers!* After a certain time he took of the perfumed powder and threw it into the brazier. The quantity thrown in must have been large, for a thick smoke issued from the fire and filled both the rooms! When it had been dissipated, I perceived the spectre, standing two paces from me, and stretching toward me its gaunt bony hand! I took it in mine, and made my *salaam, and I was extremely astonished to find it, though hard and bony, quite warm and living!*

" ' Art thou one of the ancient inhabitants of this earth?' I asked in a loud voice.

" I had not finished the sentence when the Sanskrit word (yes) appeared and disappeared on the breast of the old Brahmin, as if it had been written in the dark with a piece of phosphorus!!

" ' Wilt thou leave me something as a token of thy visit?' I continued.

" The spirit snapped the three-fold cotton thread which surrounded his loins, gave it to me, and vanished at my feet " [!!]

Subsequently, (for other things happened afterwards) he adds, " Govindaswami then rose up. *Perspiration was streaming from every part of his body, and he was thoroughly exhausted!*"[1]

He afterwards gives an account of the *fakir's* fearful end.

" About 4 years after the occurrences narrated above, I travelled, by rail, *via* Madras, Bellary, and other places, to Aurungabad, in order to visit the subterranean temple of Kali.

" The principal subterranean vault is a celebrated place of pilgrimage, and one always finds there a crowd of the followers of the Brahma, and of *fakirs* who come from India to perform their 9 days' devotion in the Cave of Evocations."

" Sitting day and night in front of a fierce fire, which the faithful (*chélas*) keep up—a tight bandage over the mouth and nose to escape from breathing the least impurity, eating nothing but a few grains of parched rice moistened with water filtered through cloth—*they are reduced gradually to a state of such emaciation as to preclude the idea of life in the body.* The moral forces rapidly diminish, and when they reach the end

---

[1] See page 85.

of this protracted suicide, life has long ceased to be active, and physical and intellectual decrepitude has supervened !

" All *fakirs* who aspire to attain the highest transformation in the upper world, *are required to submit their bodies to such horrible tortures !*

" On my arrival at Kali, a new comer, some few months ago, from Cape Comorin, was pointed out to me. *He was sitting between two braziers*, in order, no doubt, to facilitate the decomposition of his organs. He was already in a state of almost complete insensibility.

" But my astonishment was great indeed, when, from a deep cicatrix, which traversed the entire upper portion of his scalp, I was enabled to recognize in him the *Sadhu* of Trevandrum ! I drew near him, and, in that beautiful mother tongue which he loved so much to speak, I asked him if he remembered the Franguy (Frenchman) of Benares.

" A flash, as of lightning, brightened the almost extinct eyes, and I heard him mutter the Sanskrit sentence which had appeared to us in phosphorescent letters on the evening of our last séance—

(Having assumed a fluidic body.)

" This was the only sign of attention which I could obtain from him.

" The Hindus in the neighbourhood, who, though familiar with such strange sights, were so struck by his extraordinary emaciation (veritably a mere skeleton) that they had surnamed him ' *Kali-Saba*,' or the corpse of Kali !

"Thus," adds the narrator, "closes the career of a Hindu *Jogi*—in decrepitude and imbecility!"

And oh, how sad and awful an end! For the Scriptures solemnly assert, no matter how sincere a man may be in his *belief of a lie*—that "*if I give my body to be burned,*"—as the poor deluded Phoongyee did[1]—"and have not charity," or, "the love of God shed abroad in" my "heart by the Holy Ghost,"[2] (which none but those who are "born of God"[3] ever can have) "*it profiteth me nothing.*"[4]

My second and last instance, the demoniac teaching in which was nevertheless *directed to the same end—the teaching of blasphemous falsehood*—is selected from some of the séances of Mr. Eglinton, held in Bruges, in 1879. The narrator, Mrs. Florence Marryat Lean, profanely commences her narrative thus :—

"At last the dry bones in this world-renowned old city have commenced to shake. Our first '*conference,*' as they call the *séances* here (and, I think, since the latter term has fallen so much into disrepute, that it would not be a bad idea to introduce the word amongst our English Spiritualists), was held the same evening at the house of Mr. Eglinton's hostess, Mrs. M——, where we imagined all our sittings would take place. But in the course of it 'Joey' [a spirit, as it would seem, assuming that name] informed us that on the following night we were to sit at the house of Mrs. B——, the friend with whom *we* are staying. I

---

[1] See page 61.   [2] Rom. v. 5.   [3] John iii. 3, 5.   [4] 1 Cor. xiii. 3.

must premise that this house is so ancient that the date of its original building has been completely lost. A stone let into one of its walls bears an inscription to the effect that it was restored in the year 1616. And an obsolete plan of the city shows it to have stood in its present condition in 1562. Prior to that period, however, it is supposed, with 3 houses on either side of it, *to have formed a convent;* but no printed record remains of the fact. Beneath it are subterranean passages, now choked with rubbish, which lead no one can tell whither. I have stayed in this house many times before, *and have always felt strange and unpleasant influences from it, especially in a large room on the lower floor, now used as a drawing-room, but which is said* ORIGINALLY TO HAVE FORMED THE CHAPEL OF THE CONVENT! Others have felt the influence besides myself, but we have never had reason to believe that there was any particular cause for it.[1] On the evening in question, however, when we expressed curiosity to learn why 'Joey' desired us to hold our next 'conference' in Mrs. B——'s house, he told us that the medium had not been brought over to Bruges for *our* pleasure, or even edification, but that *there was a great work to be done here,* and that *Mrs. M—— had been expressly influenced to invite him over,* THAT THE PURPOSES OF A HIGHER POWER THAN HIS OWN SHOULD BE ACCOMPLISHED!! Consequently on the following evening Mrs. M—— brought Mr. Eglinton

---

[1] See pages 91, 92.

over to our house, and '*Joey,*' *having been asked to choose the room for the* '*conference,*' selected an *entresol* on the upper floor, which leads by two short passages into the bedrooms. The bedroom door being locked, a curtain was hung at the entrance of one of these passages, and '*Joey*' declared it was a first-rate cabinet ! !

"We then all assembled in the drawing-room for some conversation and music, for the time appointed for the '*conference*' had not arrived. The party consisted only of Mrs. B—— and Mrs. M——, the medium, my husband, and myself. After I had sung a few songs, Mr. Eglinton *became restless,* and moved away from the piano, saying *the influence was too strong for him !* He began walking up and down the room, and staring fixedly at the door, before which hung a *portière.* Several times he exclaimed pointedly, 'What is the matter with that door? There is something very peculiar about it.' Once he approached it quickly; Joey's voice was heard from behind the *portière* saying, 'Don't come too near.' Mr. Eglinton then retreated to a sofa, and *appeared to be fighting violently with some unpleasant influence ! He made the sign of the cross,* then extended his fingers towards the door, *as though to exorcise it;* finally he burst into a scornful mocking peal of laughter that lasted for several minutes ! As it concluded A DIABOLICAL EXPRESSION *came over his face !!*[1] He clenched his hands, gnashed his

---

[1] See also page 93.

teeth, and commenced to grope in a crouching position towards the door. We concluded he wished to go to the '*conference*' room, and let him have his way. He crawled more than walked up the steep turret stairs, but on reaching the top *came to himself suddenly* and fell back several steps. Luckily my husband was just behind, and saved him from a fall. *He complained very much of the influence, and of a pain in his head,* and we went at once into the '*conference*' room, and sat at the table. *In a few seconds the same spirit had taken possession of him!* He left the table and groped his way towards the bedrooms, listening apparently to every sound, and with his hand holding an imaginary knife, which was raised every now and then as though to strike. *The expression on Mr. Eglinton's face during this possession is* TOO HORRIBLE TO DESCRIBE!!![1] THE WORST PASSIONS WERE WRITTEN AS LEGIBLY THERE AS THOUGH THEY HAD BEEN LABELLED!! There is a short flight of steps leading from the *entresol* to the corridor, closed at the head by a padded door, which we had locked for fear of accident. When apparently in pursuit of his object *the spirit led Mr. Eglinton up to this door*, and he found it fastened; *his moans were terrible!* Half a dozen times he made his weary round of the rooms, striving to get downstairs to accomplish some end, and had to return to us, moaning and baffled. At this juncture *the medium was so exhausted* that 'Daisy' [another spirit, as it would seem, calling itself by this

---

[1] See also page 93.

name] took control of him and talked with us for some time, during which we procured the writing on the arm. 'Daisy' having taken off Mr. Eglinton's coat and bared his arm, asked me to write the name of the friend I loved best in the spirit-world on a piece of paper. I left the table, and not thinking the injunction of much importance, wrote the name of *a dear friend now long passed away*, BUT WHO IS MUCH WITH ME, and folded the paper. The medium took it as I gave it, and holding it in the flame of the candle burned it to ashes which he gathered and rubbed upon his arm. In another minute there stood out in bold characters the words '*Florence is dearest,*' and which I find was *a gentle rebuke from my dead child* [!] that I should have written any name but hers upon the paper!!

"We asked 'Daisy' what *the spirit* was like *that had controlled her medium,* and she said *she did not like him* [!!]; *he had a very bad face* [!!], no hair on the top of his head, and a long black frock [!.] From this we concluded he must have been a monk or a priest!!

"When 'Daisy' had finished talking to us, 'Joey' desired Mr. Eglinton to go into the cabinet, but as soon as he rose, *the spirit which had first controlled him got possession again,* and led him grovelling as before, towards the bedrooms! HIS OWN GUIDES *therefore carried him into the cabinet before our eyes!* HE WAS LEVITATED FAR ABOVE OUR HEADS, his feet touching each of us in turn; he was then carried past the un-shaded window, which enabled us to judge of the height he was from the ground, and finally over a large table into the arm-chair in the cabinet!

" During supper Mr. Eglinton appeared to be quite himself; but as soon as the meal was over *the old restlessness returned upon him*, and he began pacing up and down the room, walking out every now and then into the corridor! In a few minutes we perceived that *the uneasy spirit had again controlled him*, and we followed him into the corridor. He went steadily towards the drawing-room door, but on finding himself pursued turned back 3 times and pronounced emphatically the word 'Go!' He then entered the drawing-room, which was in darkness, and closed the door behind him, whilst we waited outside. In a little while he reopened it, and speaking in quite a different voice, said, 'Bring a light! I have something to say to you!' When we re-assembled we found Mr. Eglinton *controlled by a new spirit*, whom ' Joey ' has since told us, *is one of his* HIGHEST GUIDES!! Motioning us to sit down, he stood before us and said,

" ' I have been *selected from amongst the controls of this medium* to tell you the history of the unhappy spirit who has so disturbed you this evening. *He is present now*, AND THE CONFESSION OF HIS CRIME THROUGH MY LIPS WILL HELP HIM TO THROW OFF THE EARTHBOUND CONDITION TO WHICH IT HAS CONDEMNED HIM!! Many years ago the house in which we stand was a convent, and underneath it were 4 subterranean passages running north, south, east and west, which communicated with all parts of the town.'

" (I should here state that Mr. Eglinton had not previously been informed of any particulars relating to

the former history of this house, but that Mrs. B——
has told us since that, many years ago, some one said
in her hearing that, at one time, there were 4 passages
excavated beneath it.)

" ' In this convent there lived a most beautiful
woman—a nun ; and in one of the neighbouring
monasteries a priest, who, against the strictest laws
of the Church, had conceived and nourished a passion
for her. He was an Italian, who had been obliged to
leave his own country for reasons best known to himself, *and nightly he would steal his way to this house
by means of one of the subterranean passages, and
attempt to overcome the nun's scruples* and make her
listen to his tale of love ; but she, strong in the faith,
always resisted him. At last, one day maddened by
her repeated refusals and his own guilty passion, he
hid himself in one of the northern rooms in the upper
story of this house, and watched there in the dusk
for her to pass him on her way from her devotions in
the chapel, but she did not come. *Then he crept down
stairs stealthily, with a dagger hid beneath his robes,*
and met her in that hall. He conjured her again to
yield to him, but again she resisted, *and he stabbed her
within the door, on the very spot where the medium first
perceived him.* HER PURE SOUL SOUGHT IMMEDIATE
CONSOLATION IN THE SPIRIT SPHERES, BUT HIS HAS BEEN
CHAINED DOWN EVER SINCE TO THE SCENE OF HIS AWFUL
CRIME ! ! He dragged her body down the secret stairs
(still existent) to the vaults below, and hid it in the
subterranean passage. After a few days he sought it

again, and buried it. He lived many years after, and committed many other crimes, but none so foul as this. *It is his unhappy spirit* WHICH ASKS YOUR PRAYERS TO HELP IT TO PROGRESS ! ! It is *for this purpose* we were brought to this city, *that we might aid* IN RELEASING THE MISERABLE SOUL THAT CANNOT REST '! !

" I asked, ' By what name shall we pray for him ? '

" ' Pray for " the distressed being." Call him by no other name.'

" ' What is your own name ? '

" ' I prefer it to be unknown. May God bless you all and keep you in the way of prayer and *truth* [! !, *and from all evil courses* [! !] , *and bring you to everlasting life.* Amen ' ! !

" The medium then walked up to the spot he had indicated as the scene of the murder, *and knelt there for some minutes in prayer ! !* If I have failed to impress you with an idea of what a solemn scene this was, it is the fault of my pen, for it was the most thrilling manifestation that any of us have ever witnessed " ! !

The above account seems to have been sent by this lady to the editor of the " *Spiritualist* " Magazine, for publication in his columns : where I presume it first appeared. Continuing her narrative, on the 20th July, 1879, she says :—

" In order that the medium might be rested, we did not hold a ' *conference* ' yesterday ; but as we sat at dinner together loud raps came on the back of his chair, and on our calling the alphabet, the name ' Bencdetta ' was rapped out. We concluded it must have been the ' distressed being,' *who could not pronounce the Sacred Name!* In the evening I sat alone at the table with Mrs. B——, when the name ' Hortense Dupont ' was given us, and the following conversation ensued :—

" ' Who are you ? '

" ' I am the nun. *I did love him.* I couldn't help it. *It is such a relief to think that he will be prayed for ! !* '

" ' When did he murder you ? '

" ' In 1498.'

" ' What was his name ? '

" ' I cannot tell you.'

" ' His age ? '

" ' Thirty-five.'

" ' And yours ? '

" ' Twenty-three.'

" ' Are you coming to see us to-morrow ? '

" ' I am not sure.'

" This evening, *by ' Joey's ' orders* we assembled at seven. Mr. Eglinton did not feel the influence in the drawing-room to-day, but directly he entered the ' con-ference ' room *he was possessed by the same spirit!* His actions were still more graphic than on the first occa-sion. He watched from the window for the coming of his victim through the court-yard, and then recom-menced his crawling stealthy pursuit, coming back each time from the locked door that prevented his egress. With such heartrending moans that no one could have listened to him unmoved. At last *his agony was so great* as he strove again and again, like some dumb animal, to pass through the walls which divided him from the spot he wished to visit, *whilst the perspiration streamed down the medium's face with the struggle,*[1] that we attempted to make him speak to us. We implored him in French to tell us his trouble, and believe us to be his friends, but he only pushed us away. At last we felt *we must pray for him,* and Mrs. B—— and Mrs. M——, with myself, kneeled down and *repeated all the well-known Catholic prayers ! !* As we commenced the *De profundis* the medium fell prostrate on the earth, and seemed to wrestle in his agony. At the *Salve Regina* and *Ave Maria* he lifted his eyes to heaven and clasped his hands, and in the *Paternoster* he appeared to join ! ! *But directly we ceased praying the evil passions returned,* AND HIS FACE BECAME DISTORTED WITH THE THIRST FOR BLOOD ! ! It was an experience that no one who has seen could ever forget ! At last I begged Mrs. B—— to fetch *a crucifix,* which we placed in his breast ! It had not been there many seconds, before *a different expression came over his face,* and he seized it in both hands, straining it to his eyes, lips *and heart*—holding it from him at arm's length, *then passionately kissing it, as we repeated the Anima Christi ! !* Finally he held the crucifix out for each one of us to kiss—*a beautiful smile broke out over the medium's face, and the spirit*

---

[1] See page 133.

passed out of him! Mr. Eglinton awoke *terribly exhausted!* His face was as white as a sheet, and he trembled violently. His first words were, ' They are doing something to my forehead ; burn a piece of paper and give me the ashes.'

" He rubbed them between his eyes, *when the sign of the cross became distinctly visible drawn deeply on his brow!* The spirits then said that, *exhausted as he was,* we were to place him in the cabinet, *as their work was not yet done.* He was accordingly led to the arm-chair behind the curtain, whilst we formed a circle in front of him. In a few seconds *the cabinet was illu-minated,* AND A CROSS OF FIRE APPEARED OUTSIDE OF IT [! !]

" This manifestation having been twice repeated, *the face and shoulders of a nun appeared!* Her white coif and chinpiece were pinned just as the *religieuses* are in the habit of pinning them, and she seemed very anxious to show herself, *coming close to each of us in turn,* and reappearing more than once!

" ' Joey ' said, ' That's the nun, but *you'll understand that this is only a preliminary trial,* PREPARATORY TO A MUCH MORE PERFECT MANIFESTATION ! !

" I asked her if she were the Hortense Dupont who had communicated through me, and she nodded her head several times in acquiescence ! She was succeeded by a very perfect materialisation that has appeared before through Mr. Eglinton, although we have not yet recognised it. It is the spirit of a dark man, apparently an Indian; with a short black beard

10

and moustaches, who is said to have come for my
husband, and to have been connected with him in some
way when on foreign service. He returned 3 or 4
times on this occasion, *and made himself distinctly
visible to all*, seeming to be anxious to be examined
and recognized; but we have not yet discovered his
name, and 'Joey' can tell us nothing about him [!!]
This ended the '*conference*,' and I only mention it to
show what powerful sittings we are having here.
During this evening, *a watch*, which had been missed
the day before from Mrs. M——'s hands, *came floating
from the ceiling into her lap; and we were touched at
the same time by materialized hands* " *!!*

Writing again on the 22nd of July, 1879, she continues her narrative thus :—

" We came back together to Mrs. B——s' house to
supper at about 10 o'clock. During the meal loud raps
were heard about the room, and on giving the alphabet,
'*Joey*' *ordered us to go upstairs and sit*, and to have
the door at the head of the staircase (which we had
hitherto locked for fear of accident) open, which we
accordingly did! (I had remarked privately to Mrs.
B—— the day before that I felt sure *the spirit of the
monk would not feel satisfied until it had enacted the
whole of the murder*, WHICH HE HAD PROBABLY NOT
CONFESSED BEFORE HIS DEATH [!!] : but I had not
mentioned my surmises to Mr. Eglinton.) As soon as
ever we were seated at the table he became entranced,
and the same pantomime, which I have related, was
gone through. He watched from the window which

looks into the court-yard, and silently groped his way round the room, *until he had crawled on his stomach up the stairs*, which led to the padded door. When he found, however, that the obstacle that had hitherto stood in his way, was removed (by its being open), he drew a long breath, and started away to the winding turret staircase, crouching at the doors he passed, in order to listen if he were overheard. When he came to the stairs—in descending which we had been so afraid (*notwithstanding ' Joey's ' assurances to the contrary*) that he might hurt himself—*he was levitated down them in the most wonderful manner*, only placing his hands twice on the balustrades, *and being carried as in a flight to the bottom without any noise of footsteps ! !* We had placed a lamp in the hall, so that as we followed him we could observe all his actions. When he had gained the bottom of the staircase *he crawled on his stomach* [!] to the door of the drawing-room (originally the chapel), and there waited and listened ; darting back into the shadows every time he fancied he heard a sound.

" Imagine our little party of four in this sombre old house, the only ones waking at the time of night, watching by the ghostly light of a turned-down lamp the acting of this terrible tragedy ! Mr. Eglinton's face *during the possession* was a perfect study, from which Irving might have taken a lesson : but it was so awful to think that there we actually witnessed the revival of *a crime that has held its perpetrator* IN THE CONTINUED BONDAGE OF SIN *for* 400 *years* [! !], that we had no thought for anything but the solemnity of the scene! We held our breaths as the murderer crouched by the chapel door, opening it noiselessly to peep within, and then retreating with the imaginary dagger in his hand, ready to strike as soon as his victim appeared. At last she seemed to come. In an instant he sprung towards her, stabbing her once in a half-stooping attitude, and then, apparently finding her not dead, he rose to his full height, and stabbed her twice straight downwards.[1] For a moment he seemed para-lysed at what he had done, starting back with both hands clasped to his forehead. Then he flung himself prostrate on the supposed body, *kissing the ground frantically in all directions!* Presently he awoke to the fears of detection, and raised the corpse suddenly in his arms. He fell once beneath its weight, but staggering up again he seized and dragged it, slipping on the stone floor as he went to the head of the stair-case that leads to the ' cave ' below, whence the mouth of the subterranean passages is still to be seen! The door at the head of this flight is modern, and he could not undo the lock, and we, believing that if it were advisable for him to descend, *his controls would open it,* thought it best not to interfere. Prevented in dragging the body down the steps, he cast himself again upon it, kissing the stone floor of the hall and moaning. At last he dragged himself on his knees to the spot of the murder, and commenced to pray. We knelt with him,

---

[1] Here the demons evidently contradict themselves! See page 141.

and as he heard our voices, he turned on his knees
towards us with outstretched hands. I said,

"'He wants *the crucifix* again; I will go upstairs
and fetch it!'

"As soon as I had left the hall, the medium rose
and followed me. I found what I wanted in the '*conference*' room, and returning, met him at the head of
the stairs. He seized it from me eagerly, and carrying
it to the window whence he had so often watched, fell
down again upon his knees! When he had prayed for
some time, he tried to speak to us. His lips moved
and his tongue protruded, but he was unable to articulate. Suddenly he seized each of our hands in turn in
both of his own, and wrung them violently. I fancy
he tried to bless us, but the words would not come.
The beautiful smile, we had seen the night before,
broke over his countenance; [!!] the crucifix dropped
from his hands, *and he fell prostrate on the floor.* [!!]

"The next moment Mr. Eglinton was asking us
where he was, and what on earth had happened to
him, *he felt so queer.* [!] He declared himself *fearfully
exhausted,* but said he felt that *a great calm and peace
had come over him,* notwithstanding the weakness, and
he believed SOME GREAT GOOD HAD BEEN ACCOM-
PLISHED!!

"He was not again entranced, but '*Joey*' *ordered the
light to be put out, and spoke to us in the direct
voice as follows :*—

"'I've just come to tell you what I know you'll
all be very glad to hear, that THROUGH THE MEDIUM'S

POWER, AND OUR POWER, *and the great power of God* [!] *the unhappy spirit who has been* CONFESSING HIS CRIME TO YOU [!!] *is* FREED TO-NIGHT *from the heaviest part of his burden*—the being earth-chained to this spot!! I don't mean to say that *he'll go away at once to the spheres, because* HE'S GOT A LOT TO DO STILL *to alter the conditions under which he labours;* BUT THE WORST IS OVER!! This is *the special work* Mr. Eglinton *was brought to Bruges* TO DO; and Ernest and I can truly say that during the whole course of *our control of him,* we have never had to put forth our own powers, nor to ask so earnestly for the help of God, as in the last 3 days! *You have all helped* IN A GOOD WORK—TO FREE A POOR SOUL FROM EARTH, *and to set him* ON THE RIGHT ROAD, [!!] and we are grateful to you and to the medium as well as he! *He will be able* TO PROGRESS RAPIDLY NOW, *until he reaches his proper sphere,* and hereafter the spirits of himself and the woman he murdered *will work together* to undo for others the harm they brought upon themselves!! She is rejoicing in her high sphere *at the work we have done for him,* and will be the first *to help* and welcome him upwards!! There are many more earth-bound spirits in this house and the surrounding houses who are suffering like he was, though not to the same extent, nor for the same reason. *But they all ask for and need your help and your prayers,* AND THIS IS THE GREATEST AND NOBLEST END OF SPIRITUALISM—TO AID POOR UNHAPPY SPIRITS TO FREE THEMSELVES FROM EARTH AND PROGRESS UPWARDS!! After a while, when this spirit *can control the medium with calmness,* he will come himself and tell you, *through him,* all his history and how he came to fall. Meanwhile, we thank you very much for allowing us *to draw so much strength from you and helping us with your sympathy;* and I hope I shall see you to-morrow night, and that you will believe me always to remain your loving friend, JOEY.'"

I need scarcely comment upon these two last cases: as the object of the demons, who wrought these "*lying wonders,*" τέρασι ψεύδους, as the Holy Ghost calls such false miracles,[1] is sufficiently obvious from the narratives themselves: for "lying wonders," or *supernatural prodigies, wrought for the purpose of deception,* (as the Greek words import,) they certainly were! But indeed, the Editor of "Psychic Notes," has himself virtually given us his comments upon all such diabolical manifestations; not only by giving utterance to sentiments and opinions inculcating the same end and object; but also by quoting approvingly the sentiments and opinions of others like-minded with himself.

Thus, he quotes a reply of the Editor of the " *Theosophist,*" to a correspondent, who asked him, " *Is creation possible* FOR MAN ?" in which, among other things, he said :—" We must have a clear understanding as to what is meant by creation. Probably *the common idea* on the subject is that the world was 'created,' the creator accorded himself, or was some-

---

[1] 2 Thes. ii. 10.

how accorded, a dispensation from the rule *ex nihilo nihil fit, and actually made the world out of nothing—* if *that* is the idea of creation to be dealt with now, *the reply of the philosophers would be,* not merely that such creation was *impossible* TO MAN, *but that it is* IMPOSSIBLE TO GODS, OR GOD ; *in short* ABSOLUTELY IMPOSSIBLE ! ! . . . . . *Theosophist-Occultists* do not, however, use the word '*creation' at all,* but REPLACE *it by that of* EVOLUTION " ! !—upon which the Editor of "Psychic Notes" remarks :

"It is one of the many reasons *why* BUDDHIST PHILOSOPHY *refuses to admit the existence and interference in the production of the universe of a direct* CREATOR *or* GOD ! ! For once admit, for argument's sake, that the world *was* created by such a being, who, to have done so, must have been omnipotent, there remains the old difficulty to be dealt with—who then created that pre-existing matter, that eternal, invisible, intangible and imponderable something or chaos? If we are told that being 'eternal' and imperishable it had no need of being 'created,' then our answer will be that in such a case there are TWO ' Eternals ' and two ' Omnipotents ' ; or if our opponents argue that it is the omnipotent No. 1, or God, who created it, then we return from where we first started—to the creation of *something* out of *nothing, which is* SUCH AN ABSOLUTE ABSURDITY before science and logic that it does not even *require* the final UNANSWERABLE *query* resorted to by some precocious children ' and who created God ' ?" ! !

Truly do the Scriptures say, " Well spake the Holy Ghost by "[1] the mouth of the Apostle Paul, in his Epistle to the Romans, of the *so-called wise* men of Greece and Rome—whose followers these *so-called Theosophists*, (divinely illuminated ones!) really are :—" For the wrath of God is revealed from heaven against all ungodliness and unrighteousness of men, who hold the truth " (*i.e.*, as afterwards explained, " The eternal power and divinity of God ") " in unrighteousness ; because that which may be known of God " (*i.e.* the above-mentioned truth) " is manifest in them ; *for God hath shewed it to them.* For *the invisible things of Him* from the creation of the world *are clearly seen, being* UNDERSTOOD *by the things that are made, even* HIS ETERNAL POWER AND GODHEAD ; so that *they are without excuse!* "[2] Hence while " *we*," who *believe* in God, " *through faith understand* that the worlds were framed by the Word of God, so that things which are *seen* were *not* made of things which do *appear*," ἐκ φαινομένων, *i.e.*, were *not* formed out of pre-existing materials ; but were *created out of nothing :*[3] " *the fool* " *still says* " *in his heart, there is no God!* "[4] Nevertheless the day is now fast approaching, when, " Behold, the Lord cometh with ten thousand of His saints, to execute judgment upon all, and to convince all that are ungodly among them of all their *ungodly deeds* which they have ungodly committed, and of all their *hard*

---

[1] Acts xxviii 25.   [2] Rom. i. 18-20.   [3] Heb. xi. 3.
[4] Psa. liii. i.

speeches which ungodly sinners have spoken against Him."[1]

And although the Editor of " Psychic Notes," may boast that " *Old Theology* IS DOOMED, but she will struggle long in her death throes, and thousands will continue to marshall themselves in her ranks, determined to save her at any risk : but ever *the truth—i.e.,* the lying doctrine of Esoteric Theosophy ! !—" comes uppermost, and in the end *error* "—*i.e.* " the glorious Gospel of the Grace of God " ! !—" must yield "; and give his hearty approval to the opinions of a celebrated professor, who advised his hearers, " not *to invoke psychic powers* for mere wonder-working, self-aggrandisement, or evil, but *to build* A UNIVERSAL SPIRITUAL RELIGION *in which* BOTH EAST AND WEST CAN JOIN, *both* ANCIENT AND MODERN *truth* CAN BLEND : "[2] yet

---

[1] Jude 14, 15.

[2] As a sample of the *advertisements* in " Psychic Notes," I cull the following :—" W. Newman & Co., Limited, Calcutta. PLANCHETTE. An instrument which affords a fascinating interest. Two persons placing their hands upon it, *and asking it a question*, it will generally, after a little time, write an answer—both the operators being quite unconscious of in any way influencing its movements. *This effect is by Spiritualists attributed to the influence of attendant spirits ;* by others it is supposed to be accomplished by what is called Psychic Force—a force which science has not yet explained, but which is now undergoing investigation by some of the leading scientific men of the day.

" *By Spiritualists, this little instrument is considered to be a ' celestial telegraph,' and it is said to open up the secrets of the spiritual world !* Certainly some very surprising messages have been written by it, and some astonishing secrets have been revealed ! *It writes not only in the European languages,* but has been known *to write equally well in the Bengali, Nagri, Persian and Sanskrit Characters ! !*

we know, from the unerring testimony of the Divine Word itself, that the personal individual Antichrist, *who will head up these diabolical blasphemies, "shall come to his end, and none shall help him";*[1] when "Jehovah shall be King over all the earth: *in that day* shall there be one Jehovah, and His Name one;"[2] for although "there are *many devices* in a *man's* heart, *nevertheless the counsel of* JEHOVAH, THAT SHALL STAND."[3]

And here I might have introduced "*the doctrines of*" the "demons" themselves; but as it is absolutely essential, in exposing the system of "Spiritualism," so-called, that the exposure should be an effectual and a crushing one; and it is, therefore, needful to know more particularly what is going *on also in this country;* I must first, in accordance with my previous announcement,

(3) Give several extracts from a work before referred to, entitled, "Spirit Workers in the Home Circle, an Autobiographic Narrative of Psychic Phenomena in

---

"Price, complete in box, with full instructions, 3 rupees"! !

This instrument has been introduced into Great Britain; and I am sorry to say that it is being extensively used among an increasing number of people of the upper and middle classes in this country. Truly we are fast returning to Acts xix. 24, &c. And we have now *photographs of spirits* advertised for sale! I have one at this moment before me, which came from America, and which was given to me by a clergyman, who had it presented to him by some one else!

[1] Dan. xi. 45.   [2] Zech. xiv. 9.   [3] Prov. xix. 21.

family daily life, extending over a period of 20 years."
—wherein we shall not only again meet with most of
the phenomena before described ; but also be enabled
gradually to trace the development of them, from the
beginning to the close.

I have not the least doubt of the sincerity of the
writer; nor do I question his assertion, that "the
phenomenal facts in " his "book, have all been carefully and repeatedly verified by" himself "and members
of " his "household : " but that he is under an awful
delusion in supposing that, in thus communicating
with demons, he has been holding fellowship with
deceased members of his family, I have no more doubt
than I have of my own existence. In his Introduction,
he says, " I have no intention of submitting myself to
the judgment of any tribunal, and I cannot acknowledge
the authority of any judge, or council, or court, or
committee, to pronounce judicially upon the facts
which I present. *If it pleases them to do so*, that is
their affair, not mine, and whatever may be the satisfaction they find in the procedure, *I should be very
sorry to deprive them of it.*" [1]

Acting upon this permissive intimation, therefore, if
I may so call it, I shall now proceed to give extracts
from, as well as to comment upon, his book—first
premising, that he states he had " no inducement
whatever " in writing it, " but love for," what he con-
ceives to be "truth ;" and that " at the outset," he

---

[1] "Spirit Workers," &c., p. 11.

" started with a general impression that inter-communication between the visible and invisible world was possible, and under certain conditions probable."[1] What his previous views were, may be stated in his own words :—" Spiritualism is no new thing." " It is earlier than theology, earlier than ritual, earlier than ecclesiastical organization, earlier than speculation. It lies at the basis of the history of the Divine life in man : "[2] " It asserts itself in the earlier periods of most forms of religion, and doubtless is actually an essential factor in their constitution. Brahminism, Buddhism, Mohammedanism, Judaism, all start more or less avowedly from a germ of Spiritualism."[3] " Thus *modern Spiritualism*, so far as it is new, is a re-affirmation, *with added emphasis*, of *Christian* laws and facts." ! !"[4] " If," therefore, he says, " the facts here adduced are true "—two results follow :—

" First, *They* will supply a *positive* and, I may safely claim the right of calling it a *scientific, proof* of an after state.

" Second, *They* will *correct some current notions* relating to that life, its quality and occupations ! *They* will *prove* that Death does not break the continuity of individual existence, or change the individuality of those who pass away from us, *either exalting them to a state of miraculous perfection, or plunging them into an abyss of* UNNATURAL *and* UNDE-

---

1 " Spirit Workers," &c., p. 8.   2 Ib., p. 1.   3 Ib., p. 2.
4 Ib., p. 3.

SERVED *degradation!* *They* give no hint of *re-incar-nation*, or any other *fantastic changes* which men have constructed in their dreams or speculations, or reasoned out of imperfect deductions!!"[1]—conclusions which, I need hardly say, being diametrically opposed to Scripture testimony, *must of necessity be false!*

These then being the views of the writer, we cannot much wonder at what followed. "*Mediumship*, as it is familiarly called, or what would be more correctly designated *spirit-sensitiveness*," he says, "has existed in our family as far back as I can trace": but "it was in the year 1869 that the unmistakable wave of psychic power came to us *unsought*, and in the midst of family life."[2] "While we two"—his wife and himself—"after burying three little ones, sat wondering if these three whom we had lost, one after another, were lonely, and what was really the future into which they had entered, there came a sound which we had heard before, but had well-nigh forgotten. It was only like a bodkin tapping on the table—*but our little ones stood at the door and knocked!* Had we not previously been acquainted with these tiny raps we might have left them unnoticed, but we had patience with the raps as they came upon the dining-table, until they grew in number and variety, and until *each little one was recognized by his own distinct rap!!* They came at every meal and *joined in our conversation;* the table was lifted up and moved about the room, *often without physical contact,*

---

[1] "Spirit Workers," &c., pp. 9, 10.   [2] Ib., pp. 17, 18.

like a thing of life, and our four surviving children *became thus familiarized with what was to grow into mediumship in all of them! !*[1]

"The first endeavour of these little spirits seemed to be *to prove their* nearness, and *individuality*, as well as their intense interest in all that was going on among us! As we chatted at meals, their raps on the table chimed in affirmatively or negatively to our conversation"![2] "About this time it was *no unusual thing*, when I stood up to carve the joint at the dinner-table, to have the table suddenly moved completely away from my reach and, *upon my asking for it to be brought back to me*, for it to return and push me back until I was tightly pinned to the wall"![3] "It was an immense amusement to our children:" " and I am not sure that it is not *more rational* to think of *young angels thus occasionally employed*, than as sitting on a damp cloud singing hallelujahs"!!![4]

On another occasion, he says, " during the singing of a hymn, one of my children, who was joining heartily, would suddenly cease, the entire expression of face would change, and he would then speak ' as the spirit gave him utterance' !! In this state *he would narrate things entirely outside his own knowledge*, and tell of matters unknown to any one present, which I always took care subsequently to enquire into, and was gene-

---

[1] " Spirit Workers," &c., p. 19.

[2] " In spirit communications *one* rap means almost invariably No ; and *three* raps YES."—" Spirit Workers," &c., p. 21.

[3] See pages 85, 86, 87, 89 and 90.   [4] " Spirit Workers," &c., p. 22.

rally able to verify." [1]   " Nor did the children *suffer as mediums frequently do,* when their own vital force is used in the production of physical phenomena. Absolute faith and trust,"—*but not, alas! in God!*—" casting out fear, created a condition in which it seemed that ' all things were possible ' " [2]—an awful perversion of Scripture phrases indeed !

Having thus introduced the writer, as it were, to my readers ; and permitted him to explain, in his own words, how he first became a " Spiritualist ; " I shall now simply cull extracts here and there continuously from his book, to show the progress of the movement in his family and household, during the period mentioned by him.

" During the years 1871-73," he says, " the presence of our spirit children was persistent, and was frequently accompanied with communications in one form or another from *older spirits* associated with them in the spirit world, and who, while thus *ministering to us,* were at the same time *teaching them and developing their spiritual life* " *! !*   " The mediums, or sensitives, it should be borne in mind, were our own children only, carefully watched and guarded by my wife and myself, who also possess *contributive* power ! " [3]

" This is the manner in which *Louisa,* our first (still-born) child, first communicated with us "—adding in a note, " This spirit child was still-born in 1857 :

---

[1] " Spirit Workers," &c., p. 23.   See pages 52, 55, 98, 103, 107.
[2] Ib., pp. 25, 26.   [3] Ib., pp. 27, 28.

had she lived on earth she would now have been 15 years old, and *as* of such age she now came among us frequently." "One of her first requests was to have her name placed in the *family register* with the others! This we had not done, as she never breathed on earth. But *we were taught* THROUGH HER that no germ of life is ever lost, and that young children dying are frequently about our earth-life with us, learning thus through life's experiences, *until they can become in time* OUR MINISTERING SPIRITS!!![1] *Louisa* now frequently wrote automatically through my hand, and I have pages of such writing." "*Another spirit* at this sitting *came to thank us for having prayed for him;* IT HAD ASSISTED HIM TO RISE TO A BETTER LIFE!! *Here dawned upon us the truth* [!!] *that praying for the so-called dead is* ALWAYS PERMITTED, *and may be* A SACRED DUTY;[2] and that most urgent reasons on the other side for the development of modern Spiritualism may be inferred from these interesting and often tragic cases"!! Farther on, he says, "During considerable merriment, while E. was entranced, he suddenly *looked terrified*, clung to me and said most earnestly '*Pray!*' Some *dark looking spirit* had approached our circle, *probably with no evil design* [!], but rather, we may hope, *to gain some good* [!!] : but the boy at once recognized him as not of the same *sphere* as *the* HAPPY HOLY ones [!!] usually about us!!"[3]

---

[1] See Division vii., Sec. 2.   [2] See page 150.
[3] "Spirit Workers," &c., pp. 32, 33.

"Sitting *en séance* alone we used now often to put paper and pencil upon the floor under the table in order to obtain *direct* spirit writing, and we occasionally received a few words written under these circumstances, not in the handwriting of parents or children sitting around the table. This was the beginning of a phase of mediumship which some years afterwards produced most astonishing results, *more remarkable* than any I have yet given to the public"[1]—many instances of which he gives us in the book itself. Take the following as samples of spirit writing :—" Christ *helps us;* HIS HELP *to you direct* WOULD EMBARRASS, NOT HELP." " No evil spirit can draw that "! ! He adds in a note, " meaning the cross, which is often introduced into writings of *good* spirits, and appears to be used as a sort of *ritual of reverence*"[2] ! ! " Surely and certainly swells the wave of Spiritualism. It increases, and will, until it leads you on to the Second Coming of the dear Jesus "! ! " Maintain *a spirit of trust*, devoid of all fear, and your household will receive largely of spirit life—*mediumistic life* we mean"—the writer adding " (these last few words were in reply to my mental question) "! ![3]

Speaking upon " direct spirit voice and writing," he says, " We invariably at set séances commenced with a short prayer ! Lights were then put out by " the direction of the spirits, " and the cool spirit breeze very

---

[1] " Spirit Workers," &c., p. 86.   [2] See pages 144, 145, 149.
[3] " Spirit Workers," &c., pp. 40-42. See also pages 75, 101, 131.

soon was felt by all in the circle;[1] as also were very strong and delicious perfumes as of violets. Our little boy soon said, 'I see a beautiful spirit with a bowl containing four different coloured waters! Now she's throwing some over us:' and immediately we discovered a different scent—an *aromatic* one followed by others." "After lights and perfumes again in profusion, we heard the card board tube," which had been "provided at the request of the spirits"—"tapping against the ceiling. A cooler breeze came, followed by vibrations of the table and atmosphere, and suddenly the spirit, addressing F.J.T., said in a clear voice, different to any human one, and giving me the impression of a voice without *chest* force—

"'Good evening!' (F.J.T. started, at which the spirit said more softly), 'I thought you were so brave?'

"F.J.T. 'So I am, but you came so suddenly.'

"Spirit. 'I'll be more careful another time. You have friends here to-night. Introduce me'!!

"Upon this being done we all in turn had a most interesting conversation for over an hour" !

"I asked if the children might sit on another occasion.

"Spirit. 'Better not. It frightens children.'

"M.T. 'But ours are accustomed to *séances*—will you come and talk to-morrow evening to them for a short time?'

---

[1] See Division vi., Sec. 4.

" Spirit.　'I'll try.　It's getting late—I must go !'"[1]

Then he narrates how the spirit came ; and " as soon as he had established a freedom with the children, *and said one or two funny things to make them laugh,* he *suddenly in a loud voice* turned to little Nelly, who was laughing, and simply said, ' Little Nelly.'　She is naturally very shy and timid, and this was too much for her—to be addressed by a strange voice.　She began to cry.

" The spirit voice turning to F.J.T., said, ' There— I'm sorry, but *I told you so.*　I must go ' !!　And we broke up the séance."[2]

In a sitting after supper " the first spirit, on returning, said that my father and mother were together, sitting in a beautiful arbour, the seats of which were covered with crimson velvet !!　They were clothed with purple robes lined with white ; his was made of velvet, hers of satin, their usual evening dress !!　In the morning they were crimson lined with white. They had various dresses for different seasons ; *and the dresses there were all made by love*—IN THE LOVE SOCIETY—and were symbolical, as this description possibly may be " !!　And then the lying spirit told them, in reply to the question, " Was it true that Christ died ? "—that " His body died "—" part of His material body—the grosser parts, *evaporated on the cross ;* the remnant when the linen clothes were left in the sepulchre.　The body He rose with was *entirely spiritual* " ! ![3]

---

[1] " Spirit Workers," &c., pp. 45, 46.　[2] Ib., p. 48.　[3] Ib., pp. 49, 50.

In the year 1871 he built a new house at Hendon ; and subsequently by the direction of the spirits, *he " dedicated it to spirit-communion " ! !* But his health having given way, his spiritual guides directed him to leave Hendon, and settle at Blackheath ; when he adds, " alas, the home mediumship we had in such rich profusion was gone ; " and it was not until the 20th of January, 1876, that " the next *physical* manifestation of spirit presence came " : when there was again " a break of six years—until 1882." Then he adds :—" (*Louisa* who was now about to come in great power would have been, had she lived, twenty-five years of age)." " On my return home to Blackheath with my wife, I was sitting in an easy chair and in robust health, when a bad headache suddenly came upon me without any apparent reason. My daughter said, ' *Mr. L.* is standing by you, and wants you to write.' I went into my study, took the pencil, and wrote off rapidly and without a correction, as follows :—

" ' Watch and pray. We are coming in great power —you will be guarded and be *the conservators of great good to the world ! Let some regular time be appropriated* FOR SPIRIT COMMUNION, if no other time can be found *let it be* ON SUNDAY EVENINGS.—Louisa *and* L.'

" My headache was gone when this writing was finished.

" Some days after I was impressed to write as follows :—

" ' Yes, dear friend, I am here and though you cannot see me N. has eyes which you have not at present, but will soon have. . . We are all here—group spiritual as well as group earthly—*all one now* IN CHRIST, the loving minister of all ! ! *Sunday evenings* will *not be mis-spent* when you are sitting earnestly *at this work* ' " ! ! [1]

It would seem that their servant, " Mary had been a sensitive all her life. Seeing spirits about her as a child, and playing with them, she took it as the most natural thing in the world to associate with them, and thought everybody had the same privilege !"[2] And "in November, 1883, the difficulty of getting breakfast punctually at 8 o'clock," he says, "which I desired, although Mary was never remarkable as an early riser, was solved by our spirit friends": for " one morning when Mary came down—late as usual—she found the fire already alight, and the water in the kettle hot !"[3] Rather sceptical himself on this point, he watched, and *at last "saw it done !"*[4] After which it seemed to be a thing of ordinary occurrence—nay, he testified " that when the fires are lit in the morning the kettles always *left empty over night* have also been found filled with water and usually nearly boiling " ! ! Afterwards he says, " when my daughter went into the dining-room, she saw the things taken out of the sideboard cupboard *before her eyes*, and placed on the table ": while the next day, " the brass kettle, which is taken upstairs to the breakfast table, was standing *empty* on the table,

---

[1] " Spirit Workers," &c., pp. 88, 89.   [2] Ib., p. 92.
[3] Ib., pp. 97, 98.   [4] Ib., p. 101.

just put there by my daughter, and while both were looking at it, it was then and there *filled with boiling water* from the larger kettle boiling on the kitchener"!!^{1}

At length we come to *materializations*. " On *Sunday*, April 29, 1883," he records, among other things, " The cabinet was moved about the room bodily, and the wooden cap on the top lifted up and down by the power inside it. Mary on coming to her normal state said she had been looking in the cabinet, and seen four materialized spirits there. One, *not of our group*, was determined not to let *Louisa*, who was materialized, come out among us, as she wished to do. On the curtains opening at the bottom and upwards for about 2 feet, we saw white raiment or shining drapery—quite glittering. But *confusion followed;* the cabinet was banged about, turned right round before us ; and I broke up the circle. The power was unusually great, and, what was unusual to us, *so was the annoyance ! !* "^{2}

" But we tried with more success on *another Sunday* evening in July! On this occasion . . . . we heard *some questioning going on apparently among the spirits materialized who should first appear!* It was decided in favour of ' *Pocha*,' who came among us as a vivacious coloured little sprite about 3 feet high.

" She came out of the cabinet, carrying in her little arms the fairy bells—an instrument 2 feet in length and 7 inches or 8 inches wide, weighing 2½ lbs. This

---

^{1} " Spirit Workers," &c., pp. 108, 109. ^{2} Ib., pp. 117, 118.

she placed on the chair where Miss Wood had been sitting, and fingered the strings with her little dark hands as a child would to amuse itself. She then went to my wife who was sitting 4 feet or 5 feet from the cabinet, took her hand, and as my wife leaned downwards, she put her tiny arms round her neck and kissed her! Crossing over the room she took my hands, then my daughter's, and afterwards my daughter-in-law's hands—fondled them a bit, and retired to the cabinet!

"Again the curtains opened, and out came a tall female form with less power than '*Pocha*,' nor was she able to speak as '*Pocha*' had done. But she was known to our clairvoyants, who saw her through the white drapery in which she was enveloped; it was the promised form of *Louisa, her first appearance* thus materialized amongst us. Gaining power, she slowly walked up to her mother and gave her her hand, but had not sufficient power to embrace her as she tried to do! Walking then to the chair on which the fairy bells were resting, she took them up and brought them to me, leaving them in my hands. I took her hand gently, but, although fully materialized, it lacked the firm touch of little '*Pocha's*,' and seemed too ethereal to be pressed! On her retiring, another spirit—a male form—came out, but lacked the power to go to his father at the farther end of the room. . . . Then three sweet little spirits in succession were materialized, and came into our midst for the first time; delicate little forms of children radiant in light;[1] *those who*

---

[1] See page 122.

were daily among us and working with us, unseen *then* to all but the clairvoyants. . . . A hand now, seen by some favourably seated, took out the pins and threw the papers on the floor before us all! Then as the curtains opened all saw the light aura, and those on one side of the room the form of a tall spirit. '*Pocha*' said in her curious little voice, 'There's another spirit coming out with a baby;' we heard afterwards it was *Louisa* with *Dewdrop*, our last little one!! *But a thunderstorm at this moment broke over us*, disturbed the conditions, and the sitting was discontinued"![1]

From this time it would appear, that the writer kept a diary of the occurrences; and he here observes, "The phenomena are too numerous and continuous to be *all* recorded:" but "I have inserted no phenomena *without being satisfied of its actual occurrence*, and in the exact manner in which it is recorded"[2]—of which I may say, I have myself no reason whatever to doubt: for his experience exactly tallies with all that we have seen recorded before of the like phenomena.

He then proceeds to record many wonderful and extraordinary circumstances; such as spirit-writings on paper locked up in drawers, or placed between the leaves of books; writings on the wood of the cabinet, on the walls and on the ceilings, &c.—the communications being in hands-writing totally different from each other; of which he gives many fac-simile specimens—some being in languages unknown to him; one

---

[1] "Spirit Workers," &c., pp. 118-120.   [2] Ib., pp. 121, 122.

of which, on his presenting it to a learned man, turning out to be written in very ancient Greek! " On one occasion," he says, " the boy who was in the hall getting boots together for cleaning, and was going down the stairs, *was met by the tray coming up*, and would certainly have run over it had it not been put down, *to his intense consternation*, upon the *top* stair! This experience is typical of what occurred more than once, and to other members of our household " ! !¹

The spirit, who personated his daughter *Louisa*, having "neatly and clearly written" a letter to him " on lines three-eighths of an inch apart, the writing being upon *nineteen lines only* (which in *print* would occupy more than double the number)," he wrote her " as follows, leaving blank spaces on the paper for her replies " !

" ' My dearest *Louisa*,—Why shouldn't I write to you? I want you kindly to reply to the following questions, when you can do so conveniently—I am in no hurry. Please write on this paper if you can.— Your loving Pater.'

" 1. How long did it take you to write that letter for the public, as to the writing?

" 3 *seconds*.

" 2. When you breathe on pencil and paper, do you then hold the pencil or lead *over* the paper, while passing your hand over it?

" *Yes, in left hand, and hold right hand over that.*

---

¹ " Spirit Workers," &c., p. 153.

" 3. Does the lead thus become precipitated on the paper by the power ?

" *Yes, by the aid of spirit light and influence of our power.*

" 4. If so—what is the power ?

" *What was the power in the olden time but the Spirit of God,* WHICH IS IN ALL MANKIND, *but it is not the ordinary spirit power working with you all,* BUT THE TRUE SPIRIT OF GOD *working with us and you all. You will know more later on* " ! !

There were other questions and answers, which I need not quote : but the writer adds, " on the reverse side of the paper, written over the back of my own letter to *Louisa,* she [!] has written the following :

" Dear Papa,—As you write to me I will write to you, my dearest pa, and thank you for it, but don't you think it was rather a shabby letter. I have answered your questions so far as I can, but you will see more very soon, and be quite satisfied as we want to satisfy you, but we do not care about others just yet ! Your loving Big ' *Louisa.*'

" I will only remind the reader," adds the writer again, " that ' *little Louisa* ' was for a long time her pet name among us—we having never seen her other than our first *still-born* babe, more than 27 years ago ! !

" I put my letter of questions in a table drawer, and at night when I went to bed left it there. In the morning the paper was *gone,* and I found it *locked up* in my secretaire that day. The spirit writing *is so minute that it requires a strong magnifying glass to read it* " *! !* [1]

The writer seems to have had many more communications in writing, (some specimens of which he gives) from various other spirits, in different languages —some of the writers professing themselves to be his ancestors; while others said that they were Persians and Mahommedans, &c. He likewise records many more extraordinary events that took place in his residence at Blackheath and elsewhere—such as a " disturbance " in the house, which his " spirit guides " told him " proceeded from *an ignorant earth bound spirit— with no evil intention* " [!] and that they were to " *reason* with him and *assist him to rise to a higher life* " [! !]—the spirit afterwards confessing that they had THUS " *helped him to rise* " [! !] [2]—" puddings " " *made and cooked* when *all* the family were sitting on *Sunday* evening *en séance* " [! !]—" fires lit under the *eyes* of " his " daughter," and " cookery of all kinds done to the amazement and amusement of all " [! !]— " a small child's hand put out of the cabinet, which *grew* larger as " they " looked at it "—*scented* breezes, during which " the writer was stroked by a warm soft hand," &c., &c.

But I must conclude this account, with one more extract only: which details the most extraordinary phenomena recorded in the whole book—phenomena,

---

[1] " Spirit Workers," &c., pp. 156-158.
[2] Ib., pp. 202-205. See pages 111, 112, 140, 150.

which took place at a *séance* held at Blackheath in the latter part of the year 1885, where Mr. Eglinton—*the* Mr. Eglinton, I presume, referred to at pages 135-151—was the medium. This account seems to have been sent by the writer to "*Light*"; and I shall give it in his own words.

"The notes of that sitting, as now recorded, were read and approved by five of those present, three of whom have signed the report for publication.

"In an upper room carpeted all over, and opening into a smaller room, eight of us sat down at 8.20 p.m., having first carefully inspected both rooms, locked both the outer doors, and placed securely a gummed paper over the opening crack of the door in the inner room, which led on to the landing where gas was burning. The paper so gummed was initialled by Dr. M., and was found intact at the end of our sitting at 10.20. We sat in dim light, sufficient, however, to see one another and Mr. Eglinton plainly, and those who had good sight could tell the time on their watches.

"I should say that during the evening *four or five distinct female spirits came and walked among us, and also two male spirits :* probably there were 8 or 10 appearances, but some were duplicates, *i.e.*, the same spirit after retiring into the dark room returned!

"One of the female spirits came to a lady who sat next to me, and placing her hands on her shoulders drew her towards her and kissed her! In doing this I distinctly saw a beautifully-formed hand and arm, quite bare up to and above the elbow, and it was not so large as any man's arm!   Another form saluted a gentleman present and spoke to him.   A third female spirit, which appeared to have less power, approached Dr. M.   *She evidently tried to put her arms about him,* but not succeeding, she stretched out both hands towards him, and repeatedly kissed one hand *(similar to the one he had seen at our home circle)* and threw kisses to him!! This was a clearly-formed female figure, and the arms, bare to the elbow, were distinctly seen by us all!!

"One of the male forms, who appeared to have gathered up much force, was recognised at once by my wife as a near relative!   He came up to us (sitting together), shook hands with us both, then *kissed my wife on the forehead, covering her face with his beard in so doing!*   He then turned his face towards the light and to Dr. M., who observed a resemblance to his friend whom he had known during his earth-life, and shook hands with him!   We all three noticed the physical power in the hand; *bones and muscles all felt as natural as in life;*[1] there was no timidity in his grasp; he retired three times into the dark room, and coming out again walked firmly about the room, being clearly seen by all the circle!!

"The last materialization was remarkable, inasmuch as *we saw the spirit-form developed in our midst!!* The medium, Mr. Eglinton, was made to come out *in a deep trance and in evident distress;* he walked about the room rapidly, during which time *frequent bright*

---

[1] See page 132.

lights were seen flashing from his left side!! He said in urgent, excited tones : ' Talk—talk or do something.' We, at once, *sang all together, ' Shall we gather at the river,'* WHICH SEEMED TO GIVE THE NECESSARY POWER FOR WHAT FOLLOWED!! Where lights had been seen flashing *now appeared white drapery*, at first looking like a very fine white handkerchief hanging from a pocket, but higher up than Mr. Eglinton's pockets usually were! Mr. E. now *pulled away at this gauze-like drapery*, and nervously or excitedly *drew out and laid upon the floor some five yards of this light fleecy material!!* First coming out of his side as a broad ribbon, *it spread speedily over the floor just under our eyes!!* Watching intently this heap of fine white drapery, *we saw* A FIGURE FORMING UNDER IT; *a head first, then shoulders, until a full form* 6 *feet high was developed*, some two or three feet distant from the medium, who now seemed attached to the form by the drapery only!!¹ Mr. E. now pulled away at the latter, and disclosed a fine head of curly black hair and dark penetrating eyes!! The medium was apparently *thoroughly exhausted*,² and his own strength seemed as it were transmitted to the spirit-form, *who now sheltered the medium*, put his arm about him, I think, *but anyhow supported him, and gradually led him back into the dark room, and placed him on a chair!!*

" Soon after I was called into the dark room, where I found *the medium much distressed*, and after receiving a

---

¹ See page 122.   ² See pages 85, 103, 133, 138, 145.

few directions from the spirit, *in a direct voice*, I retired! Mr. E. soon returned to consciousness, and wanted water, which I gave him, and last of all a female form, of about *four feet* high, materialized, and in glistening white, stood for a few seconds at the opening of the curtains, and then faded away into darkness "!!![1]

My readers will no doubt agree with me that such a narrative as the foregoing is deeply painful: for sad indeed is it to see whole families—for this family is but a sample of but too many others—in this land of Bibles; *with the Bible itself in their hands*—for the spirits frequently requested them in the first instance to read certain portions of it—grovelling, as it were, at the feet of demons: for that these spirits were demons personating the dead, and not the dead persons whom they professed to represent, no enlightened, intelligent Bible student could for a moment doubt.[2] Indeed the doctrines taught by them, which have already been given, and others, which I shall have to give in my next Division, clearly prove them to be " doctrines of demons " — " lies spoken in hypocrisy " by the " seducing spirits " spoken of in these last days.

IV. And this at length leads me, in the fourth place, to set forth some of " the *doctrines* of the demons." The inspired Word tells us that, these demons, whose " consciences " are " seared with a hot iron "—for the

---

[1] " Spirit Workers," &c., pp. 244-247.   [2] See Division vii., Sec. 2.

original clearly shows that it is *of the demons them-selves,* that these words are spoken, δαιμονίων, ἐν ὑποκρίσει ψευδολόγων, κεκαυτηριασμένων, &c.,—are " seducing spirits," who would " speak lies in hypo-crisy ;" and would, among other things, " forbid to marry, and command to abstain from meats."[1]

Now this passage has, as I have before observed, been *exclusively* applied to Rome ; who forbids her priests to marry, and commands her members to abstain from meat on a Friday ; and to this extent, it no doubt *does* apply to Rome ; but certainly *not exclusively.* For Rome does *not* command her members to abstain from meat *altogether;* neither does she forbid marriage *entirely :* for she has even exalted it into a sacrament ! But the *advanced* teaching of the demons in America *does both.* Thus we read in the pages of " The Rainbow," for Jan. 1867 :—" Mr. T. L. Harris, a very intelligent Swedenborgian Minister, who became a Spiritualist, and lectured in Europe, said, as reported in the *London Advertizer, ' The. marriage vow imposes no obligation in the views of Spiritualists' !* Husbands who had for years been so devotedly attached to their wives, that they have said that nothing in the world but death itself could part them, have abandoned their wives, and formed criminal connections with other females, *because the spirits have told them that there was a greater ' Spiritualistic affinity' between these husbands and certain other*

---

[1] 1 Tim. iv. 1-3.

12

women than between them and their lawful wives!"
" In a speech at the Spiritualistic Convention at
Ravenna, Ohio, July 4th and 5th, 1867, Mrs. Lewis
said, '*To confine her love to one man was an abridgment
of her rights! Although she had one husband at
Cleveland, she considered herself married to the whole
human race*'!! Hundreds of families have been
broken up, and many affectionate wives deserted, by
'affinity-seeking' husbands! Many once devoted wives
have been seduced, and have left their husbands and
tender helpless children, to follow some 'higher attrac-
tion'! Many well-disposed, but simple-minded girls
have been deluded by 'affinity' notions, and led off by
'affinity hunters' to be deserted in a few months!"
" At a Convention held at Providence, Rhode Island,
in September, 1866, resolutions were adopted (1) abandoning all Christian ordinances and worship; (2) dis-
countenancing all Sunday schools; (3) declaring *that*
ANIMAL FOOD SHOULD NOT BE USED! And to crown
all 'SEXUAL TYRANNY' *was denounced*"!! And that
there has been a vast change in public opinion on the
subject of " the marriage vow " of late years even in
this country is evidenced by the tone of the many
letters which lately appeared in " The Daily Telegraph," under the head of " Is marriage *a failure?* "—
as well as from the Records of our " Divorce Courts ":
which show that from 1858 to 1887, there were no less
than 10,221 Petitions for *dissolution of marriage;*
2,693 for judicial separation; and 6,381 Decrees *made
absolute!!*

In opening out this Division of my subject, therefore, I shall (1) shew that the demons have travestied both of the Ordinances, as well as the Sacred Person, of our blessed Lord Himself; (2) give a brief summary of some of the doctrines of the demons, gathered from various sources; and (3) give several extracts from a work entitled "*Spirit Teachings*," published by an M.A. of Oxon—which is nothing more nor less, than *the "Doctrines of the Demons" themselves*, set forth, as it were, *by their own authority ;* for the *guidance* of those who have been "seduced" by them—a pregnant proof, as I have before observed, that the close of this Dispensation is at hand !

1. The demons have travestied both of the Ordinances, as well as the Sacred Person of our blessed Lord Himself.

The Rev. Cotton Mather, to whose works I have before referred, says in "An Hortatory and Necessary Address" on this subject, "that the devil is come down unto us with great wrath, we find, we feel, we now deplore. . . . The devil, exhibiting himself ordinarily as a small black man, has decoy'd a fearful knot of proud, froward, ignorant, envious and malicious creatures, *to lift themselves in his horrid service, by entering their names in a Book by him tendered unto them.* These *witches*, whereof above a score have now confessed, and shown their deeds, *and some are now tormented by the devils, for confessing,* have met in hellish Randezvouzes, wherein the confessors do say, that *they have their* DIABOLICAL SACRAMENTS, *imitating the* BAPTISM *and the* SUPPER *of our Lord!* In these hellish meetings, these monsters have associated themselves to do no less a thing than to destroy the Kingdom of our Lord Jesus Christ in these parts of the world; and in order thereto, first *they each of them have* THEIR SPECTRES, OR DEVILS, *commission'd by them, and representing of them, to be the engines of their malice*"—a description which marvellously tallies with some of the utterances and doings of the " *spectres* " and " *demons* " of modern Spiritualism—the only difference in these days being, that as the light of truth has now been more diffused, the demons have " *transformed themselves* " into " *angels of light*,"[1] instead of exhibiting themselves in their true colours, *as demons,* under " the prince of the demons "[2]—" the prince of the power of the air, the spirit that now energizeth," ἐνεργοῦντος, *i.e.,* worketh mightily, " in the children of disobedience."[3] And that the devil has now again *travestied the Lord's Supper*, I need only give the following extract from the pages of " Psychic Notes," in proof of the fact. The account follows the statement I have already quoted from that serial, that " *Old Theology is doomed*," &c. ; and is as follows :—

" On January 12th, 1880, Mr. W. Eglinton "—the same person,. I presume, as is before referred to— " read a paper before the Dalston Association of Spiritualists, of which he is an honorary member, on

---

[1] 2 Cor. xi. 13-15.   [2] Mat. xii. 24.   [3] Eph. ii. 2.

" Mediums and Mediumship," from which we extract the following :

" And here let me tell you of a *séance* held under the above-mentioned higher conditions—*one of the most beautiful* [!] it has ever been my lot either to induce or attend ! It was on New Year's Eve, 1878, and the meeting took place at the house of Mrs. Makdougall Gregory, of 21, Green Street, Grosvenor Square. There were 8 or 10 persons present, some of whom I see here to-night. After the dark *séance* manifestations, which upon this occasion were more powerful and instructive than usual, I took my seat in the back drawing-room, being separated from the sitters by a heavy curtain. I wish to strongly impress upon your minds the *séance* which I am now relating was a most unusual one, due, I firmly believe, to the fact of my having given many *séances* at the same house, and to the friendship, trust, and appreciation with which every sitter regarded me. Of course, what occurred during the materialisations was related to me afterwards by the sitters present, as, unfortunately, *during these manifestations I am kept in a deep trance.* The gas was turned on until *the room was pervaded by a dim religious light* [! !], when slowly the curtains opened, and from the cabinet came one dearly loved, long known, and always treasured by the hostess, Lady G——, widow of the late Field Marshal Sir W. G——. The form was no dummy dressed up to represent life, nor Mr. Eglinton transfigured, which will be best evidenced by Mrs. Gregory's own words :—

" ' I have no hesitation in giving my testimony to the wonderful power and satisfactory nature of your mediumship. Indeed, I, personally, have never seen it surpassed. I, with many others, have scrutinized it carefully when it occurred in my house, and we have all been satisfied with its truth. *Seven* different times my friend Lady G—— *appeared to me fully material-ized, when you were lying apparently in a trance* on my sofa in the drawing-room, visible to 5 or 6 of my friends who were with me at the time. Your sincere friend, LIZETTE MAKDOUGALL GREGORY.'

" What could be *more beautifully impressive* [! !] than this midnight scene on New Year's night? *The spirit, after requesting* CAKE AND WINE *to be brought* TASTED THE CAKE, *touched the wine, and then handed it to each of the sitters, that* THEY MIGHT PARTAKE OF THIS HOLY COMMUNION WITH HER ! !

" After this the persons present *were requested to kneel*, and in their midst, THE SPIRIT KNELT ALSO, *and pour-ing fourth a solemn invocation, asked that Almighty God would bless each friend present*, and make their new year one long to be remembered, and then vanished ! ! When the influence had left me," says Mr. Eglinton, " and I found myself fully conscious, I was persuaded the *séance* had been a failure, so restful and peaceful was my condition ; and not until I saw the tear-wet eyes of my friends, and received their grateful messages of thanks, did I fully understand this memorable event " ! !

The following account of the blasphemous imper-sonation of our blessed Lord is taken from the

"Cincinnati Enquirer;" and is quoted by Mrs. McHardie, in her " Midnight Cry."

"We have just received a remarkable document, *duly attested by seven witnesses*, giving an account of a series of *séances*, which we print *verbatim*, simply stating that these witnesses are all persons of respectability, moving in the best circles of their respective homes, and looked upon as truthful and reliable. Adventists are looking for the Second Coming of Christ, and if this wonderful story is true, He has surely come!! The attested document says, among other things :—

"'Friday morning we had a private *séance*, at which only eight persons were present, including Dr. Pence. The medium entered the cabinet, and in about twenty minutes was entranced. After a little while, during which the spirit control talked as usual, the cabinet door opened, and *a majestic form appeared, that filled us with awe :* for there in the door stood, in majestic grandeur, *Jesus of Nazareth !* the Lord of Glory! the King of Kings! the pure and holy Christ of God! *He had come according to promise* [!], and stood manifest before our eyes! He stood looking at us silently for several moments, and then said: "You are faithful soldiers, and greater wonders than these shall you yet see"!! These words He spoke in a low voice. He then beckoned each one of us to Him, took us by the hand, and *blessed us before retiring to the cabinet !!* He had stood in the door and on the platform nearly half an hour. He had a white robe and a crown upon

His head, in the centre of which glittered a beautiful gem. A faint halo was visible surrounding His sacred head. He left us awe-stricken with His sacred presence. *This was the masterpiece of materialisation !* Surely these are the days foretold by John the Revelator, when he declared that Jesus Christ should come again a second time with power and great glory, and have not the dead arisen throughout the land, and angels returned, appearing unto many! Would that every mortal could have seen and *known*, as we now *know*, this glorious truth!! The Saviour of mankind has reappeared; *the Second Advent has arrived;* the heavens are opened; the dead are raised; mortality is swallowed up in immortality; death has lost its sting, and the grave its victory!! Having examined the cabinet, the *séance* room, and the medium, we are prepared to witness to the world that *the materializations* that have occurred in our presence are true.'

" (Here follow signatures of the witnesses)."[1]

Well might Mrs. McHardie, and others, who have also noted this diabolical imposture, refer to the warning words of our Lord, " Then, if any man shall say unto you, Lo, here is Christ, or there; *believe it not.* For there shall arise *false Christs, and false prophets, and shall shew* GREAT SIGNS AND WONDERS; insomuch that, IF IT WERE POSSIBLE, *they shall deceive the very elect.* Behold, I have told you before. Wherefore *if they shall say unto you,* Behold, He is in the desert;

----

[1] The Midnight Cry, by E. McHardie, p. 474.

go not forth : behold, *He is in* THE SECRET CHAMBERS ; *believe it not.* For as the lightning cometh out of the east, and shineth even unto the west ; *so shall also the coming of the Son of Man be* "[1]—*no* " SECRET *rapture,*" as some persons delude themselves with supposing ; but " with power and great glory "[2]—when " every eye shall see Him, and they also which pierced Him : and all the tribes of the land," πᾶσαι αἱ φυλαὶ τῆς γῆς, *i.e.,* of Israel,[3] " shall wail at Him," επ'αυτον. " Even so, Amen."[4]

2. A brief summary of some of the doctrines of the demons, gathered from various sources.

The Rev. T. L. Harris, whose testimony I have before quoted, on abandoning " Spiritualism " on account of its demoralising tendency, published a sermon preached in London on the 6th of January, 1860 ; from which Lieut.-Gen. Sir Robert Phayre, writing upon " Spiritualism unveiled," in " The Silver Morn," of June, 1887, gives the following summary of *the doctrines* held by Spiritualists, and *professedly taught by spirits* from the unseen world :—" First, that according to spiritualistic tenets, *nature is God!* Secondly, that God is an undeveloped principle in progress of EVOLUTION ! Thirdly, that the Jehovah of the Bible was a ferocious human spirit who deceived ancient Medea ! Fourthly, that the Lord Jesus Christ was but a natural man, possessed of

---

[1] Mat. xxiv. 23-27.   [2] Luke xxi. 27.   [3] Zech. xiv. 1-5.
[4] Rev. i. 7.

the ordinary mediumistic faculty of spiritual clairvoyance! Fifth, that our Lord's theological and psychical teachings were but the reproductions of false mythologies! Sixthly, that he held His power, great or little, because under the influence of departed men!"

Mr. T. W. Greenwell, in his "Latter-Day Delusions," in "The Watchword," under the head of "Spiritualism;" while quoting the above, also adds to their number as under:—

"All things originate in nature, and man is a development of the animal—our first parents, born of brutes, were savages of a degraded type—All things and beings are governed by natural necessity; man possesses no freedom nor moral will—There is no retrogression, through moral disorders, either of the individual or of the species—*Vice is virtue in its unprogressed or germinal condition;* SIN IS THEREFORE AN IMPOSSIBLE CHIMERA!—Self-love is the centre and fountain-head of all human affections, and the chief inspirer of all human or spiritual actions [1]—*the spirit world* is the theatre *for the continued evolution* of human spirits, *under the perpetual force of nature* WORKING THROUGH SELF-LOVE!—lastly, *the doctrine of free-love is inculcated*"!!

---

[1] "All sin and vice," says good old Archbishop Leighton, "springeth from the property of our own will; all virtue and perfection cometh and groweth from the mortifying of it, and the resigning of it wholly to the pleasure and will of God." "For *from* SELF-LOVE *and* SELF-WILL, *spring* ALL SIN and ALL PAIN."

And the Rev. A. R. Fausset, writing in the " Silver Morn " for October, 1885, on " Spiritualism tested by Scripture," quotes from a book on spirit-manifestations by Stone, in 1852, which he says, " denies (1) the Scripture doctrine of the Trinity in one God, and the Godhead of Christ ; (2) the fall and consequent innate corruption of every man ; (3) the believer's acceptance through faith in the Lord Jesus, as our sin-atoning substitute, making reconciliation by His blood-shedding, between God and man ; (4) the need of our regeneration by the Holy Spirit, if we would enter heaven ; (5) the eternity of future punishment and hell. It represents even the worst men as entering bliss at death, *their happiness increasing progressively* AS THEY RISE IN MORALITY HEREAFTER ; (6) it denies the resurrection of the body ; and a day of judgment which will fix men's state for eternal weal or woe ; according to their works now ; and the second advent of Christ ; (7) it renders the Bible (even the New Testament) a superannuated almanack " ! !

Let me add a few more only, in confirmation, from " *Spirit Teachings* and writings," culled from " Spirit workers in the Home Circle;" and then I will pass on.

" January 31, 1871, Automatic.

" When we say keep to your boyhood faith in the old gospel *we do not intend you to believe you cannot outgrow it! The Gospel of our dear Jesus was but the beginning of* A MORE GLORIOUS DEVELOPMENT OF THE CHRIST LIFE—all that ever will remain, *but* SPIRIT-UALISM SHALL CONSIDERABLY ADD AND EXPAND IT !—

the same truths, dear Papa—do not shrink from our messages. Science *advances* and *Religion must!* It would not be worthy of God if it did not, *nor carry out Christ's promise that greater things shall ye do!* —when He has gone to the Father. Which is *the greatest*, think you? *Christ* or *His Spirit?* The former was the seed corn, *the latter will bring on the second coming in power*—the true spiritual harvest—go in and reap—shrink not—be not dismayed so long as *the spirit of Christ leads the way!*—onward ever, dear Papa. Good night." [1]   And if we have not here a " seducing spirit," with a " conscience seared with a hot iron," " speaking lies in hypocrisy," there never was such a thing !

" November, 1882.   Another automatic message " ; with a postscript, as follows :—" *The reason* is and must be *the ultimate appeal* in *all things*—where the reason cannot go nor penetrate you will be wise to refuse to follow " [2]—a sentiment which would suit " Rationalism " to perfection !

" October 22, Automatic.

" *The resurrection is* A CONTINUOUS PROCESS OF SPIRITUAL LIFE ! It may commence here with you, but will continue *yonder*, as you call it ! THERE IS NO SUCH THING AS A RESURRECTION OF FLESH, for that corrupts and cannot live apart from the spirit. . . ." [3]

" Sunday, 19th and 20th April [1885].—Had a long conversation on re-incarnation with the *direct* voice of

---

[1] " Spirit Workers," &c., pp. 251, 252.   [2] Ib., p. 255.   [3] Ib., p. 257.

E.M., who said he had been living on earth once, and *should never again*"—true enough in *the demon's case;* no doubt!—"neither he, nor *Saadi* and *Wamik*, who had been there in the spirit world hundreds of years, *ever heard of one case of re-incarnation;* he would endeavour to get at the truth of it and write fully (this he has not yet done), but on January 31st, 1866, we received the following *direct* writing upon the subject:

"We will not yet write on the subject of re-incarnation, *as you of the world are not yet ready* for it, and at the present time (it) would do more harm than good, but in due time you shall have it. E.M. and Saadi!"[1]

3. But in the work entitled "*Spirit Teachings*," published by an M.A. of Oxon, from which I shall now proceed to give extracts, we have *the authoritative doctrines*, if I may so say, *of the demons themselves;* issued for the use of the faithful: as would appear, not only from the assertions of the demons; but also from the use made of them by Spiritualists, and the reverence they seem to have for the M.A., through whom they were originally delivered.

In his introduction, which is dated March 30, 1883, the writer states, that "the communications which form the bulk of this volume, were received by the process known as automatic, or passive, writing. This is to be distinguished from psychography. In the former case the psychic holds the pen or pencil, or places his

---

[1] "Spirit Workers," &c., p. 232.

hand upon *the Planchette*, and the message is written without the conscious intervention of his mind. In the latter case the writing is direct, or is obtained without the use of the hand of the psychic, and sometimes without the aid of pen or pencil.

" *Automatic writing is a well-known method of communication with the invisible world of what we loosely call spirit.* I use that word as the most intelligible to my readers, though I am well aware that I shall be told that I ought not to apply any such term to many of the unseen beings, who communicate with earth, of whom we hear much and often as being the *reliquiæ* of humanity, the *shells* of what once were *men !* It is no part of my business to enter into these *most moot questions ! My interlocutors called themselves spirits*, perhaps because I so called them, and spirits they are to me for my present purpose.

" These messages began to be written through my hand just 10 years since, March 30, 1873, about the year of my first introduction to Spiritualism. I had had many communications before, and this method was adopted for the purpose of convenience, and also to preserve *what was intended to be* A CONNECTED BODY OF TEACHING !! The laborious method of rapping out messages, was manifestly unfitted for communications such as those which I here print. If spoken through the lips of the medium in trance, they were partially lost, and it was, moreover, impossible at first to rely upon such a message of mental passivity *as would preserve them from admixture with his ideas.*

" I procured a pooket-book which I habitually carried about with me. *I soon found that writing flowed most easily when I used a book that was permeated with the psychic aura,* just as raps come more easily on a table that has been frequently used for the purpose, and as *phenomena occur most readily in the medium's own rooms!* When Slade could not get messages on a new slate, *he rarely failed to get one on his own seasoned one!* I am not responsible for the fact, the reason for which is sufficiently intelligible!

" At first the writing was very small and irregular, and it was necessary for me to write slowly and cautiously, and to watch the hand, following the lines with my eye ; otherwise the message soon bècame incoherent, and the result was mere scribble.

" In a short time, however, I found that I could dispense with these precautions. The writing, while becoming more and more minute, became at the same time *very regular, and beautifully formed.* As a specimen of caligraphy, some of the pages are exceedingly beautiful. *The answers to my questions* (written at the top of the page) *were paragraphed, and* ARRANGED AS IF FOR THE PRESS ; and the name of God was always written *in capitals,* and slowly, and, as it seemed, *reverentially!* The subject-matter was ALWAYS *of a pure and elevated character* [!] much of it being of personal application, INTENDED FOR MY OWN GUIDANCE AND DIRECTION ! ! I may say that throughout the whole of these written communications, extending in unbroken continuity to the year 1880, there is no flippant message, no attempt at jest, no vulgarity or incongruity, *no false or misleading statement* [! !], so far as I know or could discover: nothing incompatible with THE AVOWED OBJECT, AGAIN AND AGAIN REPEATED, OF INSTRUCTION, ENLIGHTENMENT, AND GUIDANCE BY SPIRITS FITTED FOR THE TASK! ! Judged as I should wish to be judged myself, they were what they pretended to be. Their words were words of sincerity, and of sober, serious purpose "!

I have thus let the writer speak for himself, as he no doubt does, *in all sincerity :* but when my readers peruse the teaching of the demons themselves, they will be able to form their own judgment upon it.

Continuing his account, he says, " The earliest communications were all written in the minute characters that I have described, and were uniform in style, and in the signature 'DOCTOR, THE TEACHER' [! !] : nor have his messages ever varied during all the years that he has written. Whenever and wherever he wrote, his handwriting was unchanged, showing, indeed, less change than my own does during the last decade. The tricks of style remain the same, and there was, in short, a sustained individuality throughout his messages. *He is to me an entity, a personality,* a being with his own idiosyncrasies and characteristics, *quite as clearly defined as the human beings with whom I come in contact,* if indeed, *I do not do him injustice by the broad comparison! !*

" After a time, communications came *from other* sources, and these were *distinguished each by his own handwriting*, and by its own peculiarities of style and expression. These, once assumed, were equally invariable. *I could tell at once who was writing by the mere characteristics of the caligraphy!!*

"By degrees I found that *many spirits, who were unable to influence my hand themselves*, sought the aid of a spirit '*Rector*' [!!], who was apparently able to write more freely, *and with less strain on me*, for *writing by a spirit unaccustomed to the work was often incoherent*, AND ALWAYS RESULTED IN A SERIOUS STRAIN UPON MY VITAL POWERS!![1] *They* did not know [?] *how easily the reserved force was exhausted, and* I SUFFERED PROPORTIONABLY!!

"Moreover, the writing of the spirit who thus became a sort of amanuensis was flowing and easy to decipher, whereas that of many spirits was cramped, archaic in form, and frequently executed with difficulty, and almost illegible. So it came to pass as a matter of course '*Rector*' wrote: but, when a spirit came for the first time, or when it was desired to emphasize the communication, *the spirit responsible for the message wrote it himself*"!!

"Originally published in the 'Spiritualist' newspaper," he says, "*the messages have been revised, but not substantially altered*, BY THOSE WHO FIRST WROTE THEM"!!

Further on, he says:—"It is an interesting subject for speculation whether my own thoughts entered into

---

[1] See pages 85, 103, 133, 138, 145 and 175.

13

the subject-matter of the communications. *I took extreme pains to prevent any such admixture.* At first the writing was slow, and it was necessary to follow it with my eye, *but even then* THE THOUGHTS WERE NOT MY THOUGHTS! Very soon the messages assumed a character of which I had no doubt whatever that the thought was opposed to my own! *But I cultivated the power of occupying my mind with other things during the time that the writing was going on*, and was able to read an abstruse book, and follow up the line of close reasoning, *while the message was written with unbroken regularity!* Messages so written extended over many pages, and in their course there is no correction, no fault in composition, and often a sustained vigour and beauty of style. . . . *I never could command the writing!* It came unsought usually : and when I did seek it, as often as not I was unable to obtain it. A sudden impulse, coming I knew not how, led me to sit down and prepare to write ! "

" The particular communications which I received from the spirit known to me as '*Imperator*' mark a distinct epoch in my life. I have noted in the course of my remarks *the intense exaltation of spirit*, the strenuous conflict, *the intervals of peace* that I have since longed for but have seldom attained, which mark their transmission. *It was* A PERIOD OF EDUCATION *in which I underwent* A SPIRITUAL DEVELOPMENT that was in its outcome, a very original! I cannot hope, I do not try, to convey to others what I then experienced. But it may possibly be borne in upon the minds of some, who are not ignorant of *the Dispensation of the Spirit* [!] in their own inner selves, that *for me to question all the beneficent action of external spirit* [!] *on my own self* was then finally settled ! *I have never since*, even ·in the vagaries of an extremely sceptical mind, and amid much cause for questioning, *ever seriously entertained a doubt* " ! /[1]

Having given these extracts, in order that my readers may judge of the sincerity of the writer ; as well as of his own belief in the reality of the communications, of which there can, I think, be no doubt; I shall now proceed to give extracts from the " *teaching*," or " *doctrines*, of the demons" themselves ; chiefly communicated to him, in replies to questions put by him to them.

Something having been said, " as to the repeated failure of plans for man's benefit through his ignorance and obstinacy "—" I asked," said the writer, " If *these* were to be *another failure?* " in reply to which question, the spirit wrote :—

" God is giving far more than you think. *In all parts* are springing up centres from which the truth of God " —*i.e.*, spiritualistic communications—" is being poured into longing hearts, and permeating thinking minds. *There must be many to whom the Gospel of old* IS SATISFYING YET, *and who are not receptive of* FURTHER TRUTH !! WITH THESE WE MEDDLE NOT !! But many there are *who have learned what the past can teach, and*

---

[1] " Spirit Teachings," pp. 1-8.

who are THIRSTING FOR FURTHER KNOWLEDGE ! ! To *these* it is given "—*i.e.*, through the spirits—" in such measure as the Most High sees fit ! And *through them it flows to others*, and the glorious tidings spread until the day comes when we shall be called on to proclaim them from the mountain top ! And lo ! *God's hidden ones* shall start up from the lowly places of the earth to bear witness to that which they have seen and known : and the little rills that man has hid not shall coalesce, and the river of God's truth,"—*i.e.*, the teaching of the spirits—" omnipotent in its energy, shall flood the earth, and *sweep away*, in its resistless course, *the ignorance and unbelief* and folly and sin which now dismay and perplex you ! "

The writer then asks, " *This* NEW REVELATION *of which you speak* : is it *contrary to the old?* Many are exercised on that point ? " To which the spirit replies in the following intensely subtle manner :—

" Revelation is from God : and that which He has revealed at one time cannot contradict that which He has revealed at another, seeing that each in its kind is a revealing of truth, but of truth revealed in proportion to man's necessities, and in accordance with his capacities. That which seems contradictory is not in the word of God, but in the mind of man. Man was not content with the simple message, but has adulterated it with his glosses, overlaid it with his deductions and speculations. And so, as years go by, it comes to pass that *what came from God is in no sense what it was ! !* It has become *contradictory, impure, and earthy ! !*

When A FURTHER REVELATION *comes*, instead of fitting in reasonably; *it becomes necessary* TO CLEAR AWAY much of *the superstition* that has been built on the old foundation ; and THE WORK OF DESTRUCTION *must precede the work of addition! !* The *revelations* are NOT *contradictory ;* but it is necessary to destroy man's rubbish before *God's truth* can be revealed! MAN MUST JUDGE ACCORDING TO THE LIGHT OF REASON THAT IS IN HIM ! ! THAT *is* THE ULTIMATE STANDARD, and *the progressive soul will receive* what the ignorant or *prejudiced* soul will reject ! ! God's truth is forced on none. So for a time, during the previous process, THIS *must be* A SPECIAL REVELATION TO A SPECIAL PEOPLE ! ! It has ever been so. Did Moses obtain universal acceptance even amongst his own people ? Did any of the seers ? Did Jesus even ? Did Paul ? Did *any reformer* in any age, amongst any people ? God changes not. He offers, but He does not force acceptance. He offers, and *they who are prepared receive the message ! !* The *ignorant* and *unfit* reject it. It must be so ; and the dissensions and differences which you deplore *are but for the sifting of the false from the true !* They spring from unworthy causes, *and are impelled* BY MALIGNANT SPIRITS ! ! You must expect annoyances ; too, *from the banded powers of evil ! !* But cast your eyes beyond the present. Look to the far future, and be of good courage."

Then the writer, putting this question, " You have spoken of adversaries. Who are they ? " the demon replies :—" *The antagonistic spirits who range them-*

selves AGAINST OUR MISSION ; *who strive to mar its progress* by counterfeiting our influence and work, *and by setting men* and other spirits *against it ! !* These are spirits who have chosen the evil, *have put aside promptings and influences of good,* and have banded themselves under the leadership of intelligence still more evil *to malign us,* AND HAMPER OUR WORK ! ! Such are powerful for mischief, and their activity shews itself in evil passions, *in imitating our work,* and so gaining influence for a time, and most of all, in presenting to enquiring souls that which is mean and base, *where* WE *would tenderly lead* TO THE NOBLE AND REFINED ! !   They are the foes of God and man : enemies of goodness ; *ministers of evil !   Against these* WE *wage perpetual war* ” ! !

On this, he asks :—“ Have they a chief—a devil ? ” to which the demon lyingly replies :—

“ Chiefs many who govern, *but* NOT *such a devil* AS THEOLOGIANS HAVE FEIGNED ! ! Spirits good and bad alike, are subject to the rule of commanding intelligences ! ”[1]

On another occasion, he “ asks whether the marriage ties were perpetuated ” in “ other spheres of work,” *i.e.,* “ in the spirit world ; ” and he receives the reply :—

“ That *depends* entirely on *similarity of taste* and *equality of development ! !* . . . . . We know no such indissoluble ties *as exist with you.*”

---

[1] “ Spirit Teachings,” pp. 10-14.

"Then," adds the writer, "the Bible words are true, 'They neither marry nor are given in marriage, but are as the angels of God'?" to which question, he receives the reply:—

"It was truly said. We have before told you *of the law of progress*, and of *the law of association*"!![1]

Then on another occasion, the evil spirit, speaking on religion in general, says:—

"Religion, to be worthy of the name, must have its two sides—the one pointing to God, the other to man. *What has* THE RECEIVED FAITH, WHICH IS CALLED ORTHODOX BY ITS PROFESSORS, to say on this point; and *wherein* do *we differ* in *our messages;* and how far is such difference on our part in accord with reason? For, at the very outside, *we claim*, AS THE ONLY COURT *to which we can as yet appeal*, THE REASON WHICH IS IMPLANTED IN MAN!! We claim it; for it *was* BY REASON that the sages *settled the last of the writings which they decided to be the exclusive and final revelation of God!* To *reason* they appealed for their decision. To *reason we* appeal too. Do our friends claim that Divine guidance prescribed for them, what should be for all time the body of revealed truth? WE, TOO, WHO ARE THE MINISTERS OF THE MOST HIGH, NO LESS SURELY SENT THAN THE SPIRITS WHO GUIDED THE HEBREW SEERS, and who ministered to those WHOSE FIAT SETTLED THE DIVINE WORD!!

"WE are as *they:* OUR message as *their* message, ONLY MORE ADVANCED!! Our God their God, *only*

---

[1] "Spirit Teachings," pp. 45, 46.

MORE CLEARLY REVEALED, LESS HUMAN, MORE DIVINE!!
Whether the appeal be to Divine inspiration or not,
human reason (guided doubtless *by spirit agency*, but
still reason) *sways the* FINAL DECISION!! And those
who reject this appeal are out of their own mouths convicted of folly. BLIND FAITH *can be no substitute for*
REASONING TRUST!! For the faith is faith that either
has ground for its trust or not. In the former case
the ground is REASONABLE; in which case *reason* again
is *the ultimate judge:* or it is not, in which case it
would commend itself to none. But if the faith rests
on no grounds at all, we need not further labour to
shew it baseless and untrustworthy.

"To *reason* then WE *turn.* How far are WE *proved*
REASONABLY *to be* OF THE DEVIL? How far is our
creed an evil one? In what respect are WE *charge-
able with* DIABOLIC TENDENCY"!![1]

My readers will, I think, agree with me, that I have
already shewn this: but I hope to make it clearer still,
before I have done.

Certain objections having been referred to, that "the
teachings of the spirits" were "not consistent with
the received creed of orthodoxy"; the reply received
was:—"We have more to say on this subject": and
a sample of what they *did* say on the subject, I now
therefore subjoin.

" Religion, the spirit's healthful life, has two aspects
—the one pointing to God, the other to man. What
says *the* SPIRIT-CREED?

---

[1] "Spirit Teachings," pp. 51, 52.

" *In place of* AN ANGRY JEALOUS TYRANT it reveals a loving Father, who is not loving in name alone, but in very deed and truth ; into whose dealings naught but love can enter ; who is just and good and full of affection to the lowest of His creatures.

"It does *not* recognize *any need of propitiation* towards this God. It *rejects as false* any notion of this Divine Being *vindictively punishing the transgressor,* or *requiring* A VICARIOUS SACRIFICE FOR SIN ! ! Still less does it teach that this Omnipotent Being is enthroned in heaven where His pleasure consists in the homage of the elect, and in the view of the tortures of the lost, who *are for ever excluded in quenchless misery* from the light of hope ! !

" *No such* anthropomorphism finds place *in our creed ! !* As we know Him in the operation of His laws as perfect, pure, loving, and holy, incapable of cruelty, tyranny, and other such human vices: viewing error with sorrow as knowing that sin contains its own sting, He is eager to alleviate the smart by any means consistent with the immutable moral laws to which all alike are subject. God, the centre of light and love ! God, operating in strict accordance with those laws which are the necessity of *orderly existence !* God, the grand object of our adoration, *never of our dread !* " [1]

" *We* know of Him as *you* cannot know, as you cannot picture even in imagination : yet none has seen Him : nor are we content with the metaphysical

---

[1] Deut. xxviii. 58 ; Isa. viii. 13, &c.

sophistries with which prying curiosity and over-subtle speculation have obscured the primary conception of God amongst men. We pry not. The first conception with you even is grander, nobler, more sublime. We wait for the higher knowledge. You must wait too. On the relation between God and His creatures we speak at large. Yet here, too, WE *clear off many of the minute points of human inventions which have been from age to age accumulated on and over Scriptural truths! We know nothing of* ELECTION *of a favoured few!* The elect are those *who work out for themselves the salvation* ACCORDING TO THE LAWS WHICH REGULATE THEIR BEING !!

" We know *nothing* of the potency of *blind* FAITH *or credulity ! !* We know, indeed, the value of a trustful *receptive spirit, free from the littleness of* PERPETUAL SUSPICION ! ! Such is God-like, and DRAWS DOWN ANGEL GUIDANCE ! ! But WE *abjure,* and *denounce* that MOST DESTRUCTIVE DOCTRINE *that* FAITH, *belief,* assent to *dogmatic statements,* have power to erase the traces of transgression; that *the earth life-time of vice and sloth and sin can be wiped away,* and the spirit stand *purified* by a blind acceptance of a *belief,* of an idea, of a fancy, of *a creed ! ! Such teaching* has *debased more souls than anything else* to which we can point " ! !¹

At page 53 of his own Introduction, in the 3rd paragraph, the writer says :—" From this time commences that state, to which I shall often have to refer, of *great*

---

¹ "Spirit Teachings," pp. 54, 55.

spiritual exaltation, during which I was *profoundly conscious of the presence and influence of* ONE COMMANDING INTELLIGENCE, and of an action on my mind which eventuated in a *development of thought* amounting to nothing short of SPIRITUAL REGENERATION " ! !

And so having given himself up to "seducing spirits," and thus "rejected the word of the Lord,"[1] he is ready to believe the demon's lies, *on their own simple utterance of them*, although their "teaching" is diametrically opposed to the teaching of the Divine Word, and absolutely subversive of it ; and yet at the same time to imagine that he has undergone *through them*— although the Holy Ghost Himself can alone regenerate the soul—"*Spiritual regeneration*"—another diabolical travesty of the work of the Holy Ghost—and is being taught *the deep truths* OF GOD, *through their instrumentality* himself ! And this is the exercise of "*reason*" in its highest development ! What infatuation could ever equal this ! Surely it must be a "strong delusion" indeed that could ever have produced so fearful a result !

But I must hasten on to the close of the testimony. Speaking of the "mercy of God," one of the demons says :—

" Mercy is *not* a divine attribute. It is *needless ;* for mercy involves remission of a penalty inflicted, and *no such remission can be made safe* where the results have been purged away ! ! . . . . We leave to *foolish men, groping blindly in the dark their* CURIOUS QUIBBLES

---

[1] Jer. viii. 8, 9 ; Mark vii. 9 ; John xii. 48.

ABOUT THEOLOGICAL FIGMENTS!! *We* deal with *practical life;* and our creed may be briefly written :—

"Honour and love our Father, God (worship).	} Duty to God.
Help our brothers onward in the path of progress (brotherly love).	} Duty to neighbour.
Tend and guard our own body (bodily culture). Cultivate every source of extending knowledge (mental progress). Seek for fuller views of progressive truth (spiritual growth). Do ever the right and give in accordance with your knowledge (integrity). *Cultivate communion with the spirit-land by prayer and frequent intercourse!* (*Spiritual nurture*).	} Duty to self.

"Within THESE RULES are roughly indicated *most that concerns you here!!* Yield no obedience to any sectarian documents. Give no blind adherence to *any teaching* that is not *commanded by reason! Put no unquestioning faith in communications which were made at a special time,"—i.e.,* Bible statements—" and which are of *private application!* "[1]

Speaking of the after-state, one of the demons said : " *We know of* NO HELL *save that within the soul :* the hell which is fed by the flame of unpurified and untamed lust and passion, which is kept alive by remorse and

---

[1] " Spirit Teachings," pp. 56, 57.

agony of sorrow, which is fraught with the pains that spring unbidden from the results of past misdeeds; and *from which* THE ONLY ESCAPE LIES *in retracing the steps, and in cultivating the qualities* WHICH SHALL BEAR FRUIT IN THE LOVE AND KNOWLEDGE OF GOD "!!

Neither would the demon have the writer "perplexed by thoughts of *an imaginary devil!!* For the earnest, pure, and truthful soul *there is no devil, nor prince of evil* SUCH AS THEOLOGY HAS FEIGNED "!![1]

"WE *have succeeded* IN EVOLVING A SYSTEM OF THEOLOGY which you admit to be *coherent, beautiful* and *elevated* [!!], and which is acceptable to your mind! We have not ventured to do more. *We* have shewn you *a God* Who commands your adoration and respect "!![2] While on a subsequent occasion the demon, forgetting, or overlooking, his previous lying statement, that there was *no* devil, says:—" We are either of God *or the devil*"!![3]—by these very statements alone proving that he is " a *lying* spirit;" and therefore, "*of the devil*"; who is *a liar*, and *the father* of it![4]

Notwithstanding these contradictions however, the writer still consults "the evil one," through him, and asks, "Is this then the return of Christ?" when he receives the lying reply, "It is *a spiritual return.* THERE WILL BE NO SUCH PHYSICAL RETURN AS MAN HAS DREAMED OF "!![5] While further on the demon gives him his benediction, as follows:—"*I, the servant*

---

[1] "Spirit Teachings," p. 77.   [2] Ib., p. 120.   [3] Ib., p. 136.
[4] John viii. 34. See also pages 198, 200.   [5] "Spirit Teachings," p. 151.

of God, the Minister of the Most High, and THE GUIDE and *guardian of your spirit*, implore upon you the Divine benediction. The holy and loving Father bless you "!!![1]

Once more he asks, "The translation of Enoch and Elijah. What were they?" And receives for reply, "*Legendary beliefs*"!![2] And again, the demon delivers himself of this lying utterance, "*Another error even more destructive of truth is* THE FABLE *that divine inspiration*, plenarily communicated, *guided all the writers of the books of* OUR *Bible* [!] *into* ABSOLUTE TRUTH; and that, as God was in every case the author, so each individual utterance of each scribe *is of paramount and permanent authority!! This error* WE *have uprooted from your mind*, for you now know that God cannot be the author of contradictions, nor can He have said at one time what He contradicts at another!"[3]

Again, he asks, "Do *you* teach a general judgment?" —the reply being, "No. *The judgment is complete* when the spirit gravitates to the home which it has made for itself! There can be no error!"[4]

And the last utterance, which I shall quote is as follows:—"If *we* have *taken from the Christ* the halo which *the foolish and human creed* had spread round Him, *we* have shewn you the man Christ Jesus *in divinest form*, the full realization of human perfection

---

[1] "Spirit Teachings," p. 173.　　[2] Ib., p. 189.　　[3] Ib., p. 201.
[4] Ib., p. 227.

on this earth. *His body* HAS NOT indeed BEEN RAISED, but *He has* NEVER DIED, and *in spirit* He manifested Himself to His friends, walked with them, as *we* may one day walk with you, and taught them all the truth ! " [1]　While on a subsequent occasion, the lying spirit again contradicts himself by saying, " Christ *came to die* for and to save men *in the same* though in a higher SENSE, *that* ALL REGENERATORS OF MEN *have been their saviours*, and have *yielded up bodily existence* in devotion to an over-mastering idea ! ! *In this sense* He came to save *and die* for men: but *in the sense that the sin on Calvary was fore-ordained to cure* when man consummated his foul deed, HE CAME NOT ! !　And *this* is a mighty truth " ! ! [2]

The book from which I have taken these extracts, is a large 8vo volume of some 300 or 400 pages, containing much more to the same effect : but these extracts are abundantly sufficient to shew, that the " *teachings* " of these so-called " *good* spirits," are nothing more nor less than the " *doctrines of demons*," referred to by the Holy Ghost, in the passage in Timothy previously quoted : for they not only unblushingly *deny* every precious *truth* contained in the Word of God—such as the real object and purpose of the coming of Christ in the flesh—His precious death, and burial, His resurrection and ascension, &c.—His substitution and atonement, for the sins of, and the imputation of His righteousness to, His people—their eternal election,

---

[1] " Spirit Teachings," p. 245.　　[2] Ib., p. 252.

and their justification through a living faith, in Him—
their regeneration and sanctification by the Holy Ghost
—their resurrection in the body at His second coming,
and their future glorification with, and in, Him ; and
many such like precious truths : but they likewise deny
any future judgment, or Divine infliction of punishment upon impenitent sinners ; as well as strike at the
very root of all Divine revelation, by not only denying
the inspiration of the Word of God ; but asserting that,
through man's incrustations upon it, it has now become nothing better than a mass of error and deceit !

Moreover as these demons also profess to be " the
ministers of the Most High," and to be sent by Him
to bring in " *a new*" *and more complete* " *revelation ;* "
and have, *as such*, issued this *authoritative code of
doctrines* for the guidance of their deluded votaries—
which are nothing less than " *damnable heresies*," [1] and
" *hypocritical lies* ": [2]—taught by the Holy Ghost, we
may now learn from this fulfilment of the passage
before referred to, as well as others that might have
been adduced, that the close of this dispensation is at
hand.   And notwithstanding these lying doctrines of
the demons—the " profane and vain babblings, and
oppositions of science falsely so-called : which some
professing have erred concerning the faith " [3]—*we know*
and *believe* in the *truth* of the words of our Blessed
Lord, when He said, " Heaven and earth shall pass
away ; but *My Word* shall *not* pass away." [4] And it is

---

[1] 2 Peter ii. 1, 2.   [2] 1 Tim. iv. 2.   [3] 1 Tim. vi. 20, 21.
[4] Luke xxi. 33.

written in the Scriptures of truth, that "*Every* word of God is *pure.*" "*Add* thou *not* unto His words, lest He reprove thee, and thou be found *a liar* unto Him."[1] "Ye shall *not add* unto the word which I command you, neither shall ye *diminish* ought from it."[2] And the canon of Scripture closes with this awful threatening, "For I testify unto every man that heareth the words of the prophecy of this book, If any man *shall add* unto these things, God shall add unto him the plagues that are written in this book: and if any man *shall take away from* the words of the book of this prophecy, God shall take away his part out of the book of life, and out of the holy city, and from the things which are written in this book."[3] "For without are *dogs*, and *sorcerers*," φαρμακοὶ,[4] "and whoremongers, and murderers, and *idolaters*, and whosoever *loveth* and *maketh* A LIE"![5] "*Beware*," therefore, says the Apostle, "of *dogs, beware* of *evil workers*, beware of the concision. For we are the circumcision, which worship God in the spirit, and rejoice in Christ Jesus, and *have no confidence in the flesh*."[6]

And now I would ask my intelligent readers, on a review of the overwhelming evidence which I have laid before them, whether I have not convincingly de-

---

[1] Prov. xxx. 5, 6.   [2] Deut. iv. 2.   [3] Rev. xxii. 18, 19.
[4] See page 9.   [5] Rev. xxii. 15.

[6] Phil. iii. 2, 3. What I have to say upon the ecstatic feelings of the poor deluded writer, under the inspiration of the demons, I shall defer, until I come to the general reflections, which I shall have to make in the closing division of my subject.

14

monstrated, that modern " Spiritualism " *so-called*, is nothing more nor less than the *demonology, witch-craft* and *necromancy*, which have prevailed, more or less, in all ages, over the whole heathen world ; and which is so strongly denounced and so solemnly prohibited in the Word of the living God? And here perhaps some might be inclined to say, I ought to close: but when they have perused what I have further to say on the subject, I think they will then agree with me that the subject itself would not have been complete, had I not also shown *the identity* of many of *the teachings of the demons* with what is called "*modern thought ;*" as well as portrayed the *final outcome* and issue of it all, which is so clearly revealed in the Word of God itself. I come now therefore,

V.—In the fifth place, to shew the identity of many of these doctrines, with what is called "*modern thought*" : proving that they both emanate from the same source.

To show that the tendency of modern thought is in the same direction, and indeed on the same lines, as the foregoing doctrines of the demons, will not be a difficult matter : as the proofs lie at every hand : for there is no *so-called* " section of the Christian church," wherein they have not been set forth and promulgated, I might almost say, in some cases even by authority—the difficulty, if any, lying in selection and compression only.

And in opening out this subject, I shall refer, in the first instance, to that most pernicious, heretical, and misleading book, " Natural Law in the Spiritual World "—a title, which is in itself false and unscriptural : for we are expressly told in the Divine Word, that " the *natural* man receiveth *not* the things of the Spirit of God : for they are foolishness unto him ; neither *can* he know them, *because* they are *spiritually discerned.*" [1] And yet this writer, who is a professing Christian, does not hesitate to say, that " there is a *solidity* about *a law of nature,*"—by which he means, (as his book shows) such laws as he and other rationalists *suppose to be such*—" which *belongs to nothing else* in the world "—*the* " *one thing* outside ourselves, unbiassed, unprejudiced "—the " one thing that holds on its way ETERNALLY, *incorruptibly* and *undefiled :*"—a statement, I need hardly say, which not only exalts human reason above Divine Revelation ; but even if limited in its application to creation itself, would still be untrue : because it contradicts the " Scripture," which " cannot be broken ;" [2] and which declares that " *the Word of the Lord endureth for ever* "; [3] and gives the lie also to the statement of our Lord, Who assures us that, " Heaven and earth *shall pass away :* but *My Words* shall *not* pass away." [4]

But when applied to *men's crude notions*, it becomes doubly false ; for the writer's whole system is based upon the lying doctrine of " Evolution ;" which we have seen that advanced " Spiritualists," or " Theosophist-Occultists," as they delight to call themselves,

---

[1] 1 Cor. ii. 14.   [2] John x. 35.   [3] 1 Peter i. 25.   [4] Luke xxi. 33.

have substituted for "*Creation*"; which they do not
believe in—logically following out the consequences,
which flow from such a belief: for "Evolution" strikes
at the very root of the doctrine, not only of "Creation,"
but of the Creator also: for *it virtually denies both!*
Indeed at one of the meetings of the British Association held at York, in 1881, after the reading of a paper
by Professor Seeley, on "The Development of the
Plesiosaurus from the Simosaurus Pusillus," Dr.
Wright thought that "he ought to have gone
further, and shewed the audience in his illustration
the wondrous adaptations of the Creator, so that their
thoughts might be raised beyond the consideration of
dry bones;" to which the Professor replied, by stating,
"if *design* in anatomy *were accepted*, there would be
an end of all philosophical anatomy! THE WHOLE
SCIENCE OF EVOLUTION HAD GROWN OUT OF THE
ABANDONMENT OF THIS NOTION OF DESIGN"!![1]

---

[1] Archbishop Leighton, in his 3rd Exhortation to the candidates
for the degree of M.A. in the University of Edinburgh, said :—"But
you are now *philosophers*, and amidst these dismal calamities, you
comfort yourselves with the inward and hidden riches of *wisdom*, and
the sciences you have acquired. *The sciences!* Tell us, in what part
of the earth they are to be found? Let us know, pray, where they
dwell, that we may flock thither in great numbers. I know, indeed,
where there is *abundance of noise*, WITH VAIN AND IDLE WORDS, *and
a jarring of opinions between contending disputants;* I know, *where*
IGNORANCE *under the disguise of a gown and beard has obtained* THE
TITLE OF SCIENCE ; but where *true knowledge* is to be found I know
not. *We grope in the dark*, and though it is truth only we are in
quest of, *we fall into innumerable errors!* But, whatever may be
our case *with respect to the knowledge of* NATURE, as to that of *heavenly*

When men *reject the truth*, they ignore the fact, that they must thereby of necessity receive, and *believe a lie in lieu of it.* "Beyond all credulity, therefore," truly says one, "is the credulousness of Atheists, whose belief is so absurdly strong, as to believe that chance could make the world, when it cannot build a house; that chance should produce all plants, when it cannot paint one landscape; that chance should form all animals, when it cannot so much as make one lifeless watch."[1]   But why then do they not employ "chance" as their tailor, and let him make their clothes? Because "they are wise to do evil, but to do good they have no knowledge"—"they are sottish children, and they have none understanding"—"they have not known Me," saith Jehovah![2] We cannot wonder then, that the writer, having adopted this lying theory, which directly and absolutely contradicts and denies the statements of the Holy Ghost, that "Jehovah God formed man of the dust of the ground, and breathed into his nostrils the breath of life"; and that He "created" "every plant of the field *before* it was in the earth, and every herb of the field *before* it grew;"[3] is driven not only to deny, or endeavour to explain away, every statement of that Word, which strikes at the root of his own baseless theory; but that he also

---

and *Divine* things, *let us cheerfully embrace that rich present which Infinite Goodness has made us,* and be thankful, that the ' day spring from on high hath visited us.' ' *Because there was* NO WISDOM ON THE EARTH,' says Lactantius, ' *He sent* A TEACHER FROM HEAVEN. *Him* let us follow *as our guide*: for he who follows His direction, *shall* NOT *walk in darkness*' ! "

[1] Clarke, vol. i, Serm. 1.   [2] Jer. iv. 22.   [3] Gen. ii. 4, 5, 7.

necessarily likewise exalts human reason above it, and arraigns Divine truth at the bar of what the Holy Ghost calls, our natural " darkened understanding," which is " alienated from the life of God, through the ignorance that is in " us, " because of the blindness of" our " hearts " ! [1]

And all who hold *this* doctrine must *necessarily* do so : as indeed is admitted by a writer in a number of the New York " *Christian* Union " ! published in the early part of 1882 :—" Darwinism," he says, " is certainly *inconsistent* with the *ecclesiastical traditions* of *Creation* and *the fall*, founded upon the *acceptance of the Mosaic narrative* as *an infallibly accurate*, historical, and scientific record. But since *Biblical critics* are now *universally agreed* [! !] that *the first chapter of Genesis* IS NOT HISTORY, there is nothing fatal to Christian faith in conceding the *traditional* "—" *legendary beliefs*," say the demons !—" and poetic character of the immediately succeeding narrative ! The Darwinian hypothesis that man has descended *from a lower animal* is not necessarily *more degrading* to man or dishonouring to God, than *the ancient* OPINION that he has descended *from a statue of clay* [! !] into which life was breathed by a direct *creative act*" ! ! [2]

---

[1] Eph. iv. 18.

[2] Mr. Darwin himself, in writing from Down, on the 5th of June, 1879, to a young student at Jena, in whom the study of his books had raised religious doubts, among other things, said to him : " As far as I am concerned, *I do not believe that* ANY REVELATION HAS EVER BEEN MADE " ! ! And this of course *logically* follows from the adoption of his system !

This seems to be also the view of the author of "Natural Law": for he says, "No man can study MODERN *science*"—not *real* science: which is *actual knowledge,* based upon *solid facts;* but what the Scriptures brand as, "science *falsely so-called*" [1]—"without a change coming over his view of truth. What impresses him about nature is its solidity. He is there standing upon actual things, among fixed laws. And *the integrity of the scientific method* so seizes him that *all other forms of truth* begin to appear *mistakes!* He did not know before that any form of *truth* "!—evolution to wit—"could so hold him; and the immediate *effect* is to *lessen his interest* in *all* that stands on *other* bases! This he feels in spite of himself; he struggles against it in vain; and he finds, perhaps, to his alarm that he is drifting fast into what looks at first like pure Positivism! *This is an* INEVITABLE *result* of THE *scientific training*"—not of *true* scientific training, indeed; but " of *the* scientific training," which teaches the lying doctrine of "Evolution," as its *foundation truth :* for the reception of *this lie of man,* necessarily leads to the rejection of *the truth of God* Himself in the matter.

Hence he says, " *Theology* must feel to-day that *the modern world* calls for *a further proof!* Nor will the *best* theology resent this demand ; it also demands it ! Theology is searching on every hand for *another* echo of the Voice of which revelation also is the echo, that

---

[1] 1 Tim. vi. 20.

out of the mouths of two witnesses its truths should be *established!* That other echo *can* only come from *nature.* Hitherto *its* voice has been muffled. But *now* that *Science,*"—*i.e.,* the science grounded on the basis of evolution!—"*has made the world around articulate,* IT *speaks to Religion* with a two-fold purpose! In the first·place it offers to *corroborate* Theology, in the second to *purify* it "!! [1] While in a previous part of his book, he speaks of his "enunciating Spiritual Law on the exact terms of Biology and Physics"—which "meant essentially the introduction of Natural Law into the Spiritual World"—as " AN ENTIRE RE-CASTING OF TRUTH "! [2] For "the *old* ground of *faith,* AUTHORITY, is given up "!! [3]

Can we wonder after this, that he denies the Scriptural doctrine of the creation, and the fall of man—accounting this rather *a rise,* than a fall; that he sneers at the true doctrine of Christ's substitution for His believing people, and their justification by faith in Him, as degrading God into "a Great Lawyer"—an "Almighty Enemy," "from" whom "we have to get off"; and that "Jesus Christ is the One Who gets us off—a theological figure, Who contrives so to adjust matters *federally* that the way is clear"!!—referring here of course to the doctrine of Substitution which the demons also so vehemently denied!—; that he virtually denies the hell of Scripture, by asserting that, "sin, that which separates from God, which disobeys God,

---

[1] Preface, pp. xxviii. and xxix.   [2] Ib., p. vi.   [3] Ib., p. 26.

which *can* not in that state correspond with God—THIS *is hell;*" while in another place, he speaks of the gravitation of sin as " *landing* " him " in the hell of a neglected life " [1]—which is not only also, as we have seen, another of the doctrines of the " demons," but given almost in their very words !—; that he awfully travesties the doctrine of " regeneration," by contrasting it with what he calls, the " reptile-life," the " bird-life," the " dog-life," the " man-life," &c., and by describing it thus :—" There is another kind of life of which science as yet has taken little cognizance. IT OBEYS THE SAME LAWS ! IT *builds up an organism into its own form.* IT IS THE CHRIST-LIFE ! As *the bird-life* BUILDS UP A BIRD, the image of itself, *so the Christ-life* BUILDS UP A CHRIST, *the image of Himself,* in the inward nature of a man " ! !—: while he does not hesitate to speak thus of " the New Testament writers "—writers, who " spake as they were moved by the Holy Ghost "—" It is *impossible* that *they* should have been familiar with *these biological* FACTS ! ! It is *impossible* that *their views* of *this great truth*"—*i.e.,* Regeneration (that is, *his perverted view of it*) : although they had all been the subjects of spiritual vital regeneration themselves—" should have been *as clear as* SCIENCE *can make them* NOW ! !"

But enough of such revolting perversions of the truth of God. I have given these citations from this work, not so much for the purpose of confuting them, (as this

---

[1] Page 103.

has been ably done by others[1]) but in order to shew the tendency of " modern thought : " as the book itself has gone through many editions; has attained a circulation of upwards of 60,000 copies; and has been extensively read, and, I am sorry to say, greatly admired and approved of by a vast number of ministers of the Gospel of almost all denominations !

And now passing by the notorious " Essays and Reviews ; " through the judgment of the Privy Council on which, in the words of one, who has ably written on this subject, " both Romanism and Neology may be said to have attained a *recognized* standing in the Established Church of this country ; " and " the Clergy," " henceforward, have a *legalized* right to dishonour and degrade ' God's Word written ' by attributing to it *falsehood ;* "[2] and likewise passing by the infidel works of the late Bishop Colenso ; I would here give extracts from the speeches and writings of various ministers and teachers in communions, whose creeds were originally orthodox ; but from which a large, and I am sorry to say, an increasing number among them, have so lapsed ; that many of them have slidden into downright heresy itself! Not wishing, however, to be personal, I shall give no names, but content myself with simply quoting extracts from the

---

[1] See for instance, Mr. B. W. Newton's " Remarks " upon his book ; the articles upon it in " Word and Work," from Nov. 27th, 1884, to Feb. 26th, 1885, inclusive ; and the Hon. P. C. Hill's pamphlet entitled " Drifting Away," &c.

[2] Occasional Papers, by Mr. B. W. Newton. Vol. iv. pp. 71, 107.

documents in question, that my readers may judge for themselves what the character of "*modern thought*" is; and in what direction it is drifting.

And first let me quote from the utterances of an Editor of a Theological Weekly, upon *the extent* of the movement; and of a Dr. in Divinity in a manufacturing city, who has a widespread influence in the Denomination, to which he belongs, upon *the result* of the movement.

"*The real battle is over the Old Testament.* Thoroughly to understand the arguments that weigh in this question is by no means easy, and this is why the people, and many of their teachers, do not as yet apprehend the real seriousness of the situation! The argument *against* eternal punishment is *easy* and was anticipated! 'Thou thoughtest that I was altogether such an one as thyself.' But the argument for *the new view* of the Old Testament is complex, and can only be followed by those who are willing to take pains! Perhaps it can hardly be understood without some knowledge of Hebrew! But the fact is this. *In the judgment of the vast majority of scholars,* Hebrew literature did not begin before the ninth century B.C.; only one-half of the Old Testament was written before the exile, and our Pentateuch as we have it was introduced by Ezra in the year 444 B.C.!! *The Levitical legislation is the work of the exilic period,* ALTHOUGH THE AUTHORS USE EVERY ENDEAVOUR TO MAKE THEIR WORK APPEAR TO HAVE BEEN WRITTEN IN THE WILDERNESS!! The connection between *Moses* and the *Penta-*

teuch is PURELY NOMINAL!! *David wrote* NO PSALMS, *all being much later than his period!!* Solomon had nothing to do with *any* of the works that bear his name! The historical part of the Old Testament is *largely untrustworthy*, and parts of it, such as the Book of Chronicles, are 'WRITTEN WITH A PURPOSE'!! SUCH are *a few* of *the results reached!*"

The Dr. writes:—"Those of us who are in the middle life have seen THE TRADITION *of the* RELIGIOUS LIFE *and* THE TRADITION *of* DOCTRINE *melting* away together! Thirty, twenty years ago all Evangelical Christians shrank from *the habits and practices* which *the tradition of conduct* condemned, just as they shrank from *the opinions* which *the tradition of doctrine* condemned. To play at cards, or to dance, or to go to the theatre, or to get into an omnibus or cab on a Sunday was as great a revolt against an unwritten but authoritative opinion, as to reject *the Calvinistic theory* of *original sin*, or *the doctrine* of *eternal suffering. The tradition* HAS VANISHED, *or is rapidly vanishing!!* I am not discussing the legitimacy of the change, which must be obvious to all who know much about the life of Evangelical Christians [*so-called!*]; I am stating *facts* which those of us who already sustain the responsibilities of the ministry, and those of us who are anticipating them, should recognize frankly. For *good* [!] or evil *the change has come*"!!

Such being the *fact;* I will now make good my assertions, by giving various quotations from the utterances of ministers and teachers on these subjects.

Let us first take the question of *the Inspiration of the Scriptures.*

Here is the utterance of a Nonconformist minister, who had then been 12 years in the ministry :—" There are few terms in common use that have been more outraged and degraded by the petty spite of carping and ignorant criticism than the terms, ' the Gospel,' ' the Gospel of Christ,' and ' the simple Gospel.' . . . . I search the speech of Jesus in vain for systematic theology, and it is the speech of Jesus chiefly that I have to expound and enforce. I find some *rather elaborate attempts* at systematic theology in Paul: but Paul is not my master, and though I admire him and love him as a great preacher and a grander man, *I do not always agree with him,* and I do not think either *his writings* or his temper *infallible!* ' One is our Master,' even Christ, and it is Christ I have to preach and not Paul. . . . If the Bible is our sole text-book as Christian preachers, in what way do we look at the Bible ? I receive the Bible as of Divine authority, as an inspired book, as the very greatest book the world ever saw. But I do not worship the Bible. I believe there is *a very pernicious Bible idolatry* rife in our churches and fostered by the pulpit. Some people make a god of their Bible. They have a sort of *pump-handle notion of inspiration* which works only in one mechanical and perpendicular direction ! Because the Bible is a compendium of the writings of inspired men, they hasten to the belief that *all parts of the Bible* and *all of the writers of the Bible* are *equally in-*

spired" !—which we have seen, the demons also themselves vehemently contradict—" To such men *the first chapters of Genesis are of equal authority* with *the Sermon on the Mount,* and the cruel and destructive wars of semi-civilised tribes in the Old Testament are as much the acts of God as the healing miracles of Jesus ! ! . . . . The Bible is a broad *human book ;* and even its inspired men are but human after all, and therefore liable to err. I believe *there are* INSPIRED MEN NOW, *just as there were inspired men in the first age ;* but as I do not treat the inspired men of God of to-day *as infallible,* so I must refuse to treat *the inspired men of old* AS INFALLIBLE " ! !

Take again the following utterances of two other ministers of two other denominations, on the same subject.

The first says : " The theory of plenary inspiration belongs to the orthodox creeds of to-day, and although *its fallacy has been proved* CLEARLY AND INDISPUTABLY BY SCIENCE to any one who would look critically at the Book itself, yet some theologians and commentators, and the bulk of the religious people "—I wish it *were* so—" adhered to it. It was THE OLD *belief concerning inspiration !* "

The second, who is also an F.R.A.S. says :—" It is better to acknowledge frankly that our Biblical boundaries are held *subject to the rectifications of frontier* WHICH SCIENCE MAY REQUIRE ! ! So shall we save ourselves from the stultification which results from commitment to an exegesis in one age which has to be

abandoned in the next ! *Scripture writers* and readers *may err*, for they are human ; NATURE CANNOT, for IT *is* DIVINE "!! And then, referring on the next page to the Biblical account of the miracle recorded in Josh. x. 12, he dares to utter these blasphemous words :—
" It is *a wicked libel* upon the God of love to imagine that He would interrupt the harmony of the solar system for the sake of a ' great slaughter.' *It would be* A DEVIL'S DEED [!!]; and, *therefore*, in the name of the Father of all, Amorites as well as Israelites, WE DECLARE THE LEGEND FALSE "!!—a declaration, which goes far beyond what even the demons themselves have uttered !!

Let us now see what these teachers have to say upon the doctrine of *Original Sin*.

" A doctrine of original sin, or birth depravity," says a writer in a " Christian " serial, the views of the Editor of which quite coincide with his own, " seems to underlie the faith of *all* the *orthodox* churches. It is variously expressed, but the same thing is meant. . . . It is not at all difficult to see what the doctrine is which these articles and confessions "—*i.e.*, the 9th Article of the Church of England, and the Confession of the Westminster Assembly of Divines—" teach. But it may be said that *these ' frightful faiths '* are things of a long and distant past, and that *no man* SPIRITUALLY SANE *holds them now!!* The teachings of the standards of the Congregationalists, to say nothing of the Baptists, show quite to the contrary ! . . . . . All round we see that, as Dr. Payne puts it, the dogma of birth depravity, and guilt underlies the common creed of Catholic, Calvinist, and Congregationalist. Be it true or not, it is old, venerable by its prevalence, and powerful in its deep and DREADFUL INFLUENCE *over the faith and life* of millions of Christian people! *But a spirit is rising up* IN ALL THE CHURCHES, *which questions the truthfulness of this dogma*—a spirit which finds its *Inspiration*"—not as he would have it—"in the fullest faith in the love of God for all men—a love that sheds the light of *an infinite hope* upon the face of *every babe* born into the world"—but from the demons, a sample of whose "teachings" on this very subject we have already had brought before us!!

Again we are taught, "Admitting the misfortune of human birth, I repudiate," says this writer, "in the name of the Child of Bethlehem, 'who was bone of our bone, flesh of our flesh,' and had a human soul, *the atrocious caricature of Christian truth*, which has dominated the faith of 1,000 years! *The doctrine of original sin is not in any* sense, the foundation of the great system of Evangelical truth! It is the foundation of the Augustinian and Calvinistic theology. But the foundation is not the rock of Divine truth, but *a pile of semi-pagan rubbish* whose *vile exhalations have contaminated* the thoughts of men, who have mistaken the 'building made with hands'—*the cruel Theology* of Catholic and Calvinist—for the temple of God! *The dogma of original sin is* SELF-CONTRADICTORY. The fact that it sets forth, and sets forth *in its worst possible form*, that man has, from birth, an awful tendency to moral defect; instead of bringing guilt upon the little souls born into the world, greatly mitigates the sinfulness of the after-life of every man and woman of the human race !! If we are brought into this world with moral deficiencies or immoral tendencies, then that stupendous fact must be regarded by God in His judgment upon men " !! And here we may plainly perceive the same bitter enmity, and vehement denunciation, against the doctrine of God's sovereignty and electing love, as we have already seen displayed by the demons themselves !!

But what do such teachers say upon *the Atonement,* and the doctrine of *Substitution ?* Let us see.

Here is the utterance of a Congregational minister upon *the Atonement :*—" I have never had any doubt of the Atonement—though what the atonement *was* precisely, and *how made,* I do not pretend to know ! I have no theory, and no theory is required. And I demur to the demand that I must go to St. Paul for the explanation of the Atonement, instead of to Jesus ! Our modern Christianity is too much a development of Paul's Epistles instead of the Gospels ! I do not feel bound to accept *Paul's arguments and* THEORIES *concerning the Atonement as* ABSOLUTELY CORRECT !! If Paul could *make mistakes about the Resurrection,* he might make mistakes here ! At all events I do not believe that I am bound to accept *Paul's representation* of the cause, and effects, and manner of the Atonement *as infallible !* I preach a vicarious atonement [!], and I preach

15

the deity of Jesus Christ. So far as I am concerned, I could not preach a full and free salvation, I could not believe in the possibility of *universal salvation*, unless I believed in these two truths! But I should not, and *I could not*, in fact, *subscribe to the definition of these truths that is given by many theologians*, and I do not dare to say that belief in them, as I believe them, is essential to salvation "!

Hear another, an M.A. of the University of London :—" The office of Christ was not to reconcile God to man, but man to God; and *this is effected* IN PRO-PORTION *as Christ dwells in us*, bringing us more and more into harmony with the Divine! The Atonement is, indeed, the central doctrine, the pivot of Christianity; but it is an At-*one*-ment, *a making of one mind* "!!

Hence an editor of a professedly religious paper, which has an enormous circulation, who holds such views as the foregoing, thus protests against the " New Congregational Hymnal;" because it still contains *some* hymns, which set forth the true doctrine on this subject. He says :—" We claim to be in deepest sympathy with the *Evangelical*"—all these writers use the *old* terms in a *new* sense—" faith and spirit, though not with many of *the doctrinal theories* which lay exclusive claim to that name! Mr. Rogers admits that ' the letter of the old creed has changed, but its spirit still lives,' and *the great fault* of this new *Hymnal* is that it does not recognise this change of the letter! If it had, hymns *asserting the total depravity of man, or discarded* THEORIES *of the atonement, or the eternity of future punishment, or the resurrection of the physical body,* WOULD HAVE BEEN EXCLUDED!! Our contention is, that the book should have been *in harmony with the teaching of our prominent men*—such as the present Chairman of the Union—Dr. Makennal, Dr. Parker, Dr. Stevenson, and Mr. Rogers himself! If we may judge by the printed words of such men, *their teaching runs along* VERY DIFFERENT LINES *to those of the hymns to which we object!* Do these men *now teach* that 'Christ bore the curse for wretched men'; or that they are worthless worms; or that the anchor of the soul is in the wounds of Jesus; or that the Divine punishment is vindictive and *everlasting;* or that the physical body *will rise again?* If they do, they take good care never to print their words!

"We all know that during the last 25 years *the whole tone of the foremost preachers,* such as those we have named, *to say nothing of the people,* ON DOCTRINAL QUESTIONS HAS CHANGED, that whilst still filled with the *Evangelical* spirit [!]—more truly Evangelical than that of earlier days, we believe [!!]—they happily refrain from the expression of *theories* insisted upon in former times! And the new *Hymnal should have reflected this change.* It has not done this, but has included a multitude of hymns that, we venture to say, *will never be sung even in Mr. Rogers' own church!* It should have so represented the thought of such men that every hymn in it could have been sung in their congregations, and all the worshippers feel that *sermon and song* were of one spirit"!!

And what say they of *Substitution ?* Here is an extract from a sermon of a Congregational minister in a
large manufacturing town :—" I spoke a moment ago
of *the substitutionary view of the atonement as* FAST
DISAPPEARING! I can quite believe that such a statement as that must be a shock to *some* of you. And I
have no desire to produce such a result, or to speak
otherwise than tenderly and respectfully of any belief
which has been a stay and a staff to many a devout
and saintly soul. But I cannot conceal from myself
the fact, nor should I be truthful if I did not tell you
that *it is a fact*, that *Christian thinkers and preachers*,
who are not committed to a cast-iron system, *have,
many of them, discarded it*, and that it by no means
occupies the place it once did in the beliefs of
thoughtful private Christians! And the reason is not
far to seek. Each phase through which Christian
doctrine has passed has been suited for, because it has
both influenced and been influenced by, the ideas and
habits of mind which characterised the period during
which it obtained. 'Our censure of *the theology of the
past*,' says the Rev. J. B. Heard, 'begins and ends
with the remark that *it is of the past*, and that we
must *leave the dead to bury their dead!* It is no
censure to a rude and barbarous age, which held *the
wild justice of revenge*, that it regarded sin quite
consistently as a blood-feud passing on, as in Arab
tribal life, from generation to generation! It is no
censure, again, to the age of Grotius, that he reasoned
with the jurists of that day, that, provided a penalty

was exacted as a satisfaction to the broken law, it was *not* AN IMMORAL CONCEPTION *that the penalty should be borne by a substitute! The ruling ideas of* OUR AGE now detect the *non-moral* element in this *fiction* of punishment transferred from the sinful to the sinless!' This witness is true! We are coming in these days to believe that what would be unrighteousness in man can never be justice in God ; that it is *impossible* that the great fact of Atonement can rest upon *a fiction;* that God Himself is love, and that therefore the sacrifice of Christ was the *outcome* and expression and not the *procuring cause* of His love to men"—which is of course true : but this does not in the least degree militate against the doctrine of Substitution itself. "It dishonours God by representing the Son as more loving and merciful than the Father"—this is a perverted view of it: for it does nothing of the kind. "It dishonours God by representing His justice as satisfied, by what, *if it were the fact,* would be *an act of* THE GROSSEST INJUSTICE, the punishment of the innocent instead of the guilty"!! a direct contradiction of that Word, which assures us, that "*Christ* hath once *suffered for sins, the just for,*" ὑπὲρ, on behalf of, or, in the stead of, "*the unjust,* that He might bring us to God."[1] . . . "These, then, are some of the reasons for the decay of the belief in the substitutionary view of the Atonement."

Take another utterance on this subject, of an Editor of a widely-circulated *so-called* "Christian" publication.

---

[1] 1 Peter iii. 18.

Speaking of an article in the "*Nineteenth Century*," by Mr. Matthew Arnold, which he adopts, almost without alteration, he says :—The notion of the imputation of men's sins to Jesus, "is indeed *an error, entirely unwarranted by the Scriptures*"—although the Scriptures set forth the doctrine with the clearness of the sunbeam—" Mr. Arnold's substantial meaning is that Luther's interpretation of St. Paul's words is unnatural unhistorical, and unreal! *Man's sin* NEVER WAS IMPUTED TO JESUS, *and in the eternal nature of things* COULD NOT POSSIBLY BE SO !! For if there is any truth certain in morals it is the intensely personal and untransferable nature of guilt. Luther's idea, however, and the doctrine of many who are said to follow him, is that *by believing in this* UNREAL AND IMPOSSIBLE TRANSFERENCE OF OUR GUILT TO JESUS we make that transference not only possible but real, and that we are saved from condemnation thereby "—a perverted view, indeed, of the Scriptural teaching on this subject; but, nevertheless, a positive and absolute denial of the Scripture doctrine itself!

Take one more utterance—the utterance of a Dr. in Divinity, who has been the head of the Denomination to which he belongs :—" *Paganistic accretions* about the sacrifice of Christ, by which it was represented as *the appeasing of an implacable anger*, have disappeared in the radiance shining from the declaration, that God *so* loved the world that He gave His only begotten Son for its salvation." And speaking on the subject of what he calls, " Word-degeneration," he writes, " 'Depravity,' 'the fallen state,' '*inability*', '*imputation*', and kindred words and phrases, *once* voiced the surest convictions of great and earnest souls, and are still, *for some*, the clear signs of *facts;* but for *a growing host*, accepting, in essence, precisely the same facts, they have lost their primary and *spiritual* import, and are chiefly *interesting as* THE 'FOSSILS' *of a theological cabinet* " ! !

I need scarcely give many extracts from such writers, to shew their views on *Eternal Punishment ;* as the publications on this subject are numerous indeed, and wide-spreading in their influence. Nevertheless to complete the *catena* of evidence, I will give an extract from one writer only ; which fully sets forth the perverted views of most writers on this subject, in all their naked and hideous deformity. Speaking of what is now called, " The larger hope," he says :—

" The Scriptures, then, have much to teach us of the future, though not much of the *final,* estate of men. And what they teach, in so far at least as we have been able to gather it up, comes to this. *No man is wholly good, no man is wholly bad* "—although the Scriptures solemnly assure us that " there is *none* that doeth good, no, not one ; "[1] and that " the carnal mind is *emnity against God :* for it is not subject to the law of God, neither indeed can be."[2] " Still some men may fairly be called *good on the whole,* although much sin and imperfection still cleaves to them ; and others

---

[1] Psa. liii. 3.   [2] Rom. viii. 7.

may fairly be called *bad on the whole*, although there is still much in them that is good, and still more which is capable of becoming good ! When we die, we shall all receive the due recompense of our deeds, of all our deeds, whether they have been good or whether they have been bad. If by the grace of God we have been *good on the whole*, we may hope to rise into a large and happy spiritual kingdom, in which all that is pure and noble and kind in us will develop into new vigour and clothe itself with new beauty ; in which also we shall find the very discipline we need in order *that we may be wholly purged from sin and imperfection ;* in which *we may undo much* that we have done wrongly, do again and with perfect grace that which we have done imperfectly, become what we have wished and aimed to be, achieve what we have longed to achieve, attain the wisdom, the gifts and powers and graces to which we have aspired ; in which, above all, we may be engaged in errands of usefulness and compassion, by which the purpose of the Divine love and grace will be fully accomplished ! If we have been *bad on the whole* WE MAY HOPE—AND WE OUGHT TO HOPE FOR IT—to pass into a painful discipline so keen and searching that we shall be conscious of our sins and feel that we are only receiving the due reward of them ; but since there has been *some good in us*, and this good is capable of being drawn out and disentangled from the evil which clouded and marred it [!] , *we may also hope,* by the very discipline and torment of our spirits, *to be led to repentance, and,* THROUGH REPENTANCE, UNTO

LIFE ; we may hope that the disclosures of the spiritual world *will take a spiritual effect upon us,* GRADUALLY RAISING AND RENEWING US *till we too are prepared* to enter the Paradise of God and behold the presence of the Lord and the glory of His power ; *we may hope* that *our friends* who have already been redeemed will pity us and *minister to us,* bringing us not simply a cup of cold water to cool our tongue, but *words of* IN-STRUCTION AND LIFE ! ! And as for the great mass of our fellow-men, we may *hope and believe* that those who have had *no chance* of salvation *here* will have one *there* [!] ; that those who have had *a poor chance* will get *a better one ;* that those who have had *a good chance* and lost it will get *a new but a severer chance,* and even as they suffer the inevitable results of their folly and sin will feel the hands that reach through darkness moulding men "—unutterably lying and deceiving doctrines, which are almost in the very words of the demons themselves ! !

" This, *on the whole, I* take to be *the teaching of Scripture* [!] concerning the lot of men *in the age to come*—a teaching which enables us to see ' beneath the abyss of hell a bottomless abyss of love.' And if it *clash with some dogmas* that we have held and some interpretations which are familiar to us, it nevertheless *accords,* not with ' the mind of Christ ' only "—an awful lie[1]—" but also *with the dictates of* REASON *and*

---

[1] Mat. x. 28 ; xiii. 40-42 ; xxiii. 32, 33 ; xxv. 46 ; Mark ix. 43-49 ; Luke xvi. 22-26 ; &c., &c.

conscience, the voices of God within the soul!! It presents *no such sudden break in our life"*—the demons say the same; and speak of it as " *the law of* PROGRESS *and association "*—" as, *in the teeth of all probability,* we have been wont to conceive; NO HEAVEN for which we feel even *the best of us must be unfit,* NO HELL which is *a monstrous offence to* OUR SENSE *of justice "*—which is exactly what the demons themselves say!! " It promises to *every man* the mercy of justice, of a due reward for all he has been and done; and, while it impresses on us the utter hatefulness and misery of sin [!] it holds out to *every one* of us *the prospect "*—*i.e.,* in the future world—" *of being redeemed* by that just God Who is also a Saviour! Nor does it less accord with *the demands of science* than with the *dictates of reason* and the *moral sense* [!!] for it carries on THE EVOLUTION *of the human race* THROUGH ALL THE AGES TO COME!! And, therefore, let others think as they will, and cherish what trust they will: but as for *us,* with the Apostle of the Gentiles [!!], our own Apostle, ' we *trust* [!] in the living God Who is the Saviour of all men ' " [!!]—a vain and delusive trust indeed, while he is at the same time denying His Holy Name and His Word!

Such then are some of the God-dishonouring and lying doctrines of so-called " *Modern thought" :* and I would now ask my readers whether they are not *identical in every particular with the " doctrines of the demons" themselves*—nay, whether they do not in some cases *even surpass them* in blasphemous denial of the truths of God? And I would further ask, whether this does not, prove to a demonstration, that *they emanate from the same source?* And if any of my readers be inclined to think me uncharitable in so judging; I would ask them to consider well, what is written on this subject in the Divine Word itself. "It is written," of the children of God, that "*in time past*" even they "*walked according to the prince of the power of the air*, the spirit that *now energizeth* in the children of disobedience."[1] "It is written again," that "the tongue is a fire, a world of iniquity;" which "defileth the whole body, and setteth on fire the course of nature; and *it is set on fire of hell;*"[2] and that when Ananias "*lied*" unto a man, even unto Peter, he "lied to the Holy Ghost"—he "lied unto God;" and that "*Satan*" had "filled his heart," to do this![3] And if any of my readers should still be inclined to ask, "How does this affect the question?" I answer perfectly: because *all* denials of *God's truth*, are *lies unto God;* and proceed from "the devil," who "is a liar, and *the father of it.*"[4] And if they would ask again, "But can this possibly apply to any, who *may* be children of God?" I reply again, Most assuredly: for our blessed Lord Himself, after commending Peter for his noble confession of faith in Him, as "the Son of God": which, says He, "flesh and blood hath not revealed it unto thee, but My Father which is in heaven"—almost immediately afterwards, on Peter's

---

[1] Eph. ii. 2.   [2] James iii. 6.   [3] Acts v. 3, 4.   [4] John viii. 44.

having objected to the sufferings of the cross, and sought to dissuade Him from it—knowing well *who* had suggested this God-dishonouring thought to him—said unto him, " Get thee behind me, *Satan :* thou art an offence unto Me ; for thou savourest not of the things that be of *God*, but *those that be* OF MEN."[1] Surely this is decisive.

And now what *can*, what *must*, all this defection from God's everlasting truth *result in ?* This the Scriptures of truth have very plainly revealed to us: for they show us that it will issue in a vast confederacy of evil; which will ultimately lead to—

VI. The Rejection of Jehovah and His Christ, by all the nations on the platform of the old Roman Earth —ἡ οἰκουμένη, as the Scriptures term it—and the ultimate worship by all " whose names are not written in the Book of Life," of Antichrist and his image, nay, even of " the dragon "—the devil himself, who will " give him his power, and his throne, and great authority."[2] And this I shall now proceed to unfold from the Scriptures themselves.

When the Governmental power, which was committed to Israel by Jehovah, was taken from them, in consequence of their rejection of Jehovah Himself; the supreme power and authority to rule in the earth was conferred upon certain favoured Gentile nations: who will continue to exercise it, until " the time of the

---

[1] Matt. xvi. 23.   [2] Rev. xiii. 2, 4, 8, 15.

end."[1] This period is called by our Lord, " the times of the Gentiles " : which will be " fulfilled," or terminate, at His second coming.[2] And as Israel, as a nation, was found to be unfaithful in the exercise of this trust : so will the Gentile nations on inquisition be found to be so likewise. This supreme power, which was originally conferred upon Nebuchadnezzar, the King of Babylon, is now vested in the kingdoms established upon the platform of the old Roman earth : which will, " at the time of the end," consist of ten only—answering to the ten toes of the image seen by Nebuchadnezzar in his dream, as recorded in Daniel ii. —not all on *one* leg, as many expositors have imagined, but five, of course, on *each* leg, the Grecian and the Roman ; answering to the two divisions into which the old Roman Empire was originally divided. And as the " Kings of the earth," and " the rulers " generally, " set themselves," and " took counsel together, against Jehovah and against His Christ," at His *first* coming :[3] so will they, even with bitterer and more intense opposition to the truth, set themselves against Him, just before His *second* coming.

Again and again, the " rulers " and " judges " of the earth, are exhorted in the Scriptures to remember Him by whom " Kings reign, and princes decree justice "— " even all the judges of the earth : "[4] but all to no purpose. " *Be wise* now therefore, O ye Kings " : says

---

[1] See this subject largely treated upon in my " Outlines of Prophetic Truth," chaps. vi. and vii., pp. 230-341.
[2] Luke xxi. 24-28.   [3] Psa. ii. 2 ; Acts iv. 24-28.   [4] Prov. viii. 15, 16.

Jehovah : " *be instructed*, ye judges of the earth. Serve Jehovah with fear, and rejoice with trembling. Kiss the Son, lest He be angry, and ye perish from the way, when His wrath is kindled but a little. Blessed are all they that put their trust in Him."[1] " God standeth in the congregation of the mighty ; He judgeth among the gods. *How long* will ye *judge unjustly*, and accept the persons of the wicked ? Defend the poor and fatherless, *do justice* to the afflicted and needy ; rid them out of the hand of the wicked." But, alas ! God's Word having been " rejected " by them, such counsel falls upon unheeded ears ; and so the Psalm proceeds :—" They *know not*, neither *will they understand ;* they *walk on in darkness : all the foundations of the earth are out of course.* I have said, Ye are gods "—*i.e.*, ruling for, and under God, as our Lord explains[2]—" and all of you are children of the most High. But ye shall die like men, and fall like one of the princes."

And then comes up to heaven the longing heartfelt cry of the Lord's own children, for their deliverance out of the hands of the oppressor :—" Arise, O God, *judge the earth* "—*i.e.*, take back to Thyself the power and authority, which Thou hast committed unto these rulers, who have so awfully abused it—" for *Thou* shalt *inherit* ALL *nations.*"[3] And this prayer will be answered at the second coming of the Lord, when the saints will unitedly give Him thanks for it, " as it is

---

[1] Psa. ii. 10-12.	[2] John x. 34, 35.	[3] Psa. lxxxii.

written "—" We give Thee thanks, O Lord God Almighty, Which art, and wast, and art to come ; because *Thou hast taken to Thee* "—*i.e.*, into Thine own hands again the power which Thou didst before delegate to the rulers of the earth—" *Thy great power, and hast reigned.* And the nations were angry, and Thy wrath is come, and the time of the dead, that they should be judged, and that Thou shouldest give reward unto Thy servants the prophets, and to the saints, and them that fear Thy name, small and great ; and shouldest destroy," διαφθεῖραι, "them *which destroy*," διαφθείροντας, "*the earth*,"[1]—the word for "*destroy*" here used, meaning both to *corrupt* and to *destroy !*

And how had they thus "corrupted," and "destroyed" it? The prophet Isaiah, who speaks of this period, tells us :—" Behold, Jehovah maketh the earth empty, and maketh it waste, and turneth it upside down," or, as the margin has it, "perverteth the face thereof," "and scattereth abroad the inhabitants thereof." Why? Because "the earth is *defiled* under the inhabitants thereof; because they have *transgressed the laws, changed the ordinance*, BROKEN THE EVERLASTING COVENANT. *Therefore* hath the curse devoured the earth, and they that dwell therein are desolate : therefore the inhabitants of the earth are burned, and few men left." And then, after having referred to "the great tribulation"—"the fear, and the pit, and the snare "[2]—he predicts the coming of

---

[1] Rev. xi. 17, 18.   [2] Compare our Lord's words in Luke xxi. 34-36.

the Lord, which our Lord Himself tells us will be "*immediately after* that tribulation";[1] and informs us, that "it shall come to pass *in that day*, that Jehovah shall punish the host of the high ones that are on high"—*i.e.*, Satan, and his hosts, who now occupy "the heavenlies"[2]—"and the Kings of the earth upon the earth"—who will then be gathered together in the valley of Jehoshaphat, under Antichrist,[3] with the object of "cutting off" the Jewish "nation; that the name of Israel should be no more in remembrance"[4]—"and they shall be gathered together"—*i.e.*, in the valley of Jehoshaphat; where "the harvest of the earth," is to be "reaped," as we learn from Rev. xiv. 15, 16 —"as prisoners are gathered *in the pit*, and shall be shut up in the prison"—*i.e.*, in Sheol, "in the abyss," Rev. xix. 20; xx. 1-3—"and after many days shall be visited"—*i.e.*, at the close of the millennium[5]. "*Then* the moon shall be confounded, and the sun ashamed, when *Jehovah of Hosts* SHALL REIGN in Mount Zion, and in Jerusalem, and before his ancients gloriously."[6]

Before all this, however, there will have taken place in heaven, the judgment spoken of in Dan. vii. 9-14 : at which those favoured Gentile nations, to whom the supreme power in the earth had been delegated, will be proved to have utterly betrayed the trust reposed in them—the damning evidence being, that they had

---

[1] Matt. xxiv. 27-31.   [2] Eph. vi. 12.   [3] Joel iii. 1, 2, 9-17.
[4] Psa. lxxxiii., particularly v. 4, 5.   [5] Rev. xx. 11-15.
[6] Isa. xxiv. 1, 5, 6, 17, 21-23.

utterly rejected the Christ of God, and chosen as their head, and " worshipped," in lieu of Him, " the beast," and him, who dwelt in him, *i.e.*, Satan : for it is there expressly stated, that it was " *because* of the voice of the great words which the horn spake "—for " he opened his mouth in blasphemy against God, to blaspheme His name, and His tabernacle, and them that dwell in heaven "[1]—that this " judgment was set, and the books were opened." And then, judgment having been given against them, their delegated authority is taken from them, and "*the Son of man*" is re-invested with it ; " and there was given Him dominion and glory, and a kingdom, that all people, nations, and languages, should serve Him : His dominion is an everlasting dominion, which shall not pass away, and His kingdom that which shall not be destroyed." This is the period also referred to in Psa. ii. 8, 9, " Ask of Me, and I shall give Thee the Gentiles for Thine inheritance, and the uttermost parts of the earth for Thy possession." And as they will then be arrayed against Him, as is shewn in Rev. xix. 11-21, the first thing He will have to do is next declared of Him, " Thou shalt break them with a rod of iron ; Thou shalt dash them in pieces like a potter's vessel "—as the passage also just referred to likewise shows. As the scene depicted in Daniel, however, will take place *in heaven*, it will not of course be visible *on earth :* but our blessed Lord has given us an intimation *that we*

---

[1] Rev. xiii. 6.

16

may know when it has taken place : for "*immediately after* the tribulation of those days," He says—*i.e.,* at the close of Antichrist's career, Dan. vii. 11—" shall the sun be darkened, and the moon shall not give her light, and the stars shall fall from heaven, and the powers of the heavens shall be shaken : and *then* shall appear the sign of *the Son of Man* in heaven : and *then* shall all the tribes of the land," πᾶσαι αἱ φυλαὶ τῆς γῆς, —*i.e.,* of Israel[1]—" mourn, and they shall see *the Son of Man* coming in the clouds of heaven with power and great glory. And He shall send His angels with a great sound of a trumpet, and they shall gather together His elect from the four winds, from one end of heaven to the other."[2]

And this leads me to speak of Antichrist himself ; and to shew *how* the nations of the earth will thus have been deceived by him.

Many thoughtless persons, in reading the Word of God, make great mistakes, unconsciously to themselves ; by supposing that when God describes things on earth, as *He* views them, and as they must, therefore, of necessity *be* in themselves ; that they must be regarded in the same light also *by man.* For instance, when they read, that " God saw that the wickedness of man was great in the earth, and that every imagination of the thoughts of his heart was only evil continually : "[3] it would not follow, as they unconsciously

---

[1] See Rev. i. 7, where the same phrase is used, and Zech. xiv. 1-9.
[2] Mat. xxiv. 29-31.   [3] Gen. vi. 5.

suppose, that the men of *those* days, or even the men of *these* days, would have so judged. On the contrary, as the arts and sciences, undoubtedly, then greatly flourished;[1] the women of the period were beautiful and attractive; and the seductions of the world and of the flesh were so great, as even to draw the professing people of God under their baskanizing influence; the exact opposite would of course be the truth : for our Lord Himself has said, that "that which is *highly esteemed* among men is *abomination* in the sight of God."[2]

So again, when they read of God's description of the four great world-powers, as four "*great beasts*," fierce, cruel, despotic, and devouring;[3] they again unconsciously, in their own minds at the time, ignore the fact, that to the eyes of the worldling, they would have appeared in a very different light indeed! "For man looketh on *the outward appearance*, but Jehovah looketh upon *the heart*"![4] For "this great *Babylon*, that I have built," said Nebuchadnezzar, "for the house of the Kingdom by the might of my power, and for the honour of my majesty,"[5] was "the golden city,"[6] "the glory of kingdoms, the beauty of the Chaldees' excellency"![7] And we read in the Book of Esther, that "in the days of Ahasuerus," who reigned from India to Ethiopia, over 127 provinces; that when

---

[1] See Gen. iv. 21, 22: and the period above spoken of was more than 1,000 years afterwards.
[2] Luke xvi. 15.   [3] Dan. vii.   [4] 1 Sam. xvi. 7.   [5] Dan. iv. 30.
[6] Isa. xiv. 4.   [7] Isa. xiii. 19.

" the King " " sat on the throne of his Kingdom, which was in Shushan the palace, in the third year of his reign, he made a feast unto all his princes and his servants; the power of *Persia* and *Media*, the nobles and princes of the provinces being before him : when he shewed the riches of his glorious kingdom and the honour of his excellent majesty many days, even an hundred and fourscore days " ![1]

In like manner, although in Scripture, the Grecian Empire is described as a compound " beast with four heads,"[2] and we know that the Greeks themselves were voluptuous to a degree; yet their men were magnificently formed, and their women beautiful in the extreme ; while their philosophers and poets were highly intellectual; and their architecture and sculpture have never been surpassed, and have formed models for all subsequent times. While the power, authority, magnificence and far-reaching influence of the Roman Empire, which is pourtrayed in the Divine Word as a " beast, dreadful and terrible,"[3] is powerfully affecting every nation upon the platform of the Roman earth, aye, and beyond it, to this hour.

Hence in reading in the Word of God of the character of Antichrist, as therein pourtrayed, as in God's sight, as " *a scarlet coloured beast, full of names of blasphemy ;* "[4] such readers make the same mistake with respect to him, as they do in the other cases before mentioned ; and suppose that he must, there-

---

[1] Esther i. 1-4.   [2] Dan. vii. 6.   [3] Dan. vii. 7.   [4] Rev. xvii. 3.

fore, of necessity be hideous in appearance, and dreadful to look upon ; than which nothing can be more false, or misleading. For although, like Absalom of old, (who was one of the types of Antichrist,) he will be black as hell *in heart ;* yet, like him also, *in person* there will be " none to be so much praised as " he " *for his beauty :* " for " from the sole of his foot even to the crown of his head there " will be " no blemish in him " ;[1] and by " good words and fair speeches," and seducing flatteries, he will, as Absalom did in the first instance, " deceive the simple,"[2] and " *steal* the hearts "[3] of the men of this world, and mould them to his sovereign and imperious will. Moreover, as he will be unequalled in majesty of bearing and character, in commanding power of intellect, in quickness and subtlety of apprehension, and in the unlimited exercise and sway of absolute dominion and power ; and will have all the power and might of Satan himself to back him, he will not only be irresistible to the men of this world ; but likewise be *the very one,* whom they would now *hail with delight ;* and whom indeed *they are looking for !*

For thus is he described in the Divine Word.

He is to arise out of one of the four divisions of Alexander's Empire ; and as this is not to be until " the time of *the end,*" " in *the last end* of the indignation," *i.e.,* against Israel as a nation for their sins,[4]

---

[1] 2 Sam. xiv. 25.   [2] Rom. xvi. 18.   [3] 2 Sam. xv. 6.

[4] Dan. ix. 26, " with a flood," literally, " in the overflowing." Compare Isa. xxviii. 18.

and " in the *latter* time of *their* kingdom, when the
transgressors are *come to the full*,"[1] *i.e.*, when the
nations, *as such*, have cast off all allegiance to Jehovah
and His Christ; this shews, not only that these four
divisions of that Empire will *then* be in existence, as
such, and have a recognized head, in some form or
another; but also that, to this extent, Antichrist will
likewise be *a Grecian*. This is confirmed by Rev.
xiii. 2, which tells us that " the beast " " was like unto
a leopard," which was a symbol of the *Grecian* Empire;[2] and which shews also that Antichrist will, not
only be like that animal in cunning and swiftness, but
will also exhibit in himself *the beauty of form*, elegance,
and *outward* refinement, as well as possess the intellect and tastes, of that wonderful nation. It is also
to be noted, in this connection, that "Tyre and Sidon,
and all the coasts of Palestine," are charged by Jehovah just before His " sitting to judge all the Gentiles "
" in the valley of Jehoshaphat," with " *selling* " " the
children of Judah and the children of Jerusalem "
"unto the *Grecians;* that " they " might remove them
far from their own borders."[3] While in the day of
Jehovah's appearing *for* Israel, He promises to " bend
Judah," and " fill the bow with Ephraim," and " raise
up the Sons of Zion," " as the sword of a mighty man,"
against " *the sons of Greece* "[4]—passages of Scripture,

---

[1] Dan. viii. 17, 19, 23.   [2] Dan. vii. 6.

[3] Joel iii. 6, 12, 14.   See also in this connexion Zech. xiv. 2, "half
of the city shall go forth *into captivity*."

[4] Zech. ix. 11-16.

which not only prove that Tyre and Sidon, (as Babylon also,) will be restored, but that Greece will likewise, in those days, be a prominent persecutor of the children of Israel. And *if Greece proper* be the Kingdom from which Antichrist is to arise, he might well be called " a *little* horn,"[1] on his first appearing; as Greece is but an insignificant kingdom in itself; and forms a remarkable exception to all other nations, that have once lost their dominion, in having again regained it; and having at this present time a king of its own!

In the second place he is described as having a " mouth as the mouth of *a lion*,"[2] which was the symbol of the *Babylonian* Empire. Hence he will centre in himself all the power and majesty and glory of him, of whom it was said, " Thou, O King, art a King of Kings "—" Thou art this head of gold; "[3] and of whom also it was written, " all people, nations, and languages trembled and feared before him : whom he would he slew; and whom he would he kept alive; and whom he would he set up; and whom he would he put down."[4] And so we read in the Book of the Revelation, that the " ten kings " under Antichrist, " have one mind, and shall give their power and strength unto the beast ";[5] and " the dragon gave him his power, and his throne," θρόνου, " and great authority."[6]

In the third place, " his feet " are said to be " as the feet of a *bear* ":[7] which was the symbol of the *Persian*

---

[1] Dan. vii. 8.   [2] Rev. xiii. 2.   [3] Dan. ii. 37, 38.   [4] Dan. v. 19.
[5] Rev. xvii. 12, 13.   [6] Rev. xiii. 2.   [7] Rev. xiii. 2.

Empire.[1] Now "*feet*" in Scripture are used symbolically of a man's *walk.* "A naughty person, a wicked man, *walketh* with a froward mouth. He winketh with his eyes, he *speaketh* with his *feet*, he teacheth with his fingers; frowardness is in his heart, he deviseth mischief continually ; he soweth discord."[2] I apprehend, therefore, that the meaning of Antichrist, as "a beast," being described as having "the *feet* of a *bear*" intimates that his walk, or course of life, will be characterized, as that of the Persian monarchs was, by the display of oriental splendour, pomp, and magnificence.

Again, he is said to be "a king of *fierce countenance*," or, as Mr. B. W. Newton translates it, "Strong or mighty in countenance "[3]—"the same expression" being "used in Deut. xxviii. 50, of the *Romans*, when they are *first* mentioned as the appointed desolators of Jerusalem ;" and "it is an expression," he rightly says, "that seems peculiarly applicable to the crushing *iron* strength of the *Roman* power, of which Antichrist will be the last inheritor."[4]

Hence he will centre in himself *all* the power and authority of *all* the four previous kingdoms that have ruled the world—"*Roman*," as Mr. B. W. Newton again tersely puts it, "as being master of the Ten

---

[1] Dan. vii. 5.   [2] Prov. vi. 12-14.

[3] Dr. Young translates it "fierce of face." The word rendered "fierce," in the A.V. is עַז, and is applied to the *anger* of Simeon and Levi in Gen. xlix. 7 ; by Samson, to the lion which he slew, in Judges xiv. 14 ; and to Antichrist himself again in Isa. xix. 4.

[4] Prospects of the Ten Kingdoms, p. 203.

Kingdoms of the Roman world ; *Greek*, as arising from one of the four divisions of the ancient Empire of the Greeks ; *Chaldean*, as bearing the title of King of Babylon, and having that city as the centre of his power"—*Persian*, I would add, as rivalling that Empire in Barbaric magnificence and display and—" *Head of Israel* by election, or by conquest, he will thus revive and concentrate in himself past powers and past energies, to operate with more intensity than ever against God."[1]

Hence again, he is said to be " *the* King," pre-eminently :[2] who " shall do according to his will ; and shall exalt himself, and magnify himself above every god, and shall speak marvellous things against the God of gods " ; and as he is also to be so mighty a warrior, that it will become a proverbial saying, " Who is *like* unto the beast ? who is *able* to make war with him " ; " and power " will be " given him over *all* kindreds, and tongues, and nations," he will " prosper until the indignation be accomplished."[3]

But my object is not so much to give the *history* of Antichrist, (which I shall hope to open out more fully when I come to my second volume of " Outlines of Prophetic Truth,") as to shew *the ultimate issue* of the ceaseless efforts of the demons—" the spirits of demons," δαιμόνων, " *working miracles* " (as we have seen that they are now doing,) " which go forth unto

---

[1] Prospects of the Ten Kingdoms, p. 255.	[2] Dan. xi. 36; Isa. xxx. 33.	[3] Dan. xi. 36 ; Rev. xiii. 4, 7.

the kings of the earth and of the whole world, to
. gather them to the battle of that great day of God
Almighty " : in connection with the warning of which,
our blessed Lord gives His people also the animating
admonition, "Behold, I come as a thief. Blessed is
he that *watcheth*, and keepeth his garments, lest he
walk naked and they see his shame."[1]   I shall, therefore, enter no farther into his history, than will be
necessary to elucidate this point.   And that issue will
be, not the dwelling of a *demon*, or *demons*, but the
dwelling of SATAN HIMSELF, IN A MAN—even in Antichrist himself: " whose coming," we are expressly
told, will be " *after the energizing*," κατ' ἐνέργιαν, " *of
Satan* with all power and signs and lying wonders,
and with all deceivableness of unrighteousness in
them that perish ; because they received not the love
of the truth, that they might be saved."[2]   He is moreover said to be, " *the man of sin* "—the heading up,
and impersonation, as it were, *in himself, of what sin
is*, and ever must be, in its very nature and essence,
" *lawlessness* "[3] — "the son of perdition "[4] — a title,
which is only applied to one other person, and by our
Lord Himself, *i.e.*, to Judas :[5] of whom it is expressly
said, that " *Satan* ENTERED INTO HIM " ![6]   Hence
Antichrist is described as " understanding *dark sentences* "[7]—the word meaning, as Mr. B. W. Newton
again observes, " something twisted or involved, and

---

[1] Rev. xvi. 14, 15.   [2] 2 Thes. ii. 9, 10.   [3] 1 John iii. 4.
[4] 2 Thes. ii. 3.   [5] John xvii. 12.   [6] John xiii. 27.   [7] Dan. viii. 23.

therefore difficult " to unravel. " The same expression," he also observes, " is used when it is said of the Queen of Sheba that she went to prove Solomon with ' *hard questions.*' It again occurs in Psa. lxxviii. 2. ' I will open my mouth in a parable, I will utter *dark sayings* of old '—a passage applied in Matthew to the Lord Jesus. Again, we read in the Proverbs of ' the words of the wise and their dark sayings.' ' Understanding dark sentences ' is therefore a description indicative of *supernatural wisdom.* This last great Monarch of the Gentiles, described in the Scripture as one that ' cometh up out of the bottomless pit,' will rival Solomon in wisdom, and men will admire and venerate that wisdom, little caring to enquire whence it comes. *It will come from the indwelling energy of Satan.* This and the preceding clause will well explain the reason of the symbol—' a *horn having eyes* '—*i.e.*, strength and supernatural intelligence combined—but it will be intelligence that will *come from, and lead unto,* HELL. The only One," he truly adds, " who can deliver from these things is ' the great Shepherd of the sheep.' "[1]

As Antichrist is therefore described, at the commencement of his career, as " a *little* horn," who will " *pluck up* " " three of" the *then* existing " horns " or kings on the platform of the Roman earth, " *by the roots* ";[2] and will ultimately obtain such a powerful ascendancy over the whole of the ten kings as to have

---

[1] Prospects of the Ten Kingdoms, note, p. 204.   [2] Dan. vii. 8.

them entirely subject to his will:[1] it is manifest that all this will take some time to accomplish. Nevertheless, as he will be upheld and sustained by the mighty power of Satan himself, he may possibly be enabled to accomplish it in an incredibly short space of time, after the manner of Alexander of old; and with the same marvellous rapidity, with which the future confederacy of evil, which is to have " a house built in the land of Shinar "—*i.e.*, in the plains of Babylon—and to be " *established*, and set *there* upon her own base "—is represented in symbol as being *carried there* by " two women" *having* " *wings* like the wings of a stork," " *and the wind was in their wings !* "[2]

Mr. B. W. Newton has ably shewn, in his Exposition of the above Prophecy in Zechariah, that this system is essentially connected with *commerce*, of which *the* " *ephah* " is a symbol; and I entirely agree with him in this respect: but yet I think that it will not so much be *disconnected with*, as it will *grow out of*, previous Satanic systems of deceit. For " Jesuitism " is too far-reaching in its influence, and too useful an auxiliary to the Evil One, to be wholly given up, and cast aside by, him. Indeed such a result seems to me to be contrary to Scripture, to reason, and to analogy. For as " Babylonianism," or the Roman Catholic Church, *so-called*, is nothing more nor less than the devil's caricature of the future Kingdom of

---

[1] Rev. xvii. 12-14.   [2] Zech. v. 5-11.   See also Rev. xvii.

the Son[1]; and "Jesuitism," which sprang out of "Babylonianism," is the devil's caricature of the Son of the Kingdom; or, in other words, of the work of the Holy Ghost in the heart of a saved sinner:[2] so I cannot but think that Antichrist, who will be the devil's last travesty of God's truth, *i.e.*, his caricature of "*The* King," even of Christ Jesus Himself, will spring out of Jesuitism. I may be wrong in my conjectures, as I do not profess to be a "prophet," but only an "Evangelist" and "teacher:"[3] and so my readers may take my opinion on this point for what it is worth.

And as it would of course be foreign to my present purpose to enter further into this question; I would merely note in passing, that the ultimate end and object of the Jesuits is, chiefly through Rome, to obtain *universal dominion and ascendancy in the world;* and although their government is *monarchical,* and their *General* has absolute sway and dominion, not only over every member of the Order, but, I might almost now say, over the Pope himself;[4] yet they have ever sought *to enrich themselves by commerce;* and they have been marvellously skilful and successful in

---

[1] See the writer's "Babylonianism; or, The Devil's Travesty of the Kingdom of the Son."—Morgan and Scott, 6d.

[2] See also his "Jesuitism; or The Devil's Travesty of the Son of the Kingdom."—Morgan and Scott, 1s.

[3] 1 Cor. xii. 28, 29.

[4] See the writer's "Lessons from History; or Words of Warning for perilous times;" which are appearing as monthly articles in the "Protestant Echo"; commencing October, 1888.

their designs to this end. Urban VIII. issued strict
prohibitions to the Jesuit missionaries, not to engage
in commerce : but these injunctions were utterly dis-
regarded ; and the account of the voyage of M. du
Quesne gives a sample of *the unlimited commerce* which
the Jesuits carried on in Europe. Clement XII. again
issued several Bulls and Decrees against the covetous-
ness of the Jesuits *as merchants :* but all to no purpose.
The careful compiler of the " History of the Jesuits,"
in 1816, gives proof upon proof of the marvellous
success of the Jesuits as *the monopolizers of Trade* in
the countries where they had gained ascendancy!
When the Dominicans and Franciscans conducted the
Romish missions in Japan and the neighbouring
countries, the Jesuits finding these countries remarkably favourable for commerce, obtained from Gregory
XIII. the privilege of residing there alone, in exclusion
of all others, and thus secured the whole of the trade
of those countries to themselves !

Coming down to later times, M. Martin, the Governor
of Pondicherry, stated " that, next to the Dutch, the
Jesuits carry on the largest and most productive commerce with India : *their trade surpasses even that of
the English,* as well as of the Portuguese, who first
established them in India "! And that they can
readily assimilate themselves to any form of religion
or worship, which may assist them in carrying out
their designs, I might mention for example, what M.
Martin said of them in his day, on this very subject :—
" They have," said he, "*for the purposes of their*

commerce, secularized Jesuits, who have no appearance of being what they are! They are of all nations, *even Armenians and Turks.* Those Jesuits, who associate with the idolatrous Indian merchants, the Banians, dress as Banians, speak the same language, eat and drink with them, *and exercise the same heathen worship as they do :* in short, *they who do not know them,* consider them to be real Banians."[1] And Courdrette, in writing upon the commerce of the Jesuits in his day, says, " In Portugal, the Jesuits had vessels employed exclusively in their service. . . . All the accounts of travellers in the East Indies speak in the same way *with astonishment of the extent of their commerce!* . . Let us only imagine," he says, " 20,000 traders, scattered over the world from Japan to Brazil; from the Cape of Good Hope to the north; all correspondents of each other; *all blindly subjected to one individual,* and working for him alone; conducting 200 different Missions, which are so many Factories, 612 Colleges, and 423 houses of profession, noviciates and residents; and then let us form an idea, if we can, of *the produce of a commerce* of so vast an extent!"[2]

These instances, which might be greatly extended, and which of course fall far short of giving even an approximate estimate of the vast possessions of the Society in these days,[3] may serve to shew how vast

---

[1] History of the Jesuits, vol. ii. p. 380. Voyage de Duquesne, vol. iii. p 15.

[2] History of the Jesuits, vol. ii. p. 37. Courdrette, vol. iv. p. 201

[3] A correspondent of the " Standard," writing from Rome, in that paper of the 5th June, 1886, says :—" One of the most remarkable

and extensive will be that commercial system which has yet to be established on the platform of the Roman earth ; which the Scriptures seem to shew will assume an *Ecclesiastico-commercial* form; and in all probability be also of so *exclusive a character*, that all who will not conform to its evil requirements, will, as they will afterwards under Antichrist's idolatrous decrees, *be prohibited from all benefits to be derived from it ;* [1] or, in other words, according to a modern phrase, be " *boycotted !* "

And indeed some ominous signs have occurred in these days, which shew us that such an issue is not at all likely to be an improbable one : for " Word and

---

and significant social phenomena at Rome in the present day is, the truly surprising scale on which the company of Jesus has been, and is, acquiring property.　They have bought the huge Costanzi Hotel, with its annexed gardens, spaces, and buildings.　They have also acquired the whole of the adjacent large area of the barracks and extensive exercise ground of the Royal Cuirassier Guards.　They are building on the other side of the ' Vicolo Tolertino,' immediately opposite to the above-mentioned properties, a truly vast edifice.　In truth, their Establishment in this quarter will assume the importance almost of a little town !　They are also raising a vast building in the immediate neighbourhood of the railway station, which, I believe, is intended for their German College.　They have farther, I am told, secured a large area of ground in the new quarter, which is being rapidly constructed outside the Porta Pia " !

And at the close of the year 1888, there were in England, Wales and Scotland alone, no less than 2,616 Romish churches, chapels, chapels of communities, religious houses for men and women, and colleges ; 433 of which are religious houses for women, or *convents :* where poor young creatures are immured for life ; and where there is no Government inspection, nor any registration of deaths !

[1] Rev. xiii. 16, 17.

Work," in its issue of the 20th October, 1887, gave an extract from an able address of Dr. H. Sinclair Paterson, at the Evangelical Alliance Conference at Aberdeen, in that month, in which he remarked, " There are ominous signs that *the Church of Rome and scepticism will*, IN THE NEAR FUTURE, *form an alliance against the Gospel*. The present Pope does not say *non possumus*, like the last one. . . . One of the prominent Romish writers in London wrote a paper in one of our leading monthlies not very long ago, in which he said that, notwithstanding *Evolution, Darwinism, and all the other contradictions of science against Theology*, THE CHURCH OF ROME COULD EASILY ACCEPT THEM ALL! The same writer, two months ago, wrote another article, in which he stated: ' Suppose the contention of certain critics be true, and that *we have no Old Testament ;* WE CAN DISPENSE WITH IT, FOR WE HAVE THE LIVING INFALLIBLE HEAD IN THE PAPAL CHAIR AT ROME'! He has not been censured for these papers, so far as I am aware. After writing the first he remarked, ' Several of the leading members of the Roman Catholic Church *praised*, instead of blaming me.' And the second article has been sown broadcast in the same vein, and not a single whisper has been spoken against it on the part of members of that church. The fact, therefore, remains that *Rome is quite willing to accept all the conclusions of scepticism and all the speculations of science*, AND YET MAINTAIN ITS FIRM HOLD OVER THE HEARTS AND CONSCIENCES OF MEN "! !

17

For as a far-seeing student in prophecy long ago remarked, " We have had a *pagan* persecution, and a *papal* one : but the last, and most awful one of all, will be an *infidel* one ! "—of which we have, indeed, already had *a sample* in " the reign of terror," during the first French Revolution !

Now this vast confederacy of evil, Antichrist will in the first instance entirely uphold and support ; and in fact be the mainspring of its existence.[1] And this he will the more readily be able to do, in consequence of the revival of the Eastern portion of the Roman Empire ; which will then from its geographical position, its vast resources, and the fact of Babylon being the great city and seat of that part of his Empire, far out-rival the West ; and give an enormous impetus to trade and commerce. I have already incidentally shown that Antichrist will be a great patron of the arts and sciences ; and no doubt, like Nebuchadnezzar of old, he will be the chief builder of the modern Babylon : which will probably far exceed Babylon of old, both in its extent, as well as in its grandeur, glory and magnificence.[2] The account of its fall, as given in the 18th chapter of the Book of the Revelation, gives us some insight into these things, and shews us, not only the vast extent of its riches, and merchandize, but also the effect that the judgment of God upon " that great

---

[1] Rev. xvii. 3.

[2] I believe it was Mr. B. W. Newton, who first called attention to this subject in his " Second Series of Aids to Prophetic Enquiry," entitled " Babylon ; its Revival and Final Desolation."

city," will have upon "the Kings of the earth," and
"*the merchants*," "*which were made rich by her*," in
their "wailing" and "lamenting" her fall ; "because
no man buyeth her merchandise any more."[1]   It is in
consequence of Antichrist having selected Babylon as
the capital of his Empire that he is called in Scripture,
the King of Babylon ;[2] and it is in consequence of his
having resuscitated the power and energy of the East,
and thus, as it were, re-established the old Assyrian
dominion and empire, (which began with Nimrod, the
introducer of the public worship of idolatry, and will
close with Antichrist, in whom it will culminate and
end,) that he is called "*the Assyrian*."[3]

When Antichrist, therefore, has succeeded in fully
consolidating his power, he will then seek the goal of
his ambition, to reign also in Jerusalem, as the Head
of the Jewish nation : for *it is in Jerusalem especially
that he will seek to glorify himself !* It is possible that

---

[1] I have now before me the prospectus of the Mersina-Adana Construction Co., Limited, which proposes to construct a Railway in
Asia Minor, from the former to the latter place, of about 42 miles ;
and the plans accompanying it shew that it is ultimately intended
to continue the line down the Euphratean valley through Mosul
(Nineveh) and Bagdad ; and from thence, I suppose, to Babylon
and the Persian Gulf.   Dr. Sivartha, of Chicago, who has long
made it his study to develop not only all Palestine, but all the great
Euphrates valley, says that this valley is capable of sustaining
100,100,000 people, *and of again being the centre of the world's activi-
ties! Montreal Church Guardian,* quoted in "Silver Morn," of
March, 1889.

[2] Isa. xiv. 4.   [3] Isa. x. 5, 24 ; xiv. 25 ; xxx. 31 ; xxxi. 8 ;
Hos. v. 13 ; xi. 5 ; Micah v. 5, 6.

one way of ingratiating himself with that people, will
be, in his assisting them to rebuild their temple ; or,
if it be then built, of adorning it, or contributing to its
maintenance : for that the Jews, *as a nation*, will be
restored to their own land *in unbelief*, and will re-
establish the Temple services ; and that Antichrist
will be connected with them, the Scriptures themselves
most unhesitatingly declare.   That the Jews, as a
nation, will return to their own land *in unbelief*, is
proved even from one chapter only in Ezekiel, where
the Lord says, " I will take you from among the
Gentiles, and gather you out of all countries, and will
bring you into your own land. *Then* will I sprinkle
clean water upon you, and ye shall be clean. A new
heart also will I give you, and a new spirit will I put
within you. . . . *Then* shall ye remember your
own evil ways, and your doings that were not good,
and shall loathe yourselves in your own sight for your
iniquities and for your abominations," &c.[1] That the
temple will be rebuilt is also proved, from the last
chapter of Isaiah, which speaks of its being in existence, just before Israel, *as a nation*, is " born " again
" in one day,"[2] by " looking upon " Him " whom
they have pierced, and mourning ; "[3] and from the
prediction in the New Testament, that Antichrist
himself shall " sit in " it, " shewing himself that he is
God."[4] That the Temple services will be restored, is

---

[1] Ezek. xxxvi. 24, 25, 26, 31.   [2] Isa. lxvi. 5-10.
[3] Zech. xii. 10 ; xiii. 1.   [4] 2 Thes. ii. 4.

also proved from the fact, that when Antichrist breaks his covenant with the Jews, he " takes away the daily sacrifice."[1]   And that Antichrist will be received by the Jewish nation as their Messiah, our Lord long ago foretold them, when He said, " I am come in My Father's name, and ye receive Me not; if *another* shall come *in his own name*, HIM YE WILL RECEIVE."[2]

Now, the reason the Jews alleged why they would not *nationally* receive Jesus as their Messiah was, that He would not shew them a sign from Heaven,[3] which Antichrist will probably do ; and I think so for the following reasons.   When the devil was permitted to tempt our Lord, we are told that one of his temptations consisted in his " taking Him up into the holy city, and setting Him on a pinnacle of the temple," and then addressing Him thus : " If Thou be the Son of God, *cast Thyself down :* for it is written, He shall give His angels charge concerning Thee ; and in their hands they shall bear Thee up, lest Thou dash Thy foot against a stone "[4]—that is, shew the Jews this sign from Heaven ; for you see the Scriptures themselves say the angels will see to it that you are held up in so doing ; and then the Jews will acknowledge You as their Messiah at once, without any further effort on Your part to induce them to do so.   Now it is possible, that the devil *may* induce Antichrist to do this ; and

---

[1] Dan. ix. 27; xii. 11.   [2] John v. 43.
[3] Mat. xii. 38-40 ; xvi. 1; Mark viii. 11 ; Luke xi. 16, 29 ; John ii. 18 ; 1 Cor. i. 22.   [4] Mat. iv. 5, 6.

that the Jewish nation *might* receive him as their
Messiah in consequence.

Again, it is said, in the Book of the Revelation, that
Antichrist's minister, the false prophet, will " do great
wonders, so that *he maketh fire come down from
Heaven* on the earth in the sight of men, and deceiveth
them that dwell on the earth by the means of those
miracles which he had power to do in the sight of,"
ἐνώπιον, in the presence, and as the minister, of " the
beast,"[1] *i.e.*, Antichrist. Now one reason why the
Jewish sacrifices cannot now be restored, in the
opinion of the Rabbins, is, that there is *no " fire from
heaven " to kindle them :* as there was in the first
instance of old.[2] If *this* fire, then, be called down
" from heaven," as it were, *to kindle the sacrifices*, this
might seem to the unbelieving Jews, such " a sign from
heaven," as might induce them to put their trust in
Antichrist, as their Messiah ; just as such a sign had
this effect, outwardly at least, in inducing the Israelites
to acknowledge Jehovah to be the true God in the days
of Elijah.[3] But be this as it may, that they *will* do this,
is certain : for the Divine Word tells us that he will
enter into a " seven years' " covenant with them ; and
reign over them in Jerusalem as their Lord and King.[4]

---

[1] Rev. xiii. 13, 14.

[2] Lev. ix. 24 ; 1 Kings xviii. 38 ; 1 Chron. xxi. 26, &c.

[3] 1 Kings xviii. 37-39.

[4] Dan. ix. 27 ; Isa. xxviii ; Rev. xi., &c. The city spoken of in
this last chapter is *not Rome*, but *Jerusalem*. See and compare v. 8
with Is. i. 9, 10 ; Jer. xxiii. 14 ; Deut. xxxii. 32 ; Amos ix. 7 ;
Jer. ii. 18 ; xiii. 23.

This covenant is called in Scripture, a " covenant with *death*," and " an agreement with *Sheol*," [1] *the abyss*, of which Satan is " the angel : "[2] because it is made with one, who is indwelt of Satan ; and is therefore *virtually made with Satan himself !*

This covenant Antichrist will break after three years and a-half (on what pretence, or on what occasion, it would be foreign to my subject to note) ; and will then " take away the daily sacrifice," and " set up the abomination that maketh desolate," not only in the temple itself, but on one of its pinnacles[3] also, *i.e.*, an idolatrous image, no doubt of himself (as Nebuchadnezzar before him did in the plain of Dura, in the province of Babylon), for worship.[4] And *if* he had previously descended in the air, from that pinnacle, to the earth, in the sight of the Jews ; this might be one reason for his setting up his image *there also*. *That* image the Holy Ghost expressly tells us, the false prophet will have " power to give breath " (margin) unto, " that the image of the beast should both speak " —*as the demons do through their materializations now*— " and cause that as many as would not worship the image of the beast should be killed."[5]

Now our Lord solemnly warns His believing people, who may be in Jerusalem in those days, that when they shall " *see* the abomination of desolation spoken

---

of by Daniel the prophet, stand in the holy place," that they were instantly to "flee" from "Judea" "into the mountains, without so much as stopping to take any of their possessions with them:" for "then," said He, "shall be great tribulation such as was not since the beginning of the world to this time, no, nor ever shall be. And except those days should be shortened, there should no flesh be saved: but for the elect's sake those days shall be shortened."[1]

That the "abomination of desolation" here spoken of, is *not* the one mentioned in Dan. xi. 31, which refers to the idol of Jupiter Olympus, which was set up in the temple at Jerusalem by Antiochus Epiphanes, is proved from the fact, that our Lord here refers to an "abomination of desolation," which *was then*, and indeed *is still, future;* because the "great tribulation" was immediately to succeed it. And that *this* tribulation is *not* the tribulation endured by the Jews at the siege of Jerusalem by the Romans, is also proved from the fact, that "*immediately after*" *this* "tribulation," our Lord will come again. And that this coming is His second coming, and *not* a spiritual coming, is also proved from the fact, that the resurrection of the righteous dead will *then* take place: for at that very time, when " they shall *see* the Son of Man coming in the clouds of heaven with power and great glory," " He shall send His angels *with a great sound of a trumpet,* and they shall gather together His elect from the four

---

[1] Mat. xxiv. 15, 16, 21, 22.

winds, from one end of heaven to the other."[1] This is
confirmed likewise both by Daniel and Jeremiah, who
both speak of *this same tribulation, and in the same
terms*. The former says :—" And at that time shall
Michael stand up, the great prince which standeth for
the children of thy people : and there shall be a time
of trouble, *such as never was since there was a nation
even to that same time :* and at *that* time thy people
shall be delivered, every one that shall be found written
in the book. And many of them that sleep in the dust
of the earth shall awake," &c.[2] The latter says :—
" For thus saith Jehovah ; we have heard a voice of
trembling, of fear, and not of peace. Ask ye now, and
see whether a man doth travail with child? Wherefore do I see every man with his hands on his loins, as
a woman in travail, and all faces are turned into pale-
ness? Alas! for that day is great, *so that none is like
it :* it is even *the time of Jacob's trouble;* but he shall
be saved out of it. For it shall come to pass in *that*
day, saith Jehovah of Hosts, that I will break his
yoke "—*i.e.,* Antichrist's. See Isaiah xiv. especially vv.
3-5—" from off thy neck, and will burst thy bonds, and
strangers shall no more serve themselves of him : but
they shall serve Jehovah their God, and David their
King, whom I will raise up unto them." [3]

It is during this awful " tribulation " that the devil,
through Antichrist, will seek to exterminate the nation
of Israel, in consequence of their revolt against him,

---

[1] Mat. xxiv. 15, 21, 29-31.   [2] Dan. xii. 1, 2.   [3] Jer. xxx. 5-9.

by reason of his breach of covenant with them; for Satan hates *that* nation above all other nations, not only because Jehovah Jesus was born therein, but likewise because that nation, even in its dispersion, has ever been a standing witness of the truth of the words of the living God: so that even in more senses than one, it may be said of them, " Ye are My witnesses, saith Jehovah, that I am God."[1] And now is fulfilled that awful passage in Ezekiel, " Son of Man, the house of Israel is become to me dross : all they are brass, and tin; and iron, and lead, *in the midst of the furnace ;* they are even the dross of silver. Therefore thus saith the Lord Jehovah ; because ye are all become dross, behold, therefore I will gather you *into the midst of Jerusalem.* As they gather silver, and brass, and iron, and lead, and tin, *into the midst of the furnace,* to blow the fire upon it, to melt it ; so will I gather you in Mine anger and in My fury, *and I will leave you there, and melt you.* Yea, I will gather you, and blow upon you in the fire of My wrath, and ye shall be melted in the midst thereof. As silver is melted in the midst of the furnace, so shall ye be melted in the midst thereof; and ye shall know that I Jehovah have poured out My fury upon you."[2] For, as He says in another place, His " fire is in Zion, and His furnace in Jerusalem."[3] And that both these passages relate to this particular tribulation, is proved from the fact, that the " melting " in Jerusalem mentioned in Ezekiel,

---

[1] Isa. xliii. 12.   [2] Ezek. xxii. 18-22.   [3] Isa. xxxi. 9.

will not take place, until the "gathering" again of Israel after their "scattering among the heathen," and "dispersion in the countries":[1] while the "fire" and "furnace" mentioned in Isaiah, is connected with "the Assyrian," *i.e.*, Antichrist, just before the Lord's deliverance of His people out of his hand.

It is during this period, in consequence of Israel, *as a nation*, having rejected their Messiah, and put their trust in an "idol Shepherd," *i.e.*, Antichrist, that he is permitted to "eat the flesh of the fat," and to "tear their claws in pieces;"[2] and as the "Assyrian, the rod of" the Lord's "anger," "sent" by Him "against an hypocritical nation," "to take the spoil, and to take the prey, and *to tread them down like the mire in the streets.*"[3]   And that this tribulation will greatly exceed the one inflicted upon the Jews by the Romans, is proved from the fact, "that *in all the land*," *i.e.*, of Israel, "*two parts therein shall be cut off and die;* but the third shall be left therein.   And I will bring the third part *through the fire*, and will *refine them* as silver is refined, and will try them as gold is tried: *they* shall call on My name, and I will hear them: I will say, It is My people; and they shall say, Jehovah is my God"[4]— a time which is also referred to in Mal. iii. 1-6.

But as it would be foreign to my purpose, to pursue the matter farther in this respect; I would only now

---

[1] Ezek. xxii. 15.   [2] Zech. xi. 16, 17.
[3] Isa. x. 5, 6.   [4] Zech. xiii. 8, 9.

mention, that this tribulation, and the feelings and prayers of repentant Israel during it, are frequently set forth in the Psalms and the Prophets; where Antichrist is called, " the man of the earth," who " terrifies" (margin) the people;[1] "the enemy," pre-eminently, who " does wickedly in the sanctuary,"[2] *i.e.*, by setting up there the abomination of desolation; " the boar out of the wood," and *" the wild beast,"* who " devours " all before him;[3] " a cruel lord " " and a fierce King;"[4] " the lion," and " the destroyer of the Gentiles;"[5] and " the wicked one,"[6] pre-eminently, whom " Jehovah " " shall slay with the breath of His lips,"[7] or, as it is rendered in 2 Thes. ii. 8—a passage manifestly referring to the same person, and the same event —" with the spirit of His mouth, and shall destroy with the brightness of His coming," or, as it is in the original, " with the epiphany of His Parousia," or Personal Presence. There are also clusters of Psalms, if I might so say, which depict the whole period from the beginning to its close; as for instance, the 7 Psalms, in the Levitical Book of Psalms, which relate to the " Sanctuary," commencing with Psalm lxxix., and ending with Psalm lxxxv.

During this awful tribulation, therefore, Antichrist " opposes and exalts himself above all that is called God, or that is worshipped; so that he as God sitteth in the temple of God, shewing himself that he is

---

[1] Psa. x. 18.   [2] Psa. lxxiv. 3.   [3] Psa. lxxx. 13.   [4] Isa. xix. 4.
[5] Jer. iv. 7.   [6] So in the Hebrew.   [7] Isa. xi. 4.

God."[1] "And he opens his mouth in blasphemy against God, to blaspheme His Name, and His tabernacle, and them that dwell in heaven. And it " will be " given unto him to make war with the saints, and to overcome them: and power " will be " given him over all kindreds, and tongues, and nations. *And all that dwell upon the earth* SHALL WORSHIP HIM, *whose names are not written in the book of life of the Lamb slain from the foundation of the world.*" "*And all the world* wondered after the beast. And they WORSHIPPED THE DRAGON which gave power unto the beast."[2] So that *this*, and this truly, will be *the final issue* of the " apostacy " of the nations from God! For, as I have shewn in my " Outlines of Prophetic Truth," as well as in my " Personality and History of Satan," that, inasmuch as God is " only wise "—a statement no less than three times repeated in the Scriptures of truth [3]—there can but be one infinitely holy, Divine, and all-perfect will, the will of God Himself: for to assert otherwise would be to say, that God is not God, and that things might, therefore, be ordered better than they are, or have been. Hence it follows also, as a consequence, that the least conceivable departure from that will, has a necessary tendency, and unless God prevent, most assuredly will, as in the case of all those who are not saved, issue in eternal separation from His presence, irremediable ruin, and black eternal death.

---

[1] 2 Thes. ii. 4.   [2] Rev. xiii. 6-8, 3, 4.
[3] Rom. xvi. 27; 1 Tim. i. 17; Jude 25.

Moreover, as sin originated with Satan, he must of necessity be the exact opposite of God Himself, as I have also therein shewn. " For *rebellion* is as the sin of *witchcraft*," Keh'-sem,[1] " and stubbornness is as iniquity and *idolatry* "[2]—two " *works of the flesh*,"[3] which we have seen *began* with the devil, and which *must*, as we also see, *end* in *the worship of him*, and of his creature, Antichrist likewise !

And now if any of my readers should be disposed to think that God does not mean what He says; and, therefore, to question the *literal* words of the Scriptures, which I have set forth, so as to put a *non-natural* interpretation upon them, by explaining them away to signify something fanciful or mystical, on the assumption that they cannot possibly suppose that men could ever be brought to worship the devil himself; I would only remind them,

1. That this Scripture, Rev. xiii. 4, is not isolated in its statement : for every other worship offered to any other than God Himself, is virtually a worship of Satan ; as the following, among other Scriptures, plainly declare—1 Cor. x. 20; Lev. xvii. 7 ; Deut. xxxii. 17 ; Psa. cvi. 37 ; Rev. ix. 20.

2. The North American Indians, the Africans, and many other nations, have worshipped, and still worship, *evil spirits, as such, knowing them to be evil spirits !*

---

[1] See page 7.   [2] 1 Sam. xv. 23.   [3] Gal. v. 20.

3. Nay, many nations have worshipped, and some even still worship, *the devil, as such :* as the following extracts from reliable authors clearly prove. Thus, Mr. Ives, in his Travels through Persia gives the following account of *devil-worship :*—"These people (the *Sanjacks, a nation inhabiting the country about Mosul, the ancient Nineveh*), once professed Christianity, then Mahometanism, and last of all, *devilism !* They say it is true that the devil at present has a quarrel with God, but the time will come when the pride of his heart being subdued, he will make his submission to the Almighty ; and as the Deity cannot be implacable, the devil will receive a full pardon for all his transgressions, and both he *and all those who paid him attention in his disgrace* will be admitted into the blessed mansions ! *This is the foundation of their hope, and* THIS *chance for heaven* they esteem to be a better one than that of trusting to their own merits, or the merits of the leader of any other religion whatsoever ! *The person of the devil they look on* AS SACRED, and when they affirm anything solemnly, *they do it* BY HIS NAME ! ! All disrespectful expressions of him THEY WOULD PUNISH WITH DEATH, did not the Turkish power prevent them ! Whenever they speak of him, *it is with the utmost respect ;* and they always put before his name a certain *title corresponding to that of* HIGHNESS OR LORD " ! !¹

The celebrated traveller, Niebuhr, also *found the worshippers of the devil in the same country,* in a

____

¹ Travels, page 306.

village between Bagdad and Mosul, called Abd-el-asis, on the great Zab (a river which empties itself into the Tigris). This village, he says, is entirely inhabited by people who are called Isidians, and also Danâsins.[1] There are also devil-worshippers even now in many other parts of the world, as for instance in several of the countries bordering upon Koordistan, &c.

4. Nay, if the sceptical writer of " *Aut Diabolus aut nihil*," in Blackwood's Magazine for October, 1888, is to be believed (and he assures his readers that the account he gives, is " the *true* story of a hallucination ") : then *the* SECRET *worship of* SATAN *has already commenced!* The writer, in concluding his narrative, says : " Such is the *true* story of *a meeting with the devil* in Paris not many years ago—*a story* TRUE IN EVERY PARTICULAR, as can be easily proved by a direct application to any of the persons concerned in it, *for they are all living still!* The key to the enigma we cannot find, for we certainly do not put faith in any one of the theories of *Spiritualists;* but that *an apparition*, such as I have described, *did appear* IN THE WAY AND UNDER THE CIRCUMSTANCES we have related IS A FACT, and we must leave the satisfactory solution of it to more profound psychologists than ourselves " !

The chief persons named in the narrative are a Russian Prince, named Pomerantseff, and a French Abbé, named Girod, who was a sceptic! The conversation at a dinner party at the Duc de Frontignan's, at

---

[1] Travels, part ii., page 244.

which both the Russian Prince and the Abbé were present, having turned upon "Spiritualism"; the Duke said that he had "seen the Spirit of Love:" whereupon the prince said, that *he* "had seen *the devil!*"

"'Mon ami, you are insane,' cried Girod. 'Why, *the devil does not exist!*'

"'I tell you *I have seen him*—the God of all Evil, the Prince of Desolation,' cried the other, in an excited voice, 'and, what is more, *I will show him to you!*'"

This offer, the Abbé at first firmly rejected; but on further conversation with the Prince, he seemed fascinated, and accepted it—the Prince imposing only one condition upon him, that he should trust himself entirely to him, until they reached the place of meeting. And "so the matter was now arranged, and he, the Abbé Girod, the renowned preacher of the celebrated —— Church, was to meet that very night by special appointment, at half-past nine, *the Prince of Darkness;* and this in January in Paris, at the height of the season, in the capital of civilization,—*la ville Lumière!*"

"At half-past nine o'clock precisely the Prince arrived. He was in full evening dress, but—contrary to his usual custom—wearing no ribbon or decoration, and his face was of a deadly pallor."

The Abbé "remarked, with some surprise, that the carriage awaiting them was not the Prince's.

"'I have hired a carriage for the occasion,' said Pomerantseff, quietly, noticing Girod's glance of sur-

18

prise. '*I am unwilling that my servants should suspect anything of this.*'

"They entered the carriage, and the coachman, evidently instructed beforehand where to go, drove off without delay. The Prince immediately pulled down the blinds, and taking a silk pocket-handkerchief from his pocket, began quietly to fold it lengthwise.

"'I must blindfold you, *mon cher*,' he remarked simply, as if announcing the most ordinary fact.

"'Diable!' cried the Abbé, now becoming a little nervous. 'This is very unpleasant; I like to see where I am going. I believe, Pomerantseff, you are the devil yourself.'

"'Remember your promise,' said the Prince, as he carefully covered his friend's eyes with the pocket-handkerchief, and effectually precluded the possibility of his seeing anything until he should remove the bandage.

"'I wish I had not come,' the Abbé murmured to himself. 'Of course the whole thing is folly; but it is a great trial to the nerves, and I shall probably be upset for many days.'

"On they drove; the time seemed interminable to the Abbé.

"'Are we near our destination yet?' he inquired at last.

"'Not very far off now,' replied the other in what seemed to Girod a most sepulchral tone of voice!

"At length, after a drive of about half an hour, but which seemed to the Abbé double that time, Pomerantseff murmured in a low tone, and with a profound sigh, which sounded almost like a sob, ' Here we are ;' and at that moment the Abbé felt the carriage was turning, and heard the horses' hoofs clatter on what he imagined to be the stones of a courtyard.

" The carriage stopped, Pomerantseff opened the door himself, and assisted the blindfolded priest to alight.

" ' There are five steps,' he said, as he held the Abbé by the arm. ' Take care.'

" The Abbé stumbled up the five steps. They had now entered a house, and Girod imagined to himself it was probably some old hotel like the Hôtel Pimodan. . . . When they had proceeded a few yards, Pomerantseff warned him that they were about to ascend a staircase, and up many shallow steps they went. . . . When at length they had reached the top of the stairs, the Prince guided him by the arm through what the Abbé imagined to be a hall, opened a door, closed and locked it after them, walked on again, opened another door, which he closed and locked likewise, and over which the Abbé heard him pull a heavy curtain. The Prince then took him again by the arm, advanced him a few steps, and said in a low whisper :

" ' Remain quietly standing where you are. I rely upon your honour not to attempt to remove the pocket-handkerchief from your eyes until you hear voices.'

" The Abbé folded his arms and stood motionless, while he heard the Prince walk away, and then suddenly all sound ceased.

" It was evident to the unfortunate priest that the room in which he stood was not dark; for although he could of course see nothing owing to the pocket-handkerchief, which had been bound most skilfully over his eyes, there was a sensation of being in strong light, and his cheeks and hands felt as if they were illuminated!

" Suddenly a horrible sound sent a chill of terror through him—a gentle noise as of naked flesh touching the waxed floor—and before he could recover from the shock occasioned by the sound, the voices of many men—voices of men groaning or wailing in some hideous ecstacy—broke the stillness, crying—

" ' Father and Creator of all Sin and Crime, Prince and King of all Despair and Anguish! come to us, we implore thee! '

" The Abbé, wild with terror, tore off the pocket-handkerchief.

" He found himself in a large old-fashioned room, panelled up to the lofty ceiling with oak, and filled with great light shed from innumerable tapers fitted into sconces on the wall—light which, though by its nature soft, was almost fierce by reason of its greatness and intensity, proceeding from these countless tapers.

" He had then been, after all, right in his conjectures; he was evidently in a chamber of some one of the many old-fashioned hotels which are to be seen still in the Ile Saint Louis, and indeed in all the antiquated parts of Paris.

" All this passed into his comprehension like a flash of lightning, for hardly had the bandage left his eyes

·ere his whole attention was riveted upon the group before him.

" Twelve men—Pomerantseff among the number—of all ages from five-and-twenty to fifty-five, all dressed in evening dress, and *all*, so far as one could judge at such a moment, *men of culture and refinement,* LAY NEARLY PRONE UPON THE FLOOR WITH HANDS LINKED!

" They were bowing forward and kissing the floor—which might account for the strange sound heard by Girod—and *their faces were illuminated with a light of* HELLISH ECSTACY,—*half distorted, as if in pain, half smiling, as if in triumph!*

" The Abbé's eyes instinctively sought out the Prince.

" He was the last on the left-hand side, and while his left hand grasped that of his neighbour, his right was sweeping nervously over the bare waxed floor, as if seeking to animate the boards. His face was more calm than those of the others, but *of a deadly pallor,* and the violet tints about the mouth and temples showed *he was suffering from intense emotion!*

" They were *all*, each after his own fashion, *praying aloud,* or rather moaning, *as they writhed* IN ECSTATIC ADORATION!

" ' O Father of Evil! come to us! '

" ' O Prince of Endless Desolation! who sitteth by the beds of Suicides, WE ADORE THEE! '

" ' O Creator of Eternal Anguish! '

" ' O King of cruel pleasures and famishing desires! WE WORSHIP THEE! '

" ' Come to us, thy foot upon the hearts of widows! '

" ' Come to us, thy hair lurid with the slaughter of innocence !'

" ' Come to us, thy brow wreathed with the clinging chaplet of Despair !'

" ' Come to us !'

" The heart of the Abbé turned cold and sick as these beings, hardly human by reason of their great mental exaltation, swayed before him, and as *the air, charged with a subtle and overwhelming electricity,* seemed to throb as from the echo of innumerable voiceless harps !

" Suddenly—or rather the full conception of the fact was sudden, for the influence had been gradually stealing over him—*he felt a terrible coldness, a coldness more piercing than even any that he had ever before experienced even in Russia,*"—an experience, I may here add, which has been noted, and described, over and over again, at Spiritualistic séances, previous to some manifestation, or "*materialization,*" as they call it—"*and with the coldness there came to him the certain knowledge of the presence of some other being in the room!*

" Withdrawing his eyes from the semi-circle of men, who did not seem to be aware of his, the Abbé's, presence, and who ceased not in their blasphemies, he turned them slowly round, and as he did so, they fell upon *a new-comer, a Thirteenth, who seemed to spring into existence from the air,* and before his very eyes !

" He was a young man of apparently twenty, tall, as beardless as the young Augustus, with bright golden hair falling from his forehead like a girl's.

" He was dressed in evening dress, and his cheeks were flushed as if with wine or pleasure ; but from his eyes there gleamed a look of inexpressible sadness, of intense despair !

" The group of men had evidently become aware of his presence at the same moment, for *they all fell prone upon the floor* ADORING, and their words were now no longer *words of* INVOCATION, but *words of* PRAISE AND WORSHIP !

" The Abbé was frozen with horror : there was no room in his breast for the lesser emotion of fear ; indeed the horror was so great and all-absorbing as to charm him and hold him spellbound !

" He could not remove his eyes from the Thirteenth, who stood before him calmly, a faint smile playing over his intellectual and aristocratic face,—a smile which only added to the intensity of the despair gleaming in his clear blue eyes !

" Girod was first struck with *the sadness*, then with *the beauty*, and then with *the intellectual vigour* of that marvellous countenance !

" The expression was not unkind or even cold ; haughtiness and pride might indeed be read in the high-bred features, shell-like sensitive nostrils, and short upper lip ; while *the exquisite symmetry and perfect proportions of his figure* shewed suppleness and steel-like strength : for the rest, the face betokened, save for the flush upon the cheeks, only *great sadness !*

" The eyes were fixed upon those of Girod, and he felt their soft, *subtle*, intense light *penetrate into every nook and cranny of his being!* This terrible Thirteenth simply stood and gazed upon the priest, as the worshippers grew more wild, more blasphemous, more cruel!

"The Abbé could think of nothing but the face before him, and the great desolation that lay folded over it as a veil! He could think of no prayer, although he could remember there were prayers.

" Was this Despair—the Despair of a man drowning in sight of land—*being shed into him from the sad blue eyes?* Was it Despair or was it Death?

"Ah no, not Death! Death was peaceful, *and this was violent and passionate!*

" Was there no refuge, no mercy, no salvation anywhere? Perhaps, nay, surely, but while those sad blue eyes still gazed upon him, *the sadness*, as it seemed to him, *intensifying every moment*, he could not remember where to seek for and where to find such refuge, such mercy, such salvation. He could not remember, and yet he could not entirely forget. He felt that help would come to him if he sought it, and yet he could hardly tell how to seek it.

"Moreover, by degrees *the blue eyes,*—it seemed as if their colour, the great blueness, *had some fearful power,*—BEGAN POURING INTO HIM SOME MORE HIDEOUS PLEASURE!! It was *the ecstacy of great pain becoming a delight, the ecstacy of being beyond hope,* and of being *thus enabled* TO LOOK WITH SCORN UPON THE AUTHOR OF HOPE!! And all the while the blue eyes still *gazed* SADLY, *with a soft smile* BREATHING OVERWHELMING DESPAIR UPON HIM!!

" Girod knew that in another moment he would not sink, faint, or fall, but that he would,—oh! much worse!—he would smile!

" At this very instant a name,—a familiar name, and *one which the infernal worshippers had made frequent use of*, but which he had never remarked before,— struck his ear ; *the name of Christ !*

" Where had he heard it ? He could not tell. It was the name of a young man ; he could remember that and nothing more.

" Again the name sounded, ' Christ.'

" There was another word like Christ, which seemed at some time to have brought an idea first of great suffering and then of great peace.

" Ay, peace, *but no pleasure*. NO DELIGHT LIKE THIS SHED FROM THOSE MARVELLOUS BLUE EYES !!

" Again the name sounded, ' Christ.'

" Ah ! the other word was cross—*croix*—he remembered now ; a long thing with a short thing across it.

" Was it that as he thought of these things the blue eyes lessened in intensity ? We dare not say ! but as some faint conception of what a cross was flitted through the Abbé's brain, although he could think of no prayer—nay, of no distinct use of this cross—he drew his right hand slowly up, for it was pinioned as if by paralysis to his side, and feebly and half mechanically made the sign across his breast.

" The vision vanished."

Now if this had been an impersonation of Satan himself, or a " *materialization* " produced by him, the object in either case was the same—to produce in the mind of the beholder, a sympathizing pity, if I might so say, for Satan himself; with a corresponding stirring up of the " enmity " of " the carnal mind "[1] against the Christ of God, on the lying assumption that God had dealt hardly with Satan himself—an awful, and a hellish temptation, which only those who have gone down deep into their nature's evil, and understand something of " the depths of Satan,"[2] have ever been subject to![3]

The writer concludes his narrative thus : " The men adoring ceased their clamour and lay crouched up one against another, *as if some strong electric power had been taken from them and great weakness had succeeded,*[4] while, at the same time, the throbbing of the thousand voiceless harps was hushed!

" The pause lasted but for a moment, and then the men rose, stumbling, trembling, and with loosened hands, and stood feebly gazing at the Abbé, who felt faint and exhausted, and heeded them not. With extraordinary presence of mind the Prince walked quickly up to him, pushed him out of the door by which they had entered, followed him, and locked the door behind them, thus precluding the possibility of being immediately pursued by the others.

---

[1] Rom. viii. 7.   [2] Rev. ii. 24.

[3] See the writer's " Outlines of Prophetic Truth," p. 300; and his " History and Personality of Satan," pp. 53-55, 215, 216.

[4] My readers will have noticed, in several previous accounts of séances, that this effect was produced over and over again.

" Once in the adjoining room, the Abbé and Pomerantseff paused for an instant to recover breath, for the swiftness of their flight had exhausted them, worn out as they both were mentally and physically; but during this brief interval the Prince, who appeared to be retaining his presence of mind by a purely mechanical effort, carefully replaced over his friend's eyes the bandage which the Abbé still held tightly grasped in his hand. Then he led him on, and it was not till the cold air struck them, that they noticed they had left their hats behind.

" ' *N'importe !* ' muttered Pomerantseff. 'It would be dangerous to return;' and hurrying the Abbé into the carriage which awaited them, he bade the coachman speed them away—' *au grand galop !* '

" Not a word was spoken; the Abbé lay back as one in a swoon, and heeded nothing until he felt the carriage stop, and the Prince uncovered his eyes and told him he had reached home; then he alighted in silence, and passed into his house without a word.

" How he reached his apartment he never knew; but the following morning found him raging with fever and delirious.

" When he had sufficiently recovered, after the lapse of a few days, to admit of his reading the numerous letters awaiting his attention, one was put into his hand which had been brought on the second night after the one of the memorable séance.

" It ran as follows :—

" ' Jockey Club, January 26, 18—.

" ' Mon cher Abbé,—I am afraid our little adventure was too much for you—in fact, I myself was very unwell all yesterday, and nothing but a Turkish bath has pulled me together. I can hardly wonder at this, however, for *I have never in my life been present* AT SO POWERFUL A SEANCE, and you may *comfort* yourself with the reflection that SA MAJESTE [i.e., Satan] HAS NEVER HONORED ANYONE WITH HIS PRESENCE FOR SO LONG A SPACE OF TIME BEFORE !

" ' Never fear, *mon cher*, about your illness. *It is purely nervous exhaustion*, and you will be well soon ; but *such evenings must not often be indulged in* if you are not desirous OF SHORTENING YOUR LIFE. I shall hope to meet you at Mme. de Metternich's on Monday.—*Tout à vous*, Pomerantseff.'

" Whether or no Girod was sufficiently recovered to meet his friend at the Austrian Embassy on the evening named we do not know," adds the writer, " nor does it concern us ; but he is certainly enjoying excellent health now."

And now I will conclude with

VII. Some admonitions and exhortations, which naturally arise out of the subject itself.

1. As we have seen that " Spiritualism," *so-called*, is nothing more nor less than ancient *necromancy ;* which springs from those " works of the flesh," " witchcraft " and " idolatry," with which it is essentially connected ; and that these practices are strongly condemned in the Word of God : while those persons who

engage in them in these days, are branded by the Holy Ghost as "*apostates from the faith,*" and are said thereby to "give heed to seducing spirits," "speaking lies in hypocrisy;" and that they are under such "strong delusion," as to "believe" in their "lies:" it is manifest that *the system itself must of necessity be essentially evil and devilish;* and that God's curse must rest upon it! Nay, even Spiritualists themselves have discovered that they have been, *occasionally* (as *they* suppose) imposed upon by *evil* spirits: for William Howitt said, "There is need of *caution* in *consulting* spirits; for *some* spirits *personating the departed,* have confessed themselves *devils,* when adjured in Jesu's name!" This we have also seen in some of the instances before referred to;[1] and *the demons themselves* in their "teachings," have likewise asserted the same thing.[2] But *how* then do Spiritualists suppose *that they are able to distinguish* between good and evil spirits? Simply, by the *testimony* of the lying demon himself! Can infatuation equal this: when the Holy Ghost solemnly assures us, that such *practices* are *diabolical in themselves;* and that *all* such spirits are "*lying,*" "*seducing*" spirits—demons, under the direction and control of "the Prince of the demons," Satan himself! For thus speaketh the Holy Ghost in the Old Testament:—"When they say unto you, Seek unto them that have *familiar spirits,*" the *Ohvoth,*[3] "and unto *wizards,*" *Yid-d"goh-neem,*[4] "that peep and

---

[1] See pages 107-112. [2] See pages 197, 198. [3] See page 4. [4] See page 5.

that mutter: should not a people *seek unto their God?*
for the living to the dead?"—*i.e.*, Should the *living* seek
unto the *dead!* What inconceivable folly! "To the
law and to the *testimony :* if they speak *not* according to
this word, it is *because there is no light in them.*"[1] And
thus also speaketh He in the New:—"Let no man
beguile you of your reward in a voluntary humility and
*worshipping of angels, intruding into those things which
he hath not seen, vainly puffed up* BY HIS FLESHLY
MIND, and NOT *holding the Head*, from which all the
body by joints and bands having nourishment ministered, and knit together, increaseth with the increase
of God."[2] Surely these Scriptures are even, of themselves, *alone* sufficient to settle the whole question!

But can we wonder, when men are so deluded as to
reject such precious storehouses of Divine wisdom and
experience, as are treasured up in God's Word ; and to
think that their own natural " darkened understanding " is sufficient to guide them in such matters ; that
they should, in the judgment of God, be given over to
believe in lies ! "O Jehovah, I know that the way of
man is not in himself: it is not in man that walketh
to direct his steps."[3] "Yea, also the heart of the sons
of men is full of evil, and madness is in their heart
while they live, and after that they go to the dead."[4]

And I would solemnly warn my unbelieving readers,
that if they once yield themselves up to the power of
the demons—and, in *consulting* them, they *do* this by

---

[1] Isa. viii. 19, 20.   [2] Col. ii. 18, 19.   [3] Jer. x. 23.   [4] Eccl. ix. 3.

yielding up their *will* to them—they will ultimately find it impossible to free themselves from them : as many a poor deluded creature has subsequently discovered to his cost.[1]　"I know," says the Rev. A. R. Fausset, in the "Silver Morn," for October, 1885, "from the testimony of a strong-minded Christian witness in London, that the spirits haunt, and are with great difficulty driven from, persons who, and places which, have for a time been given up to them"; and I have been told the same thing by several other persons also myself.　Indeed, there is only one infinitely blessed One, who *can truly* "cast out demons"—He who was "anointed" "with the Holy Ghost, and with power," and "Who went about doing good, and healing all that were oppressed of the devil."[2]　And if the Lord, in sovereign mercy, pardoned a Manasseh, who "caused his children to pass through the fire in the valley of the son of Hinnom ; " and " observed times, and used enchantments, and used witchcraft, and dealt with a familiar spirit, and with wizards ; " and " wrought much evil in the sight of Jehovah, to provoke Him to anger : "[3] I doubt not that if such persons, when "in affliction," would, as he did, under the Spirit's influence, also "humble themselves greatly before God," confess their iniquity, and "beseech" Him for mercy, that He would in sovereign grace restore and pardon them likewise.

---

[1] See page 94.　　[2] Acts x. 38.　　[3] 2 Chron. xxxiii. 6.

2. I have before referred to the text in 1 Cor. x. 19, 20; as teaching that the Gentiles in their worship did in fact *worship demons :* but I must now open it out more fully, in connexion with another text, in order to shew the bearing of both of these passages of Scripture also upon modern Spiritualism. "As concerning therefore," says the Apostle, "the eating of those things that are offered in sacrifice unto idols, we know that *an idol is nothing in the world*"—that is, that *the supposed being* worshipped under *the image* of the idol, *i.e.,* Jupiter, Juno, Mars, Venus, Adonis, Diana, &c., *has no real existence—*" and that there is none other God but one. For though there be that are *called* gods, whether in heaven or in earth, (as there be gods many, and lords many,) but to us there is but one God, the Father, of Whom are all things, and we in Him; and one Lord Jesus Christ, by Whom are all things, and we by Him."[1]　"What say I then? that the idol is anything, or that which is sacrificed unto idols is anything;" No: I do not say this : but I say that "there *are* beings, *behind* these idols, *who have an existence,*" *i.e.* "seducing spirits"! And *this* "I say, that the things which the Gentiles sacrifice they sacrifice *to demons,*" δαιμονίοις, " and NOT *to God :* and I would not that ye should have fellowship with demons."[2]

Now these texts have a very important bearing upon the matter in hand: for just as *the demons* in

---

[1] 1 Cor viii. 4-6.　　[2] 1 Cor. x. 19, 20.

those days, *personated the individuals* whom they *re-presented* themselves to be; when there were *no such persons in existence :* so do they, in *these* days, *person-ate the deceased relatives and friends* of those who consult them: when such persons *are* not, and *cannot* be, present themselves on such occasions![1]

For "what saith the Scripture?" Speaking of the wicked dead, it says :—"For to him that is joined to all the living there is hope: for a living dog is better than a dead lion. For the living know that they shall die; *but the dead know not anything,*" *i.e.,* of what transpires on earth; "neither have they any more a reward; for the memory of them is forgotten. Also their love, and their hatred, and their envy, is now perished; *neither have they any more a portion for ever in anything under the sun.*"[2] And so Job speaks :—"His sons come to honour, *and he knoweth it not;* and they are brought low, but *he perceiveth it not of them.*"[3] Again, when our Lord represents Dives and Lazarus in Hades; and the former "seeing Abraham afar off, and Lazarus in his bosom," besought him to "send Lazarus, that he might dip the tip of his finger in water," to "cool his tongue," Abraham replied, that there was "a great gulph," $\chi\acute{a}\sigma\mu a$, a chasm, "fixed" between them, "so that they that would pass" from one to the other could not do so. And when he further besought him, that he "would send" Lazarus to his "father's house," "to testify

---

[1] See also page 107.   [2] Eccl. ix. 4-6.   [3] Job xiv. 21.

19

unto them," "lest they also should come into" that "place of torment," his request was refused.[1]   Nay, we are told that such persons, on dying, "in a moment go down to Sheol";[2]   and that they will not again come up from thence until their day of judgment, at the close of the Millennium.[3]

But some of my readers may perhaps remark, " But do not the first four texts you have quoted in this connexion, refer to a time, *anterior* to our Lord's descent into Hades; when He took out from thence all His own loved ones, and placed them in the third heaven, where Paradise now is ? "   They do : but this does not affect the question, *quoad* the *wicked dead*, for *they* are in Hades yet.[4]   And as to the *righteous* dead, we have a text in Isaiah lxiii. 16, which throws light on this subject : for there repentant Israel is heard praying, just before the second coming of the Lord, " Look down from heaven, and behold from the habitation of Thy holiness and of Thy glory : where is Thy zeal and Thy strength, the sounding of Thy bowels and of Thy mercies towards me ? Are they restrained ?   Doubtless Thou art our Father, though *Abraham* be *ignorant of us*, and Israel," *i.e., Jacob,* "*acknowledge us not : Thou, O Jehovah, art our Father; Thy name* is from everlasting."   Moreover the false

---

[1] Luke xvi. 23-31.   This case is fully gone into in my " Outlines of Prophetic Truth," under the Section " Sheol."

[2] Job xxi. 13.   [3] Rev. xx. 11-15.

[4] See the whole subject of Sheol, or Hades, dealt with in my " Outlines of Prophetic Truth," Chap. xi., sec. 2, pp. 625-667.

doctrine that *all* men have " ministering spirits " attending them, and that the departed become ministering spirits to their surviving relations, is confuted by Heb. i. 14 : which states that " *angels only* " are " ministering spirits ; " and that their ministry is confined to those, " who shall be heirs to salvation " ; and that the righteous dead will not become " equal to the angels " ; and take their place, *in this respect,* until after their " resurrection."[1] Moreover, as there is not the slightest hint in the Word of God, that God Himself has ever sent any of the righteous dead on any such errand ; and as the doings of the demons are diametrically opposed to everything that is said in that Word, touching the character, and work, of the righteous—on these grounds alone (were there no other), we would give the lie direct to any such hallucination whatever.

Moreover, Spiritualists have furnished abundant evidence *themselves,* to confute their own baseless assumptions : for they tell us, over and over again, that they have seen the " *materializations,*" as they call them, of their supposed departed relatives, *formed before their very eyes ;* sometimes out of gauzy matter lying in a heap on the floor, and sometimes out of similar material, drawn out of the side of the medium himself; shewing most conclusively that *such materializations could not possibly be the spirits* of the departed : for *the bodies* of such are, as we know, still lying

---

[1] Luke xx. 35, 36 ; Heb. ii. 5 ; 1 Cor. vi. 2, 3.

mouldering in the grave ! [1]   And yet *such a materiali-zation* was blasphemously said to be, and worshipped as, Christ Jesus Himself, the Saviour ! ! [2]

3. But let us test the movement itself *in its entirety.* Our Saviour says, " *Beware* of false prophets, which come to you in sheep's clothing, but inwardly they are ravening wolves.   Ye shall know them *by their fruits.* Do men gather grapes of thorns, or figs of thistles ? Even so every *good tree* bringeth forth *good fruit ;* but a *corrupt tree* bringeth forth *evil fruit.*   A good tree *cannot* bring forth *evil fruit*, neither can a *corrupt* tree bring forth *good* fruit.   Every tree that bringeth not forth good fruit is hewn down, and cast into the fire. Wherefore by their *fruits* ye shall *know them.*"[3]   And surely the evidence I have furnished in these pages of the " *evil fruits* " of " Spiritualism," is proof enough of the *corruptness* of the tree from which they spring ! Nevertheless, I will give two more extracts from the confessions of those who were once Spiritualists, but who were afterwards emancipated from its thraldom ; not only in proof of this fact, but also to shew that the *design* and *purpose* of the demons, is to bring about *the very result*, which I have shewn, from the Scriptures, that it will eventually end in.   The Rev. T. L. Harris, after having set forth the summary of the teachings of the demons, which I have before quoted,[4] concludes his

---

[1] See pages 122, 175.   [2] See pages 183, 184.   [3] Mat. vii. 15-20.
[4] See page 185.

scathing testimony in the following words :—" I pledge myself, and stand committed to the assertion that, *through mediumistic channels,* all these things are taught *as emanating from the spirits, and* WORSE IS TAUGHT, if possible, to those who penetrate the inner circles of the gloomy mysteries where *the old magic is born again!*

" Spiritualists seek *professedly* TO PULL DOWN AND DESTROY ALL EXISTING INSTITUTIONS. *Their creed* seeks to lay its fiendish hands on *all* the safeguards of social life, and to remove *every* barrier to the gratification of their prejudices or passions. GOVERNMENTS are to become *a babel of ruins,* Church and State are to become true yoke fellows, *religious organisations* are to *crumble at its touch, and* A BEAUTIFUL STRUCTURE *full of dead men's bones* IS TO TAKE THEIR PLACE " ! [1]

Dr. Hatch, of America, also says : " Having for several years been a public advocate of the doctrine of *universal salvation, I was prepared to accept* the claims of Spiritualism as being angelic, and it is well known that for several years I did much to establish it *on this basis.* For a while its real character and nature were hid amid extravagant pretensions of the blessings to result from these heavenly messengers visiting earth's inhabitants, and in its early development we saw little comparatively *of the mischievous effects that are now so conspicuous everywhere.*

" Suffice it to say that *the horde of damned spirits,* which still lingers among the scenes of their former

---

[1] See also pages 154, 185-187.

wickedness, Proteus-like, *assuming* ANY *and* EVERY *form to accomplish their hellish purpose*, soon demonstrated, not only *the falsity of my previous faith*, but also *the terrible danger* of carrying on *a forbidden intercourse* with the unseen world; and now the drama of *the basest iniquity* is freely, and in many instances openly, enacted before the bewildered gaze of the public! In fact its *mischievous* and *corrupting effects* are only limited by the capability of human depravity! There is now a class of *necromancers*, or *earthly devils*, whose secret crimes excel in real wickedness those of Messalina and the Borgias! This statement, extravagant as it may appear, I stand pledged as a man of honour to demonstrate, whenever called upon to do so."[1] And it is a very significant fact, that one of the leading medical organs of the United States, asserted that of the 24,000 cases of insanity in that country in the year 1873, no less than 7,500 of them were believed to be directly attributed to Spiritualism.[2]

4. But there are some points, which I have not touched upon even yet; and as these may have some

---

[1] This last quotation is from an article on " Spiritualism unveiled," by Lieut.-Gen. Sir Robert Phayre, K.C.B., in the " Silver Morn," of August, 1887.

[2] London Weekly Review, pp. 131, 282. A young man was lately found, in an apparently dying condition, on the floor of a Paris church. When he was restored to consciousness it was discovered that his mind was wandering, and he was accordingly conveyed to an asylum. It has been since ascertained that the poor fellow *was the victim of* THE SPIRITUALISTS OR THEOSOPHISTS, *who had been* USING HIM AS A MEDIUM *in order to find out what General Boulanger was doing at a certain time!!*

weight with a certain class of minds, I shall now proceed to dispose of them. From what I know of the
vagaries of the human mind, I can quite conceive,
notwithstanding the overwhelming mass of evidence
which I have adduced against Spiritualism, that there
may still be some persons, who may think there is
some good in it: because they suppose, that they, or
some of their friends, who have consulted the spirits,
may have derived some real substantial benefit from
them—a vain and false notion, which I shall endeavour
to dissipate from their minds.

The excellent Matthew Pool, in his Commentary on
the Scriptures, which was written between 200 and 300
years ago, has some admirable remarks on Matt. xii.
25, 26 ; which exactly meet, and dispose of, this objection. He says :—" The sum of the argument is,
The devil is so wise, that he will look to the upholding
of his own kingdom in the world. This will require *an
agreement* of the devils "—rather, demons—" among
themselves, for if they be *divided* they cannot uphold
their kingdom, nor stand, any more than a house, city,
or kingdom in the world so divided can stand ; therefore the prince of devils "—demons—" will not forcibly
cast out the inferior devils "—demons. " There is but
one imaginable objection to this : Do we not see the
contrary to this in people's going to cunning men for
help against them that are bewitched, to get help for
them ? and is there no truth in those many stories we
have of *persons that have found help against the devil
for some that have traded with the devil ?* "—which

shows that " Spiritualism " had manifested itself in his days also ! " I answer, *it is one thing for the devils* "—demons—" *to play with one another*, another thing for them *to cast out one another*. One devil "—demon —" may yield and give place to another, *to gain a greater advantage for the whole society*, but one never quarreleth with another ! *The first may be for the enlarging of Satan's kingdom*. This must be to destroy it. When a poor wretched creature goeth *to one who dealeth with the devil for help for one who is vexed with some effect of the devil*, one devil "—demon—" here doth but yield and give place to another *by compact, voluntarily, and for the devil's greater advantage ; for it is more advantage to the devil (who seeks nothing so much as* A DIVINE HOMAGE) TO GAIN THE FAITH OF ONE SOUL, *than to exercise the power to afflict many bodies !*[1] In such cases as these, the devil, for the abatement of a little bodily pain, gains a power over the soul of him or her who cometh to implore his help, and exerciseth a faith in him. This is an establishing, promoting, and enlarging his Kingdom. But *Christ* FORCED THE DEVILS "—demons—" OUT OF PERSONS ; they did not yield voluntarily, for a greater advantage, but forcibly, for no advantage. *He did not* pray the devils to come out, nor *make use of any of the devil's sacraments, upon the use of which, by some original compact*, he was obliged to come out *upon a soul's surrender of itself by faith to him ;* but they came out unwillingly, UPON THE

---

[1] See pages 279-281.

AUTHORITATIVE WORDS OF CHRIST, *without the use of any magical rites and ceremonies testifying the least homage done to him"!*

A butcher was once driving a pig to the slaughter-house ; and, as is often the case under such circumstances, he could not get it to move on. Happening to have some beans in his pocket, he pulled a few out from time to time, and placed them on the road before the animal; and thus succeeded in his object. But could any one but a fool ever have supposed, that he meant this *in kindness to the pig ?* The Scriptures tell us, that " man being in honour abideth not : he is *like the beasts that perish.* This their way is their folly : yet their posterity approve their sayings. Like sheep they are laid in Sheol ; death shall feed on them ; and the upright shall have dominion over them in the morning," *i.e.,* in the resurrection ; " and their beauty shall consume in Sheol from their dwelling." [1] While it is said of " the simple one " " among the youths," who was seduced by the " harlot," that " he goeth after her straightway, *as an ox goeth to the slaughter,* or as a fool to the correction of the stocks ; till a dart strike through his liver ; as a bird *hasteth to the snare,* and knoweth not that it is *for his life."* For " her house is the way to Sheol, going down to the chambers of death." [2] Yea, " the dead are there ; and her guests are IN THE DEPTHS *of Sheol."* [3]

In the years 1863 and 1864, during which I was Undersheriff of the county of Lincoln, and had to be

---

[1] Psa. xlix. 12-14. [2] Prov. vii. 7, 22, 23, 27. [3] Prov. ix. 18.

present at the Assizes; while attending one of the Judges in the Crown Court, on one occasion, my position was close to two murderers, man and wife, who were arraigned for poisoning the mother of one of them, (the wife, I believe,) with the object of getting possession of her property. It was a most wicked cold-blooded murder: as the evidence shewed that they poisoned her by slow degrees ; while at the same time, they outwardly shewed kindness to her, and professed to be doing all they could to alleviate her sufferings! The Judge, who tried them, took, as it seemed to me, a most perverted view of the case ; and to the intense surprise of every one present in Court, as well as the great disgust of the Chief Constable, he summed up elaborately in favour of the prisoners, and almost urged the Jury, if they convicted the prisoners, to bring in against them only the modified verdict of manslaughter. The Jury could not agree, and were locked up all night in consequence; and in the morning, to the surprise of everyone, they acted on the Judge's suggestion, and brought in a verdict against the prisoners of man-slaughter only! The solicitor, who had the conduct of the case, told me some years afterwards, that most of the witnesses against the prisoners were then dead; and from the mode in which they pined away, he had a strong suspicion that they had been previously poisoned by the prisoners themselves!

Now *can* there be anything more diabolical than the murder of a parent by a child, who at the same time is blinding that parent by professing towards her the

most tender and devoted affection! Alas! there can.
For as there are *degrees* of wickedness among *men :* so
likewise are there among *the demons* themselves! For
our Saviour has told us, that " when the unclean spirit
is gone out of man," *i.e.*, voluntarily, for his own
purposes, " he walketh through dry places seeking rest,
and findeth none. Then he saith, I will return into
my house from whence I came out : and when he is
come, he findeth it empty, swept, and garnished.
Then goeth he, and taketh with himself seven other
spirits *more wicked than himself*, and they enter in and
dwell there : and the last state of that man is worse
than the first "—a prediction, which our Lord applies
primarily to the Jewish nation, as such, in the days of
Antichrist—" Even so shall it be unto this wicked
generation "[1]—which is now freer from crime than
any other nation : but which, the prophetic Scriptures
assure us, will *in that day* be as one possessed of seven
devils!

And is it not infinitely more awful, when " lying,"
" seducing " spirits, whose " consciences " are " seared
with a hot iron," by such *apparently* kind attentions
and thoughtful provisions for the wants and comforts
of a family, as are described over and over again in the
pages of " Spirit Workers in the Home Circle,"[2] thus

---

[1] Mat. xii. 43-45.

[2] Hence, he speaks of them, *in consequence*, at pp. 61, 72 and 109,
as " our spirit *friends ;* " at p. 105, " as righteous as *beneficent ;* " at
p. 150, as " the intelligence invariably used for *good* purposes ; " &c.,
&c. : and at p. 18, he actually speaks of this " unmistakable wave of
psychic power," as " streaming " " its *benign* and *celestial* radiance "

seek to lure those who are deceived by them, into " the blackness of darkness for ever!"[1] For the Word of God expressly states, that "*sorcerers*," φαρμακεῦσι,[2] " and *idolaters*, and all liars, shall have their part in the lake which burneth with fire and brimstone : which is the second death."[3] And our Lord tells us that "the thief" — here representing Satan himself, either mediately, or otherwise—" cometh *not*, BUT FOR *to steal, and to kill, and to* DESTROY."[4] And rightly is his " name in the Hebrew tongue, therefore," called " *Abaddon*"—*destruction*—" but in the Greek tongue" he " hath his name *Apollyon* "[5]—*destroyer !*

Yes, " we may be fully assured of this, that all the baskanizing and seductive influences, that Satan and his hosts can bring to bear upon the lusts and passions of men, are brought to bear upon them, *for the one hellish purpose* OF THEIR DESTRUCTION AND DEATH ! . . . . . All the mighty instrumentality which Satan has at his command, ' the principalities and powers in the heavenlies,' ' the hosts of wicked spirits ' under him, and the innumerable ' legions ' of ' demons ' over whom he reigns as ' the prince,'—all, all are straining their utmost energies"—especially in these days, when they know that their time is now but " short "—"*for the same diabolical end*—DESTRUCTION AND DEATH !"[6]

" through " his " life's chequered experiences as *one of the gifts* promised to the early disciples when the Comforter should appear ! ! "

[1] Jude 13.   [2] See page 10.   [3] Rev. xxi. 8.   [4] John x. 10.   [5] Rev. ix. 11.

[6] Extracted from the writer's " Personality and History of Satan," pp. 41, 42.

5. But even yet, I can quite suppose, that there may still be some, who may think that the marvellous light, strength, intellectual vigour, apparent wisdom, and even, what they suppose to be, *heavenly consolation*, which have sometimes flowed into their spirits, through this influence, could not *possibly* have proceeded from *evil spirits;* but must, of *necessity*, have emanated from *good spirits;* and must, therefore, be *of God!* To "cut off" all "occasion," therefore, "from them which," I might so say, "desire occasion"[1] thus to delude themselves; I will fully meet, and reply to, this objection likewise.

The Rev. A. R. Fausset, in the "Silver Morn" for September, 1885, remarks, "I have letters from a pious London lady who has found, *she thinks, great comfort* from Spiritualistic communications with her beloved mother deceased, and who firmly believes *they come from the Lord!*" And he rightly replied to her, "God's commandment is (Deut. xviii. 11), 'There shall not be found among you *a consulter with familiar spirits nor a necromancer*,' *i.e.*, a consulter of the dead. You do consult the dead. You are not on God's ground, but on Satan's. *You put yourself in Satan's power.* Your prayer is a self-deceiving mockery; when you fly in GOD's face in the very act of praying to GOD, GOD *gives you up to your own delusion*, as GOD gave up Ahab to the lying demon who undertook to persuade him to go to his own Kingdom (Old Testament lesson). So GOD saith to all who 'set up

---

[1] 2 Cor. xi. 12.

idols in their hearts, and put the stumbling block of their iniquity before their face,' 'I the LORD will answer him that cometh to Me according to the multitude of his idols.' When once Satan has *beguiled religious professors into forbidden practices by religious masks,* HAVING GOTTEN THEM INTO HIS POWER, he will soon throw off the mask " !

It is against such delusions as these, that the Holy Ghost has expressly warned us, when he tells us that as "false apostles" and "deceitful workers," can "transform themselves into the apostles of Christ:" so "*Satan himself* is" ofttimes "*transformed into* AN ANGEL OF LIGHT";[1] and so appears, *in this form,* to the deluded children of men, who put their trust *in him.* And as my subject would be incomplete, without an unmasking, and exposure, of *this* device also ; I shall now proceed to expose it accordingly.

The late Dean Goode several years ago, published a very valuable work, entitled, "The modern claims to the possession of the extraordinary gifts of the Spirit, stated and examined;" in which he gives many instances, both ancient and modern, of Satan having deluded even Christian men, as well as others, by assuming the character of "an angel of light:" some few of which I shall now transcribe.

"In the year 1625, Comenius," who was then "travelling as one of a deputation from the United Brethren in Moravia, to some of their brethren in

---

[1] 2 Cor. xi. 13-15.

Poland," relates how, " on his way back," he paid a
visit to " one Christopher Kotter, a pious man, an
inhabitant of Sprottau in Silesia," who was reputed
to be *a prophet;* and " he says, he cannot but mention,
to the praise of God, *what delightful emotions his mind
experienced,*" while he was translating his prophecies
into Bohemian. And yet the event shewed, that he
was utterly deceived: for the prophecies were *proved to
be false;* and "Kotter" himself " was banished from
his country as a false prophet ! "[1]

Again in the spring of 1688, there arose in Dauphiny,
in France, " the Camisars," who laid claim to the gift
of prophecy; " one of the first " of whom was " a poor
shepherd's daughter of 14 or 15 years old, as ignorant
and untaught as one could imagine."   A Mr. Lacy, an
Englishman, who investigated their claims, and who
seems to have completely believed in them, and actually
became " one of their principal supporters and *prophets
in this country,*" published a book about them in 1707 ;
from which the following is an extract—" When I
came to the Assembly, there was *a girl* preached with
an eloquence and fluency to me most admirable. . .
The spirit fell upon her, and she made a long prayer :
*methought I heard an angel, so charming were the
words that came from her mouth !* After prayer she
set a psalm, and tuned it melodiously; then she gave
us a discourse *so excellent, so pathetic, so well digested,*
with that *holy gracefulness* and ardent zeal, that we

---

[1] " Modern Claims," &c., pp. 162-164.

could not but believe it was more than human that spoke in her. . . . . *She quoted many texts of the Old and New Testament as if she had the whole Bible by heart,* . . . and she applied them so aptly that affected us strangely. . . She *promised* also . . . *after a manner very powerful, exact, and pressing, that religion in its purity should be re-established in the kingdom!*"[1]

And then, after having entered into several other particulars, he continues :—"Everything was done by inspiration. . . . It was in fact *by the spirit's express direction* that they took up arms against the King's troops. 'It was only,' says Elias Marion, 'by the *inspirations* and their repeated orders, that *we began the war* for the enjoyment of our holy religion.' And yet, notwithstanding these injunctions, interferences, and revelations of the spirit, as they supposed"—a great many of which he *particularly enumerates*—both prophets and people, "were in a few years miserably exterminated by the King's troops, and ALL *their prophecies* respecting the *speedy* downfall of Babylon, by which they meant the Romish Church, and the establishment of Christ's kingdom, left to the present hour unaccomplished!"[2]

Another company of prophets also arose in England in 1707, who were so gifted by the spirits, that they deceived many. "Sir Richard Bulkley informs us, that he heard one of them, who did not know one

---

[1] "Modern Claims," &c., pp. 169-172.　　[2] Ib., p. 181.

Hebrew letter from another, utter with great readiness and freedom complete discourses in Hebrew, for near a quarter of an hour together, and sometimes much longer."[1] He seems himself to have been completely deceived by them; but Dr. Josiah Woodward, who thoroughly tested their pretensions to *Divine* inspiration, came to a very different conclusion: for in a tract *he* wrote on the subject, he says:—"The Holy Scriptures inform us, that the devil sometimes transformeth himself into the likeness of an angel of light: *and perhaps he scarce ever acted that part more exquisitely than in this case!* Persons are brought to put up prayers and make exhortations, which are in most points *very good and pious;* humility, meekness, and charity, are recommended, and many other parts of religion duly represented."[2] How then were they discovered to be *false* prophets? "We may see," says Mr. Henry Nicholson, in his "Falsehood of the new prophets manifested," "and all the world may be satisfied, that these new prophets are *not* from God, by their *contradicting* one another in ecstasies by turns; *in which, also, they upbraid and condemn one another as* FALSE *and* SELF-EXALTING"![3]

"Another still more remarkable case is that of Joanna Southcott, which lasted for many years, and whose followers, at the time of her death in 1814, amounted to about 20,000, pervading every county in England, and numbering among them many persons

---

[1] "Modern Claims," &c., p. 188.   [2] Ib., p. 193.   [3] Ib., p. 196.
20

of the highest respectability, piety, and intelligence, including 5 clergymen of the Established Church, and many dissenting ministers; and had 5 chapels in and near the metropolis alone. She herself died under the delusion, which was so firmly rooted in the minds of a vast number of her followers, that they did not abandon it for several years after her death, *expecting her speedy resurrection*" ! [1]

I might also refer to Swedenborgianism, which has greatly extended in England of late years; to Prince's Agapemone; to the Jezreelites, and their huge temple: which is in course of construction at Gillingham; and which is to cost £25,000; as well as to the mad delusions of the followers of King Solomon, so-called, at Brighton; and other demoniacal delusions.

The case, however, which I particularly wish to refer to, and which remarkably meets the point in question, is that of Mr. Robert Baxter, a pious solicitor, who was for a time led away by the Irvingite delusion. In his " Narrative of Facts," which was first published in 1833, and which I have now before me, he thus describes how he first got entangled in this snare.

" I had heard," he says, " many particulars of the extraordinary manifestations which had occurred at Port Glasgow, in Scotland;" and being " conscious that nothing but an abundant outpouring of the Spirit of God could quicken the church into active life " ; he says, he " longed greatly, and prayed much for *such* an

---

[1] " Modern Claims," &c., p. 216.

outpouring and testimony" himself. "When I saw," therefore, he says, "as it seemed to me proof that those who *claimed the gifts* were walking honestly, and that *the power manifested in them* was *evidently super-natural*, and moreover bore testimony to Christ come in the flesh, *I welcomed it at once as the work of God*."[1]

Accordingly he attended one of the prayer meetings, which were then being held in London; and hearing a Mr. T. "speak two or three words very distinctly, and with an energy and depth of tone which seemed to" him "extraordinary," "it fell upon" him "as a supernatural utterance, which" he "ascribed to the power of God"! "In the midst of the feeling of awe and reverence which this," and some other utterances "produced," he was himself "*seized upon by the power;* and in much struggling against it, was made to cry out, and" himself "to give forth a confession of" his "own sin in the matter, for which" the congregation had been "rebuked; and afterwards to utter a pro-phecy."[2]

"I was overwhelmed," he says, "by this occurrence. The attainment of the gift of prophecy, which this supernatural utterance was deemed to be, was, with myself and many others, *a great object of desire!* I could not, therefore, but *rejoice* at having been made the subject of it. . . . There was in me, at the time of the utterance, very great excitement; and yet I was distinctly conscious of *a power acting upon me* beyond

---

[1] Narrative, pp. 3, 4.   [2] Ib., pp. 4, 5.

the mere power of excitement. . . . Conceiving, *as I had previously done*, that the power speaking in the speakers *was of God*, I was *convinced the power in me was the same power!* "[1]

And then referring to certain circumstances, which I need not mention here, he adds, "I am thus particular in explaining these circumstances, that I may accurately show how unequal we are, in our own strength, to stand before God; and *how rapidly we may fall from all our convictions and views of truth*, if our God should see fit, in judgment for our sins, *to leave us for a season* TO THE INFLUENCE OF A SEDUCING SPIRIT "![2]

"On another occasion," he says, when at church, "the whole of the ordinary services passed without any visitation of power; but after the sacrament had been administered, when kneeling to return thanks, *the power came upon me largely*, though the impulse was not to utterance—my tongue was riveted as I was repeating the response, and MY SOUL FILLED WITH JOY AND THANKSGIVING, AND SUCH A PRESENCE OF GOD, *as it seemed to me*, AS EXCEEDED ANY PEACE AND JOY I HAD EVER BEFORE TASTED AT THAT HOLY SACRAMENT! When reporting to friends the proofs of the power being of God, *this has always occurred to me*, and has generally been *felt by them* AS CONFIRMING THE WORK; since, as we argued none but the Spirit of God would, at such a season, be permitted to enter in, and none

---

[1] Narrative, pp. 5, 6.   [2] Ib., p. 8.

but the Spirit of God could produce such fruits in the mind. It is certainly very mysterious ; *but if I was unfaithful to God* in forgetting my Lord's injunction to *watch* as well as pray ; AND HAD ADMITTED THE CLAIMS OF THIS SPIRIT, without trying it strictly by the doctrines, as we are enjoined to do ; was it not just and gracious in God to show me, *that I was utterly incapable* BY ANY OTHER TEST *of trying the spirits ?* " [1]

Still continuing to believe in the spirit, he continues, " The power which then rested on me was *far more mighty than before*, LAYING DOWN MY MIND AND BODY IN PERFECT OBEDIENCE, and carrying me on without confusion or excitement. . . . Every former visitation of the power had been very brief ; but now it continued, and seemed to rest on me all the evening. The things I was made to utter, flashed in upon my mind without forethought, without expectation, and without any plan or arrangement : all was the work of the moment, and *I was as* THE PASSIVE INSTRUMENT OF THE POWER WHICH USED ME "! And then, speaking of interrogating the spirit who spoke through the medium in power, he says, " I have been since much struck with *the inconsistency* (whenever any doubt is entertained whether a spirit speaking or working in any one is of God) *of consulting with the spirit, or seeking explanation from the person who has the spirit!* So doing, WE AT ONCE PUT OURSELVES UNDER THE POWER OF THE SPIRIT, *and are*

---

[1] Narrative, pp. 10, 11.

deceived, unless God graciously interpose ! One method God has given us for trying the spirits, and in order to do this faithfully we must stand, resting in faith upon our God ; and in the name of our God, reverently towards our God, but *without at all bowing before the spirit we are trying*, set out Christ come in the flesh, and demand a confession. We are *not faithful to our God* if we *bow to* or *consult any spirit* before we have tried it ! *When we once bow*, WE WORSHIP IT, *and give it* POWER OVER US TO DECEIVE US "! ![1]

Again, he says, "To those who have been used to watch over the workings of their own minds, and who have never been visited with the temptation of yielding to impressions ; nor visited with any power beyond the mere vagaries of excitement ; it may seem inexplicable how persons can be brought to surrender their own judgment, and act upon an impulse, or under a power working in them, without daring to question that power. The process is, however, very simple, and the reasons supporting it are very plausible, and—the premises admitted—perfectly logical. My own case may be an example : accustomed to try the powers and weaknesses of my own mind in public and in private ; in business and in religious meetings ; in speaking and in prayer ; in reasoning, and in exposition ; I found, on a sudden, in the midst of my accustomed course, *a power coming upon me which was altogether new*—an unnatural, and in many cases, a

---

[1] Narrative, pp. 13-15.

most appalling utterance given to me—matters uttered by me in this power of which I had never thought, and many of which I did not understand until long after they were uttered—*an enlarged comprehension and clearness of view* given to me on points which were really the truth of God (*though mingled with many things which I have since seen* NOT TO BE TRUTH, *but which* THEN HAD THE FORM OF TRUTH)—great setting out of Christ—GREAT JOY AND FREEDOM IN PRAYER—*and seemingly*, GREAT NEARNESS OF COMMUNION WITH GOD, IN THE MIDST OF THE WORKINGS OF THE POWER—the course of the power quite contrary to the course of excitement.—It was manifest to me *the power was supernatural;* it was *therefore a spirit.* It *seemed* to me to bear testimony to Christ, and to work the fruits of the Spirit of God. The conclusion was inevitable, that *it was the Spirit of God;* and if so, the deduction was immediate, that IT OUGHT IN ALL THINGS TO BE OBEYED. . . . Awful, therefore, is the mistake, if a *seducing* spirit is entertained as the Holy Spirit of Jehovah. . . . Looking back upon it now, I can only say, all this *seeming demonstration* of *truth* and *holiness* would not have been permitted to deceive us, *if we had not forgotten the text,* ' SATAN HIMSELF IS TRANSFORMED INTO AN ANGEL OF LIGHT.' " ! ! [1]

The writer was, by the blessing of God, ultimately delivered " as a bird out of the snare of the fowler," [2] by having had clearly revealed to him, the *lying* and

---

[1] Narrative, pp. 21-23.　　[2] Psa. cxxiv. 7.

contradictory nature of the utterances themselves ; as well as *the false doctrines* which were taught, and confirmed *in power by the spirits uttering them !* And he states, in the preface to his second edition, that his " Narrative " had, under God, been " made instrumental to the opening of the eyes " of some who had been " under the delusion." May the Lord grant His blessing on this brief summary of it likewise.

And here I would note, that the power of Satan is such, that he not only can deceive men, by appearing to them as " an angel of light ; " but that he can also *confer special gifts upon them*, and increase those natural gifts, which they already possess: which he *will do*, if he can only induce them to employ these gifts in his service: and as the Rev. Edward Payson, D.D., long ago also discovered, he can moreover " *counterfeit* every mark of a real Christian, except " one—and that is, " *a growing acquaintance with the desperate wickedness and surpassing deceitfulness of the heart !* " [1] For it is the Holy Ghost alone, Who can truly " convince " the sinner of his " sin." [2] And I will, therefore, conclude this Section, by giving an

---

[1] Life of Payson, p. 208.

[2] John xvi. 7-9. It is quite true, that when it suits Satan's purpose, he can make sin appear very terrible to the sinner, in order to drive him to despair of mercy, or induce him to believe that he has committed the unpardonable sin : but this is only conviction of the *guilt* of sin, which natural men may have *under the law :* but the conviction of sin *under the Gospel* by the Holy Ghost, is the conviction of sin in its *nature and essence,* as *being against God,* &c. Psalm li. 4, 5, 17.

example in point, under each of the above heads, by way of a final admonition on this all-important subject.

Colonel Meadows Taylor, in his " Story of My Life," from which I have already quoted, says, on one occasion, that " there were great rejoicings on the recovery of the Rajah, and among other entertainments a Hindoo Play, which I had never seen before, taken from the Bhagwat, or recitation of the poem relating to Krishna.

" The chief performer was a handsome young girl, who was a capital actress and singer, very richly dressed. She personated one of Krishna's wives, lamenting his absence from her ! The text was given in recitation, with here and there an air and chorus, the language, Canarese, which I could not follow. One plaintive air with a chorus was excellently given, and I wish I had been able to take it down. Her acting was admirable : grief, sadness, hope, jealousy, despair, all depicted in turn, and her joy at the last when she found she had been tormenting herself for nothing after all ! Yet the whole was performed by stone-cutters, who could neither read nor write ; and the plays had been learned by rote ; and were traditional in their families " ! ![1]

Dr. Payson, writing to his mother, on the 10th of August, 1808, says :—" One person who was esteemed by Mr. K., and the whole church, and by myself too, not only as a Christian, but a very eminent one, *of*

---

[1] Story of my Life, vol. i., pp. 319, 320.

whose religion I had not the least doubt, and who appeared very humble and broken-hearted, and in short, to be everything we could wish, *has discovered that she was building on the sand!* She had been a professor some time, but had never heard of, or suspected, the difference between *holy* and *selfish love,* and is now fully convinced that all her love was of the latter kind! As she possesses good sense and information, the accounts she gives of her experience, while destitute of religion, are very profitable, and *open to the view new ways in which persons may be deceived, of which I had scarcely any conception!*"[1]

And he says again :—" The manner in which people obtain a false hope, is generally this : they first believe that God is reconciled to them, and then are reconciled to Him on that account ; but if they thought that God was still displeased with, and determined to punish them, they would find their enmity to Him revive. On the contrary, the Christian is reconciled because he sees the holiness of the law which he has broken, and God's justice in punishing him; he takes part with God against himself, cordially submits to Him, and this when he expects condemnation. *He* is reconciled, because he is pleased with the character of God ; the *false convert,* because he hopes that God is pleased with him."[2] And he adds :—" One mark of the true convert is, that he continues to repent of his sins, after he hopes that they are pardoned. All that the hypo-

---

[1] **Life of Edward Payson, p. 147.**   [2] **Ib., p. 269.**

crite desires, is salvation from punishment; and when he thinks this end secured, he feels no concern respecting his sins. But the true Christian desires to be saved from sin; and his hatred of sin, and repentance for it, increase in proportion as his assurance of heaven increases. Another mark is, that all disposition to make excuses is taken away. The repentant sinner feels willing to lie at God's feet, and confess his sins, without even wishing to excuse them."[1]

"Wherewithal," then, "shall a young man cleanse his way? By taking heed thereto according to Thy word."[2] For "the entrance of Thy words giveth light; it giveth understanding to the simple."[3] "O send out Thy light and Thy truth: let them lead me; let them bring me unto Thy holy hill, and to Thy tabernacle."[4] "Thy word is a lamp unto my feet, and a light unto my path."[5] "Trust," therefore, "in the Lord with all thine heart; and lean not unto thine own understanding"—*which we have seen, that it is the special object of the demons to induce those who have been deceived by them to do!*[6]

"In *all* thy ways acknowledge Him, and *He* shall direct thy paths."[7] "If," therefore, "any of you lack wisdom, let him ask of God, that giveth to all men liberally, and upbraideth not; and it shall be given him. But let him ask in faith, nothing wavering.

---

[1] Life of Edward Payson, p. 273.   [2] Psa. cxix. 9.   [3] Psa. cxix. 130.
[4] Psa. xliii. 3.   [5] Psa. cxix. 105.
[6] See pages 162, 188, 199, 200, 202, 204, 206.   [7] Prov. iv. 5, 6.

For he that wavereth is like a wave of the sea driven
with the wind and tossed. For let not that man
think that he shall receive anything from the Lord.''[1]
And when men wilfully, and persistently, reject the
truth of God, their doom is sealed; and their " blood "
will " be upon " their "own head."[2] And it is sad
indeed, when God has to say of those who are set
apart to teach others, " They which lead thee *cause
thee to err*, and *destroy the way of thy paths.*"[3] " And
if the blind lead the blind, both shall fall into the
ditch."[4] And "the man that wandereth out of the
way of understanding *shall remain in the congregation
of the dead.*"[5] " An ignorant and unfaithful ministry,"
says Matthew Pool, "is the greatest plague God can
send among a people." " And what will ye do,"
says John Bunyan to such unfaithful preachers, " *when
your congregation comes bellowing after you into hell ?*"

6. And what has *occasioned* all these deadly evils,
and laid us open, as a nation, to the seductive influences
of such God-dishonouring blasphemies? Our *national
rejection* of Jehovah and of His Christ, by the introduction of Romanists, Jews, *as Jews*, and atheists, into
our Parliament ; by the exclusion of God's Word from
our Government Schools ; and by the *national recog-
nition*, and *state support*, of idolatry, both Romish and
heathen, as well in this country as in our Colonial

---

[1] James i. 5-7.   [2] Acts xviii. 6.   [3] Isa. iii. 12.
[4] Mat. xv. 14.   [5] Prov. xxi. 16.

dependencies ! [1] *These things* have "*provoked*" God to withdraw His gracious influence from us, as a nation, and to leave us to our own devices. For " what saith the Scripture ? " Deprecating in the strongest possible terms, the notion that *any* Christian should *ever* give the least countenance to *idolatry*, the Apostle says, in a passage, which I have more than once before quoted, " Ye *cannot* drink the cup of the Lord, and the cup of *demons:* ye *cannot* partake of the Lord's table, and of the table of *demons*. Do we *provoke the Lord* to jealousy ? Are we *stronger than He ?* " [2]

And can there be a greater curse, either to an individual, or to a nation, than to be left of God, to their own devices—" Ephraim is *joined to idols : let him alone* " [3]—for it is a sure presage of ruin. " They have chosen *their own ways*, and their soul delighteth in their abominations. I also will choose *their delusions*, and will bring their fears upon them." [4]

Archbishop Leighton, in " A Fragment upon Ezra ix." truly says :—" ' Our transgression is grown up to heaven.' *It hath had a long time to grow in, and all that time hath been incessantly growing,* AND THEREFORE GROWN SO HIGH. ' Since the days of our fathers we have been in this trespass.' *Generations pass,* BUT YET YOUR SINS ABIDE. When the succeeding genera-

---

[1] See the writer's " National Idolatry," John F. Shaw & Co., 1d. ; and his " Lessons from History ; or, Words of Warning for 'Perilous Times,' " before referred to, page 258.
[2] 1 Cor. x. 21, 22. [3] Hos. iv. 17. [4] Isa. lxvi. 3, 4.

tion follows on in it, *the former sins are reserved*, AND THE LATTER ADDED TO THEM, and so, they are kept alive. *Thus* they GROW! *This fills up the measure,* AND RIPENS A PEOPLE FOR JUDGMENT, that is filling and growing all the while suitable to the sin, *till it be poured out!* Hence, public calamities, and long-lasting judgments on people!" For, as our blessed Lord Himself says, the sins of former ages, if followed, and unrepented of, although often warned against, are all ultimately visited upon the nation finally disregarding such warnings: as He said to that nation, which rejected Him, "that upon you may come *all* the righteous blood shed upon the earth, from the blood of righteous Abel unto the blood of Zacharias, son of Barachias, whom ye slew between the temple and the altar. Verily I say unto you, *All these things shall come* UPON THIS GENERATION."[1]

I have already pointed out many of *the effects* of the withdrawal of God's favour from us, as a nation, in the tendency of " modern thought "; but passing by the cases of Romanists and Ritualists, as well as of Rationalists; who virtually reject the Gospel altogether: I would now rather refer to what I might call *the reflex action* of such withdrawal upon the so-called *Evangelical* portion of the community; who still profess to *believe* in "the *Gospel* of the *grace* of God."[2] And, alas! what can be said of the great mass of these, truly now called, *neo*-evangelicals? That they

---

[1] Mat. xxiii. 35, 36.   [2] Acts xx. 24.

have utterly lapsed and gone from the doctrines of grace; and that they are now setting forth "another," ἕτερον, *i.e.*, a *different* "Gospel: which is *not another*" ἄλλο; for there is *but one true Gospel:* but a perversion of "the Gospel of Christ."[1] For the Gospel that is presented by the greater number of Evangelical preachers, *so-called*, to the men of to-day is a *universal Gospel*, which unconverted men are said to have the ability to make their own, whenever they choose: so that the "salvation," which these preachers and teachers preach to sinners, is no longer "*of the Lord*"; but *of men!* For have we not heard over and over again, at so-called Gospel services, such exhortations to all the hearers present, without exception, as *these?*—"Come to Jesus: come to Jesus *now.* You know Jesus *can't* save you, unless you'll *let* Him!—Christ died *for all:* therefore, you see He must have died *for you;* and you have only to believe in Him, and to be saved. He can't *believe* for you: you must believe *for yourself*—your sins were laid *on Jesus;* therefore they *cannot be on you;* for they can't be in *two* places at the same time. You see you have only to believe in Him, and you will be at peace— when Jesus died on the cross, every person in the world died on that cross with Him. You have therefore only to see this, and just trust yourself in His hands, and you will be saved!" I pledge my word, that I have heard such lying statements as these, at

---

[1] Gal. i. 6, 7.

so-called Gospel addresses again and again. Nay I once heard an open air preacher, who was a member of a band of preachers, reckoned to be Evangelical, preach upon Rom. x. 9, in which he told his hearers, that of course, they all "*believed* in their *hearts*" that God had "raised" Jesus "from the dead": all that was requisite, therefore, was that they should now come out, and "*confess* Him with their *mouths*"; and they would be "*saved*"!

And even among those, who are better taught in these things, there is a growing and increasing number of Christian professors, who not only deny that the Gentiles were ever under the moral law: but likewise actually account those who hold the Scriptural doctrine, that the obedience and sufferings of the Lord Jesus in life and in death were on account of His elect people only; and that the righteousness that He thus wrought out for them, is imputed to them on their believing in Him, *as heretics*—although the Scriptures set forth these precious truths, as with the clearness of a sunbeam; and they have always been held and taught by sound divines from the beginning. Hence *the old theology* (as we have seen) is completely going out of fashion; and is being rapidly supplanted by an emasculated form of *sentimental religion*, and by *sensational religious tales*, which are being sold by hundreds of thousands! Calling at the Depository of the Religious Tract Society some time ago, and enquiring for a copy of that admirable little Exposition by the Rev. John Venn, of Luke i. 68-79, entitled, "Mistakes in

Religion Exposed," I was informed that it had long since been out of print! "Then are you not going to *reprint* it?" I enquired. "Oh, no:" I received for reply, "*this class* of theology is now *never enquired for*"! Then I say, the more the pity: and the greater the shame. Not long after this, I purchased a beautifully, and even expensively, bound copy of Archbishop Leighton's whole works in 5 vols., at a second-hand bookseller's, for 7s. 6d., when he offered me a magnificently bound copy of Owen's whole works, in 21 vols, for 22s.! And I actually saw another complete copy of Leighton's works, offered in another bookseller's catalogue, for 9d.!

All these things are truly signs of the times; and they indicate but too clearly the end to which we are drifting. And all this apparent show of Gospel earnestness and success, and the circulation of so much supposed Gospel knowledge and instruction, only serves to blind people to the true nature of the dangers to which we are exposed: for they induce people to think that things are becoming *better*, instead of *worse*; and that the Gospel is making *progress* in the world; and as some vainly even still imagine, will ultimately convert it to Christ! although the Scriptures plainly inform us, that "God *at the first* did visit the Gentiles" only "*to take out of them* a people for His name."[1]

---

[1] Acts xv. 14. The so-called "Holiness movement," likewise, which in many cases is but the teaching of the lying doctrine of "perfection in the flesh;" and the Israelitish craze that *we are*

21

Moreover the " more sure word of prophecy," which is intended by the Holy Ghost, to be " a light that shineth in a dark place, until the day-dawn, and the day-star arise,"[1] has been so corrupted by the false glosses and unsound systems of men ; that, in many cases, it is being used rather to " *hide* counsel without knowledge,"[2] than to enable men truly to " *discern* the signs of the times." [3]

How often, for instance, have the false prophecies of "the time of the end," occasioned by the belief in the unscriptural doctrine of the year-day system, been " a snare and a trap " to the unwary ; and by thus throwing contempt upon the Prophetic Word, have resulted in some minds, not only in a disgust of the whole subject, but in the rejection of that Word as *any guide* in the matter whatsoever ! I remember several years ago reading a work by a Captain Baker, entitled " The Day and The Hour ;" in which he predicted that the last day would be on the 20th of September, 1878 !—a day which has already passed,—and the day of judgment on the 11th of February, 1922 ! He also predicted that the Queen would abdicate on the 9th of October, 1867 ; and the fall of Rome would take place on the 6th of December following ; while the resurrection of the saints was to occur about 1 a.m. on the

---

Israelites, and must therefore be *blessed as such,* are likewise working much mischief amongst Christian professors. See the Writer's tractate, " Christian Perfection, so-called : shewing what it *is,* and what it *is not.*" S. W. Partridge & Co., 2d.

[1] 2 Peter i. 19.   [2] Job xlii. 3.   [3] Mat. xvi. 3.

night of 24-25 January, 1875! Time, therefore, has already proved him to be a "*false prophet.*" Nevertheless, there are such prophets amongst us still; who, notwithstanding the positive assertion of our blessed Lord, that "of *that* day and hour *knoweth no one,*" οὐδεὶς, "no, not the angels of heaven, but My Father only,"[1] still dare to predict the very day and hour itself, when the Lord Himself shall come!

What mischief, likewise, has resulted from the so-called "secret rapture" theory: for which there is not even the shadow of a text in proof, in the Divine Word.[2] For the belief in this false doctrine, by inducing professing Christians to think that they will of course escape *all* the evils that are coming upon the earth, has led them to look upon the persecutions of the days preceding, as well as those during, the reign of Antichrist, as things which could only affect *other people*, and with which *they* could not possibly have anything to do: although the Scriptures most positively assure us that Antichrist is to "make war with *the saints,*" *i.e., as such,* and to "*prevail against them;* UNTIL the Ancient of days," *i.e.,* Jehovah Jesus, "came, and judgment was given to the saints of the Most High; and the time came that the saints possessed the Kingdom."[3] Hence the study of the sub-

---

[1] Mat. xxiv. 36.

[2] See the Writer's "Can the Parousia of the Lord be separated from His Epiphaneia, or from His Apokalupsis?" S. W. Partridge & Co., 1d.

[3] Dan. vii. 21, 22. See also Rev. xiii. 7.

ject, in *this* connexion, has assumed quite a *sensational*
aspect; and numbers of people, instead of approaching
it with the awe and reverence that is due to it, and
which it ought ever to awaken in the heart of a
Christian, can read about these things, and even converse upon them, as " *coming wonders;* " as they would
read or converse upon the stirring incidents of a novel!
Numbers of little tracts and books likewise, some of
them most offensive in their details, depicting as in a
drama, what *the writers* think would be *likely* to take
place on earth, &c., *after* the rapture of the church,
&c., are eagerly read and circulated, by such persons:
while those religious periodicals, whose editors enter-
tain these erroneous views, and parade them before
their readers in the most sensational manner, have a
circulation in what is called *the religious world*, which
is truly astonishing! Not long ago, I saw an announcement that a Company had been formed to pur-
chase from the Editor one of these periodicals, and
two others of the like character, also owned by him;
whose capital was to be £70,000! And how terrible
will be the effect upon the minds of deluded professors,
who believe in these things; when they are undeceived
by the taking place of the events themselves! Well
would it be for such, if they would even now take heed
to the warning cry of the Holy Ghost in Amos v. 18-
20. " Woe unto you that desire the day of Jehovah!
to what end is it for you? The day of Jehovah is
darkness, and not light. As if a man did flee from a
lion, and a bear met him; or went into the house, and

leaned his hand on the wall, and a serpent bit him. Shall not the day of Jehovah be darkness and not light? even very dark, and no brightness in it?"

Truly such things as these have intensified the evil of these days, by shutting people's eyes to the real nature of the coming crisis: so that they do not see where we are in the prophetic chart; and not clearly "discerning the signs of the times,"[1] are much more liable to be caught in the "snare," which our Lord has told us, "shall come on all them that dwell," $\kappa\alpha\theta\eta\mu\acute{\epsilon}\nu\upsilon\varsigma$, literally, are "seated," *i.e.*, settled, "on the face of the earth." Let us then, who are but "strangers and pilgrims"[2] in the land, take heed to the solemn warning, which He gives us, in connexion with this subject, "Watch *Ye* therefore, and pray always, that ye may be accounted worthy to escape all these things that shall come to pass, and to stand before the Son of Man."[3] "*Ye*, therefore, beloved," says the Apostle, "*seeing ye know these things before, beware lest* YE *also*, being led away with the error of the wicked, fall from your own steadfastness. But grow in grace, and in the knowledge of our Lord and Saviour Jesus Christ. To Him be glory both now and for ever. Amen."[4]

7. And now, am I asked, in conclusion, "What remedy, then, do you propose for the evils, which you

---

[1] Mat. xvi. 3.   [2] 1 Peter ii. 11.   [3] Luke xxi. 35, 36,
[4] 2 Peter iii. 17, 18.

thus deplore?" I answer at once: I have *no remedy*
to propose. *All* remedies, (as salvation itself is,) *are
in the hands of God alone.* If *He* should see fit, in
sovereign grace and mercy, to stir up His people to
plead with Him for "a lengthening of" our "tran-
quillity," He will grant it; and then, there will be a
"breaking-off of our" national "sins by righteousness";[1] and "the evil day" may be deferred for a
time: but if not, come it must to a certainty; and as
it seems to me, (though I am free to admit, I may be
wrong in this conjecture,) *speedily !*

Should the Lord, however, again interpose on our
behalf, as He has before so frequently done, I am quite
sure of this, that His blessed Spirit would bow us
down under a deep sense of our national apostacy from
Him; and that very many of us would have to go
down much deeper into our nature's evil, than we
have ever done yet; and have experimentally to acknowledge, that " we have *no might* against this great
company that cometh against us; neither know we
what to do: but our eyes are *upon Thee.*"[2] And *then,*
I doubt not, the Lord would raise up a far greater
number of faithful preachers to witness for Him, than
we now have: who would give us again the good wine
of the Old Theology; and truly set forth " the glorious
Gospel of the Blessed God:"[3] and His Spirit accompanying the Word spoken, we should have a blessed
revival of religion; and many would no doubt, in *that*
case, be truly converted and blessed.

---

[1] Dan. iv. 27.   [2] 2 Chron. xx. 12.   [3] 1 Tim. i. 11.

And if any of my readers would enquire " What *is* the good wine of the Old Theology; and what is it *truly* to set forth ' the glorious Gospel of the Blessed God' "? As the reply to this two-fold question, is needful to be given, not only in consequence of my having touched upon the *spurious* Gospel, but also as *an antidote to it*—I will endeavour to give it in as brief a form as I am able.

In the first place, the Word of God would have to assume its rightful place in man's estimation, as a direct revelation from God Himself—Divinely inspired; and, therefore, true in every particular, and holy as He is holy—the infallible rule of faith and practice: and therefore the Divine *test* and touchstone of all truth; to which, man must bow down his reason; and to whose authority, therefore, he must submit his conduct. For " the words of Jehovah are pure words: as silver tried in a furnace of earth, purified seven times " [1]—words, which do *not* mean, as certain self-sufficient theologians have falsely asserted, that the words of Jehovah are to be *found* in the Bible; but that they have to be *eliminated* from other words in it, by a so-called " verifying faculty " in man: an assertion which only demonstrates but too clearly the surpassing ignorance, presumption, and deceit of the human heart. But they mean, that *the Scriptures themselves*, which are the words of Jehovah, are words *belonging* to earth, or *taken from* the words of earth;

---

[1] Psa. xii. 6.

but so *purified from* them, as silver that has been tried in the fire, has been purified, by passing through a furnace of earth seven times.[1] For if the *words* of the Bible be *not* inspired, as the Scriptures themselves over and over again assert them to be, then we have *no* revelation from God at all![2]

Now this revelation from God, distinctly sets forth the Unity of the Godhead in a Trinity of Persons, in Father, Son and Holy Ghost, Who are alike interested the Divine Covenant of Grace—the Father, in electing, the Son, in redeeming, and the Holy Ghost, in regenerating and sanctifying, the elect people of God; who were all " chosen " "in Christ," "before the foundation of the world ; that " they " should be holy and without blame before Him in love "[3] and " whose names " were then " written " " in the Lamb's Book of life."[4]

---

[1] See the Writer's tractate, "The Words of Jehovah." S. W. Partridge & Co., 2d.

[2] See proof of the *verbal* inspiration of the Scriptures in the Writer's preface to his book of " Outlines of Prophetic Truth." Dear old John Newton truly says, in one of his Sermons, on Matt. xi. 28 : " When the eyes of the understanding are opened, we begin to see every thing around us *to be just so as the Scriptures have described them. Then,* and *not till then,* we perceive, that what we read in the Bible concerning the horrid evil of sin, the vileness of our fallen nature, the darkness and ignorance of those who know not God, our own emptiness, and the impossibility of finding relief and comfort from creatures, *is exactly true. . . . From hence,* we may assuredly conclude, that *the Book which gives us such just views of everything that passes,* MUST BE GIVEN BY INSPIRATION FROM HIM, *Who is the searcher of hearts. This proof* is equally plain and conclusive *to all capacities that are spiritually enlightened, and* SUCH ONLY ARE ABLE TO UNDERSTAND IT."

[3] Eph. i. 3, 4.   [4] Phil. iv. 3 ; Rev. xiii. 8 ; xx. 15 ; xxi. 27.

In setting forth these truths, therefore, the old Theology sets them forth, *as they are revealed to us in the Divine Word.* It shews us, that the fall of man from God, was not the superficial thing that men imagine; but that it was *an awful fall,* resulting in *spiritual death;* from which man has no more power to awaken himself to " newness of life,"[1] than a dead body has to rise again from the tomb. It shews us— what even so many Theologians, who are *reckoned* orthodox, deny—that *Adam's sin* was *imputed* to his posterity; because they stood or fell in him, as their federal head; and that it was *this imputation* of Adam's sin, that " *constituted* " *them sinners;* and thus corrupted their nature: thereby rendering it " earthly, sensual, and devilish."[2]   God only, therefore, now recognizes two men, Adam and Christ: and all men are either in the one, or in the other. " The *first* man Adam was made a living soul; the *last* Adam was made a quickening spirit." " The *first* man is of the earth, earthy: the *second* man is the Lord from heaven. As is the earthy, *such are they* also that are earthy: and as is the heavenly, *such are they* also that are heavenly."[3] " For as by one man's," *i.e.,* Adam's, " *disobedience* the many," οἱ πολλοὶ, *i.e.,* all those, who stood in him, as their federal head, " *were constituted,*" κατεστάθησαν, " *sinners,* so by the *obedience* of One," *i.e.,* Christ Jesus, " shall the many," οἱ πολλοὶ, *i.e.,* all those, whom He represented in the Covenant of Grace,

---

[1] Rom. vi. 4.   [2] James iii. 15.   [3] 1 Cor. xv. 45, 47, 48.

and who, therefore, stood in Him, " *be constituted,*" καταϲταθήϲονται, " *righteous.*"[1]

In setting forth the work of Christ for His people, the old Theology, therefore, utterly rejects man's crude thoughts on this subject; and still keeping close to the Scriptures of truth, teaches us, that in consequence of the very nature and being of God, and the fact of man's being under wrath and curse, by reason of sin, that there could not by any possibility be reconciliation to God, nor any recovery of covenant peace with God, *without a mediatorial atonement by suffering for sin :* for " where a covenant is, *there must also of necessity be the death* of the appointed,"[2] *i.e.*, sacrifice. For Christ Jesus became the sin-offering and substitute of all His redeemed people : so that when Christ died, they died, representatively, *in Him ;*[3] when Christ was buried, they were buried in Him ;[4] when Christ rose from the dead, they rose from the dead in Him ;[5] and now " sit " representatively likewise, " in the heavenlies " *in Him :*[6] our " life " being " *hid with Christ in God :* " so that " when Christ, who is our life, shall be manifested," φανερωθῇ, " then shall " we " also be manifested *with Him* in glory."[7]

The Old Theology, therefore, teaches what Scripture also teaches, that the Lord Jesus Christ alone accomplished the whole work of atonement and redemption;

---

[1] Rom. v. 19.   [2] Heb. ix. 16.
[3] 2 Cor. v. 14, ἀπέθανον ; Rom. vi. 6-8.   [4] Rom. vi. 4.
[5] Col. ii. 12 ; iii. 1.   [6] Eph. ii. 6.   [7] Col. iii. 3, 4.

and that when He took our nature into His glorious
Godhead, and in the sinless "body," which the Holy
Ghost had "prepared for" Him,[1] "put away sin by the
sacrifice of Himself;"[2] "by" that "one offering,"
"He perfected for ever them that are sanctified,"[3] *i.e.,*
all His believing people: "for both He that sancti-
fieth and they who are sanctified are all of one: *for
which cause* He is not ashamed to call them brethren."[4]
Moreover, as He was circumcised, and thus "made
Himself a debtor to do the whole law,"[5] not of course
for Himself, (as He was ever in Himself infinitely
righteous, and divinely perfect,) but for those whom
He represented in the Divine covenant of grace, He
thus wrought out a righteousness for them, which is
infinitely and divinely perfect. Hence He is said, to
have "magnified the Law, and made it honourable,"[6] by
such an obedience to it, as no mere created intelligence
could by possibility have rendered: and He is, therefore, said to be, "the end of the Law for righteousness
to every one that believeth" in Him.[7] And this obedience, having been performed by no less a person than
the Son of God Himself, must infinitely have over-
valued every other obedience that could possibly have
been rendered to God by all creatures together; even
had they all continued in their original integrity and
uprightness. Hence, the atonement and righteousness
of Christ are *inseparable;* and the offering made by

---

[1] Heb. x. 5.   [2] Heb. ix. 26.   [3] Heb. x. 14.   [4] Heb. ii. 11.
[5] Gal. v. 3.   [6] Isa. xlii. 21.   [7] Rom. x. 4.

Him on behalf of His people, was *of Himself wholly*, both in life and in death ; for He was pre-eminently a living sacrifice, capable, only while His soul dwelt in the body, of either suffering, or acting in the great work of the Redemption of His people : and this was *fully accomplished*, when He said, "It is *finished;*"[1] and yielded up His spirit on the cross. For He is expressly said, to have "given *Himself* for us,"[2] *i.e.*, believers ; to have "*learned obedience* by the things which He *suffered;*"[3] and to have "become *obedient* unto," μέχρι, "*death*, even the death of the cross"[4]—the Greek word used, most clearly implying that *He was obedient both in doing and suffering all the will of God, even from His birth until His death.* Moreover, it is expressly said to believers in Christ—"And *you*, that were some time alienated and enemies in your mind by wicked works, yet now *hath He reconciled* IN THE BODY OF HIS FLESH THROUGH DEATH, *to present you holy and unblameable and unreproveable in His sight.*"[5] For He "was delivered," διὰ, "on account of our offences," which had thus been laid upon Him ;[6] "and was raised again," διὰ, "on account of our justification,"[7] which He had thus accomplished.

The old Theologians likewise truly taught, that this Divinely perfect life and death of Christ, and the spotless righteousness He wrought out thereby, was solely on behalf of His elect people : for whom He

---

[1] John xix. 30.   [2] Titus ii. 14.   [3] Heb. v. 8.   [4] Phil. ii. 8.
[5] Col. i. 21, 22.   [6] Isa. liii. 6.   [7] Rom. iv. 25.

then acted as their Head, Representative, and Substitute ; and that they obtain the benefit of it, when quickened by the Holy Ghost, they plead guilty, as sinners, under the curse of the Law, which they have broken, and trust alone in the finished work of Jesus, for their acceptance before God : when they are " justified freely by " God's " grace through the redemption that is in Christ Jesus " ;[1] and His all-perfect righteousness is " *imputed* " *to them*, or reckoned to them *as theirs*, for their perfect standing *in Him* before God. For thus it is written of His redeemed ones, " For He hath made Him, Who knew no sin, to be *sin for us ;* that we might be made *the righteousness of God* IN HIM."[2] Hence the Scriptures clearly shew, on a comparison of Psa. xxxii. 1, 2, with Rom. iv. 5-8, as well as in other places, that as the Law demands a perfect obedience to its requirements, as well as contains the most absolute prohibition against disobedience ; it follows that *the sinner's* justification before God, comprehends, *not only his acquittal from having broken the Law, but his acceptance also as having fulfilled it, i.e.*, in his Substitute, Surety, and Representative, Christ Jesus the Lord.[3]

These old Theologians, therefore, never made the mistake of offering the Gospel to dead sinners, *as such ;* or of dishonouring the Holy Ghost, by telling their hearers that they had the power to repent and

---

[1] Rom. iii. 24.   [2] 2 Cor. v. 21.

[3] See the Writer's tractate on " Justification." S. W. Partridge & Co., 2d.

believe the Gospel, whenever they pleased. No. They
exalted the majesty and glory of the ever-blessed God ;
they thundered out the threatenings of the law against
impenitent sinners ; they laid them low, by setting
forth, from the Divine Word, their awful ruin by the
fall—the natural " blindness of their understanding,"[1]
the hellish perversion of their will,[2] the " enmity "
of their " carnal minds " against God,[3] and the fearful
" deceitfulness of" their " hearts " ;[4] and that they
were moreover, as " transgressors of the law," under
the curse and wrath of God ; and had no natural
ability, or desire to turn unto God ; or, to believe in
the Saviour whom He had provided for the lost,
without His special grace preventing them.[5] And was
not this the very method pursued by our Blessed Lord
Himself, as well as by His Apostles after Him ? Nay,
is it not the very method that ought, and *must* ever
be pursued, if we would expect our testimony to receive a blessing from on high? For God will bless
such teaching as this : not only because it gives Him
glory ; but also because it is in strict accordance with
the teaching of His own most blessed Word.

And so, when men were thereby convicted of sin by
God the Holy Ghost,[6] and their hard " hearts " had
been " broken in pieces " by " the hammer " of His
" Word,"[7] these old Theologians *then* set " the Gospel

---

[1] Eph. iv. 18 ; Acts xxvi. 18.   [2] Isa. liii. 6 ; Job xxi. 14, 15 ; xi. 12.
[3] Rom. viii. 7 ; John iii. 19.   [4] Jer. xvii. 9.
[5] James ii. 9-11 ; Gal. iii. 10 ; John iii. 18, 36 ; vi. 44.
[6] John xvi. 8, 9.   [7] Jer. xxiii. 29.

of the grace of God " before them ; and told them that
" the Son of Man came to seek and to save that which
was *lost* " :[1] for " this is a faithful saying, and worthy
of all acceptation, that Christ Jesus came into the
world to save *sinners*."[2] For then they knew that
this would *truly* be " Gospel," or *good news* to such as
these : for Christ "came not to call the righteous, but
sinners to repentance."[3] Are there then any righteous
persons out of Christ ? No indeed: " there is none
righteous, no, not one ":[4] but, alas ! there are
many out of Him, who vainly imagine themselves
to be so. Well, with these, Christ will have nothing
to do. And what folly is it to suppose, that any but
the broken-hearted, and the self-renouncing, sinner,
to whom the Gospel truly has been sent, will welcome
it, and believe in it, to the saving of his soul !

Indeed when our Blessed Lord Himself first preached
the Gospel, in the Synagogue at Nazareth ; and set
forth the sovereign and electing love of God, Who
" hideth these things from the wise and prudent, and
revealeth them unto babes " ;[5] His hearers in that day,
(as such hearers are, on the setting forth of such doctrines in the present day,) were scandalised at His
utterances, and " were *filled* with wrath, and rose up
and thrust Him out of the city, and led Him unto the
brow of the hill, whereon their city was built, that they
might cast Him down headlong."[6] And what *was* the

---

[1] Luke xix. 10.　　[2] 1 Tim. i. 15.　　[3] Mat. ix. 13.　　[4] Rom. iii. 10.
[5] Mat. xi. 25.　　[6] Luke iv. 28, 29.

Gospel which He preached unto them? "The Spirit of the Lord is upon Me, because He hath anointed Me to preach the Gospel to *the poor ;* He hath sent Me to heal *the broken-hearted*, to preach deliverance to *the captives*, and recovering of sight to *the blind*, to set at liberty them that are *bruised*, to preach the acceptable year of the Lord."[1] Ah! yes: these are they, who will welcome, and believe in " the Gospel of the *grace of God* ": for as broken-hearted sinners they will fully have realized their misery, and have deeply felt their need of the remedy provided for them, in the adorable Person and all-perfect Work of their Sin-offering and Substitute, Christ Jesus Himself. " The *sacrifices of* God are *a broken spirit :* a *broken* and a *contrite* heart, O God, Thou wilt not despise."[2] Why? Because it is *His Spirit's doing.* Yes:

> " The Holy Ghost must give the wound ;
> And make the wounded whole."

For none but He can truly " convince " the soul " of sin, and of righteousness, and of judgment ":[3] and when *He* does this, it is an effectual, and a saving work, and *never unless.*

And as such old Theologians might almost be considered fierce, when they denounced God's judgments against impenitent sinners : so, on the other hand, were they loving, and tender, and gracious, when they dealt with such broken-hearted, convicted ones, as these. And herein again, they did but follow the

---

[1] Luke iv. 18, 19.   [2] Psa. li. 17.   [3] John xvi. 7-14.

example of Christ, as well as that of His Apostles also. And in thus dealing with these anxious souls, they did not, (as so many do in these days,) urge them to try to manufacture a faith out of their own hearts, wherewith to lay hold on Christ; but knowing that "faith cometh by hearing, and hearing by the Word of God," [1] and that the Lord Himself had bidden them to "take up the stumbling block out of the way of" His "people;" [2] they endeavoured to do this, by trying to take the eyes of such troubled ones off from themselves, and to direct them to "*look off* unto," ἀφορῶντες, "Jesus, the Author and Finisher of our faith." [3]   For when souls are thus "quickened" by the Holy Ghost, and the light of Divine truth shines into their hearts, they sometimes have a fearful revelation of their nature's evil; and then realising for the first time that they are *truly* "*lost*," they imagine that it is all over with them, and "write bitter things against themselves"—foolishly imagining in their heart of hearts, (though they do not know it at the time,) that the salvation of the Lord is for *righteous* persons, and not, as it really is, and ever must be, *for sinners only !*

Hence such Theologians, in dealing with these anxious souls, then set before them "*the Gospel of* THE GRACE *of God*"; and directed them to the many *gracious promises* in the Divine Word, held forth to such troubled ones as these—"Look unto Me, and be ye saved, all the ends of the earth: for I am God, and

---

[1] Rom. x. 17.   [2] Isa. lvii. 14.   [3] Heb. xii. 2.

22

there is none else "[1]—"Behold the Lamb of God, which taketh away the sin of the world"[2]—"As Moses lifted up the serpent in the wilderness, even so must the Son of Man be lifted up: that whosoever believeth in Him should not perish, but have eternal life"[3]—"He was wounded for our transgressions, He was bruised for our iniquities: the chastisement of our peace was upon Him; and with His stripes we are healed"[4]—"Who His own self bore our sins in His own body on the tree, that we being dead to sins, should live unto righteousness: by whose stripes ye were healed"[5]—"Be it known unto you therefore, men and brethren, that through this man is preached unto you the forgiveness of sins: and by Him all that believe are justified from all things, from which ye could not be justified by the law of Moses"[6]—"Come unto Me, all ye that labour and are heavy laden, and I will give you rest"[7]—"Wherefore He is able also to save them to the uttermost that come unto God by Him, seeing He ever liveth to make intercession for them."[8]

And in thus instructing them out of the Divine Word, when they saw the buddings of a divinely-wrought faith in their hearts, they would tenderly encourage them, by opening out the promises, and applying them in a practical manner to their case. For instance, if they perceived, that any soul, en-

---

[1] Isa. xlv. 22.   [2] John i. 29.   [3] John iii. 14, 15.   [4] Isa. liii. 5.
[5] 1 Peter ii. 24.   [6] Acts xiii.   [7] Mat. xi. 28.   [8] Heb. vii. 25.

lightened by the Divine Spirit, had really ventured upon Christ, although in much weakness, and might nevertheless be still staggering through unbelief; in opening out such a promise as Isa. xlv. 22, they would do it somewhat after this manner :—You see these words contain, first a Divine command, " Look unto Me ; " and this command extends itself to "all the ends of the earth," to sinners at the greatest distance ; in obedience to which the quickened soul ought, as the man with " the withered hand " did, when Christ commanded him to " stretch forth his hand " :[1]—for *God's biddings* to such are *enablings*—in the strength of the Holy Ghost, to " venture," or attempt a *direct act of faith*, or, an immediate look to Christ, as the only Saviour of the chief of sinners. And then it would find, that upon this direct act, it might straightway attempt a *reflex act*, or a taking of Christ at His word as to its salvation *in so looking*. For you see, that as the first clause of the words, " Look unto Me " contain a Divine command of *faith*, so the next " Be ye saved," a glorious grant of *salvation* to every true believer in Jesus. For it is as much your duty, as a quickened soul, to *believe* the grace and faithfulness of Christ in the one, as to *obey* Him in the other ; and if the blessed Spirit enable you so to do, you will no more question your *salvation*, than the *faithfulness* of Him that promised it. See in this light also that word in Isa. xlix. 6, " That thou mayest be My salvation unto

---

[1] Mat. xii. 13.

the end of the earth : " from whence you may see, that
as Christ was lifted up as the *Father's Salvation* for
poor lost sinners, even to the end of the earth, it will
be as impossible for *you to perish*, LOOKING TO HIM AS
SUCH, as for *God Himself* to be unfaithful. And *thus
believing*, you will surely enter into rest. Nay, by the
light that will thus spring into your soul, *through fresh
acts of faith*, you will see far more clearly to read your
past experiences with comfort to yourself.

So, likewise, when these Theologians would " build
up believers on their most holy faith,"[1] they did not
direct them to look into the dungeon of their own
hearts for light ; but up to " the Sun of Righteousness "[2] Himself. And so keeping to the directions of
the Divine Word, they taught them, " As ye have
therefore *received* Christ Jesus the Lord, so *walk* ye in
Him ; rooted and built up in Him, and stablished in
the faith, as ye have been taught," *i.e.*, by the Holy
Ghost, when He first enabled you to " lay hold upon
the hope set before " you in the Gospel ;[3] " abounding
therein with thanksgiving."[4] And how *did* you receive
Christ Jesus as your Lord ? Was it not as a poor
needy sinner, with the empty hand of a living faith,
receiving out " of His fulness " that which you *then*
needed ?[5] So then, *walk* ye in Him : for " in the
Lord " have you " righteousness *and strength*."[6] For
you are to be " strong in the *grace* that is *in Christ*

---

[1] Jude 20.   [2] Mal. iv. 2.   [3] Heb. vi. 18.   [4] Col. ii. 6, 7.
[5] John i. 16 ; Col. i. 19.   [6] Isa. xlv. 24.

Jesus "[1]—" strong *in the Lord*, and in the power of *His* might : "[2] for now you are to " walk *by faith*," and " not by sight."[3]

And accordingly such Theologians would instruct such souls, that when Satan would assault them, and strive to obstruct their progress in the Divine life, by attacking their faith, and stirring up their natural unbelief; if the Lord saw that, to meet these assaults they would fall back upon past experiences, and try to gain comfort from thence, He might, to cause them to die to a life of sense and to lead them up to a higher life of faith on the Son of God, be pleased to draw a veil over His work in their souls. Whereupon, instead of " fainting "[4] under the Lord's dealings with them, they were to *cast themselves anew upon His faithful promises*, and to *stay themselves upon their God*, even while they walked in the dark ;[5] and in the end they would find that the blessed Spirit would reveal Christ Himself more and more to them, as the *only source* of their comfort, and the *true foundation* of their *faith*, and *peace*, and *joy*. And so if, when assaulted by Satan and unbelief, they would *fly immediately to Christ*, they would get the victory far sooner than by disputing with Satan upon past experiences ; and that which was " lacking " in their " faith," would thus be " perfected ;"[6] and they would the sooner become " strong in faith, giving glory to God."[7]

---

[1] 2 Tim. ii. 1.   [2] Eph. vi. 10.   [3] 2 Cor. v. 7.   [4] Heb. xii. 5.   [5] Isa. l. 10.   [6] 1 Thes. iii. 10.   [7] Rom. iv. 20.

But I must not pursue this subject farther; only I would observe, lastly, that as these sound old Theologians thoroughly understood the nature and object of "the Everlasting Covenant,"[1] which is well "ordered in all *things* and sure,"[2] "to all the seed," who are interested in it;[3] they set it forth with great power and clearness—shewing from the Scriptures that, as Christ was the substance of it,[4] the Messenger of it,[5] and the Mediator of it;[6] and that it was confirmed in Christ,[7] fulfilled in Christ,[8] and ratified by the blood of Christ;[9] that it was a Covenant of peace,[10] *unalterable*,[11] and *everlasting*,[12] "to the praise of the glory of His grace, wherein He hath engraced," ἐχαρίτωσεν, "us in the Beloved."[13] Consequently all who are interested in it, as the Scriptures assert, have the same standing before God as their Head and Surety has; and being "saved in the Lord with an everlasting salvation";[14] they will finally be "presented faultless" by Him "before the presence of" God's "glory with exceeding joy."[15] Salvation from first to last, therefore, *is of the Lord;* and the regeneration, sanctification and final preservation of elect and redeemed sinners *is wholly the work of the Holy Ghost,* Who alone begins, continues, and will carry it on in each elect and redeemed "vessel of

---

[1] Heb. xiii. 20.　[2] 2 Sam. xxiii. 5.　[3] Rom. iv. 16; Heb. vi. 17-20.
[4] Isa. xlii. 6; xlix. 8.　[5] Mal. iii. 1.　[6] Heb. viii. 6; ix. 15; xii. 24.　[7] Gal. iii. 17.　[8] Luke i. 68-79.　[9] Heb. ix. 11-14, 16-23.
[10] Isa. liv. 9, 10; Ezek. xxxiv. 25; xxxvii. 26.
[11] Psa. lxxxix. 34; Isa. liv. 10; lix. 21; Gal. iii. 17.
[12] Psa. cxi. 9; Isa. lv. 3; lxi. 8; Ezek. xvi. 60-63; Heb. viii. 10.
[13] Eph. i. 6.　[14] Isa. xlv. 17.　[15] Jude 24.

mercy,"[1] until " this corruptible " shall " put on incorruption, and this mortal " shall " put on immortality,"[2] at " the resurrection of the just : "[3] when our blessed Covenant Head in glory will say to His Father, " Behold I and the children " whom " Thou hast given Me "[4]—they are all here, my Father, not one of them is wanting, not one of them is lost.[5] For " *all* that the Father giveth Me," said Jesus, " shall come to Me ; and him that cometh unto Me I will in no wise cast out. For I came down from heaven, not to do Mine own will, but the will of Him that sent Me. And *this* is the Father's will which hath sent Me, that of *all* which He hath given Me I should lose *nothing*, but should *raise it up again at the last day.* And this is the will of Him that sent Me, that everyone which seeth the Son, and *believeth* on Him, may have *everlasting life :* and I will *raise him up at the last day.*"[6]

Moreover, as these Theologians held and taught, according to the Scriptures, the infinite security of all elect believers in Christ, and their *eternal* blessedness in the world to come : so they likewise held and taught the equally Scriptural doctrine, that the finally impenitent have no interest in the Divine Covenant of grace ; " being aliens from the commonwealth of Israel, and strangers from the covenants of promise, having no hope and without God in the world ; "[7] and that

---

[1] Rom. ix. 23. [2] 1 Cor. xv. 53. [3] Luke xiv. 14.
[4] Heb. ii. 13. [5] John xvii. 12. [6] John vi. 37-40.
[7] Eph. ii. 12.

their doom will not only be final and irreversible at death; but that their punishment also will be *everlasting*.[1]

This then is the briefest possible Outline of some of the main doctrines of the Old Theology: and sure I am that if we are ever to have a thorough revival of true religion amongst us again, upon an extended scale, it could only be by the setting forth, in the power of the Holy Ghost, of such faithful Scriptural testimony as this: for none but such preaching can give glory to God, or be blessed of the Holy Ghost, either in the conversion of sinners, or to the edification, or comfort of the children of the living God themselves. And if the Lord raise *not* up more preachers such as these, amongst us; or, if such preachers die out, or be persecuted, and their faithful testimony to the truth of God be *silenced* in the land; I cannot but think that the judgments of God will then be nigh unto us, yea, even at our very doors!

Am I asked again, "Are you so presumptuous then, as to hope that *you*, and such teachers as you, will be able to *stem* the torrent, which you say is rolling in upon us; or to *hinder* the fulfilment of the Prophetic Word, which you have expounded to us?" Most assuredly not; but when I read in the Divine Word, that "when the enemy shall come in like a flood, the Spirit of Jehovah will lift up a standard against him";[2] that even in the days of Antichrist, the Lord has promised

---

[1] Mat. xiii. 49, 50; xxv. 46; 2 Peter ii. 17; Jude 12, 13; 2 Thes. i. 7-9.
[2] Isa. lix. 19.

to " give power to " His " two witnesses " (whoever they may be,) and that " they shall prophesy " during the whole period of the " great tribulation," and thus "torment them that dwell" on the platform of the Roman " earth " ;[1] and that many Scriptures show us that, notwithstanding the " perilous times " of " the last days," there will still be a number of faithful witnesses to the truth : and when I read also in His Word, that He has *commanded* His believing people, who are able to do so, to " *contend earnestly for the faith*, which was *once* delivered to the saints,"[2] but which is now fast dying out of Christendom; and to " *put the brethren in remembrance of these things;* "[3] and has also assured us that He " hath chosen the *foolish* things of the world to confound the wise," and " the *weak* things of the world to confound the things that are mighty," and " *base* things of the world, and things which are *despised*," and " things which *are not*, to bring to nought things that are: that no flesh should glory in His presence " ;[4] I am encouraged to hope that He will accept this attempt to expose the deceit of the adversary; and, by the setting forth of His truth therein, will deliver some precious souls thereby also out of his hands.

And for the encouragement and comfort of the weak and timid believer, I would only add, that he cannot be more secure, than *in the Lord's hands :* for the Lord has pledged Himself to bring him safe unto glory ;

---

[1] Rev. xi. 3, 10.   [2] Jude 3.   [3] 1 Tim. iv. 6.   [4] 1 Cor. i. 26-29.

having moreover, told us that " there hath no temptation taken you but such as is common to man : but
God is faithful, who will not suffer you to be tempted
above that ye are able; but will with the temptation
also make *a way to escape,* that ye may be able to bear
it."[1]   Ah ! but what about the "babes in Christ"?[2]
You may rest assured of this, that *God's babes* are
quite safe *in God's keeping.* And is it not written,
" Whosoever shall confess that Jesus is the Son of
God, *God dwelleth in him,* and he in God?"[3]   And
who can touch that soul, *that is enclosed in God Himself?* "Ye are of God, *little children, and have overcome them; because greater* is *He* that is *in you* than
he that is in the world."[4]   And is not *this* enough to
comfort you? "For *all* the promises of God *in*" *Christ
Jesus* " are *Yea,* and in Him *Amen,* unto the glory of
God by us."[5] "For *of* Him," as their source and
fountain, " and *through* Him," as their sustainer and
preserver, " and *to* Him," as their end and issue," are
all things : to whom be glory for ever. Amen."[6]

APPENDIX.

At page 36, I have given an account of some Bengal jugglers, who, amongst other things, "in a moment *covered a pond with ice sufficiently strong to bear an elephant.*"

In connection with this case, I might note what took place at a "Séance with the Spiritual Society of Florence," communicated by a Mr. Guppy, to "The Committee of the London Dialectical Society," in which he says :—"The room, at my request, had been made very warm, as at the previous *séance* we were shivering. Some of the most eminent Florentine literati were present. . . . The light was put out again, and in ten minutes, *an awful crash was heard on the table*, as if the chandelier had fallen down. On lighting the candle, we found *a large lump of beautiful ice*, about a foot long and one and a half inches thick, which had fallen on the table with such force that it was broken. *It began to melt immediately*, and was put into a dish. This was more than an hour after the beginning of the *séance*, in which time the ice would have melted had it been in the room."

As the closing sheets of this work were passing through the press, the following ominous paragraph appeared in the *Graphic* of the 11th of May instant, which I here also subjoin :

" SPIRIT-RAPPING *in China* is being devoted to a highly useful purpose—raising funds for the famine-stricken ! At Moukden, in the North, *a Fairy named Hu* is supposed to dwell, who confers many favours on his neighbours *in response to their prayers and offerings! A planchette table* FOR HIS UTTERANCES is erected close to the telegraph office, *and he often condescends to signify his wishes and advice!* Lately, *by the aid of the mediums* who interpret his remarks, *the Fairy issued a lengthy exhortation to charity* [!], and the local relief committee printed his exhortation and distributed copies broadcast ! Accordingly funds flowed in rapidly, so that a relief soup-kitchen has been established and clothing bought for the destitute. *Hu requests that each donor should write the amount of his gift on a slip of paper* TO BE BURNT IN THE INCENSE BRAZIER AT THE FAIRY'S SHRINE [1] [! !], while sending the gift to the telegraph-office. Then, on the fifteenth of every month, *he will audit the accounts and present the balance-sheets to the higher spirits,* WHO WILL LAY IT BEFORE THE EMPEROR OF HEAVEN ! ! Donors *should also ask some petition on the paper to be burnt,* WHICH WILL CERTAINLY BE GRANTED ! ! *The Fairy finally recommends* THAT A GUILD *should be formed* IN HIS HONOUR to contribute money to the relief fund—the guild to be called *the 'Incense Tithe' ! !* A most practical and business-like Fairy, this Hu ! "

We have now, therefore, seen, that the demons in these days, not only blasphemously travesty the Or-

---

[1] See pages 139, 145.

dinances of the Lord, and impudently personify even the Lord Himself; but that they at the same time also (1) inculcate the false worship of the ancient *Egyptian* goddess, Isis;[1] (2) the false worship of the ancient, as well as modern, *Hindoo* god and goddess, Vishnu and Kali;[2] the false worship of the ancient, as well as modern, *Chinese* and *Tibetan*, god, Buddh; combined with the *mediæval* cult of the Fairies;[3] (3) while they also inculcate the equally false worship and doctrines of the so-called *Church of Rome ! !*[4]

We have also seen *the identity* of the origin both of Buddhism and Romanism;[5] and the following additional extract from M. Louis Jacolliot's "Experiences," (from which I have before largely quoted[6]), will likewise prove that *the several demons*, who are inculcating *these various false forms of worship, are all in close league with one another;* and that for the purpose of bringing in, what Theosophists are also seeking to effect—"*a* UNIVERSAL SPIRITUAL RELIGION *in which* BOTH EAST AND WEST CAN JOIN, *both* ANCIENT AND MODERN *truth* CAN BLEND!"[7]—that *out of this* they may bring forth the last great apostacy from the truth—the worship of Antichrist as well as of the devil himself!

This writer, after having given an account of the levitations of the *Sadhu*, as recorded by me at pages 125, 126 of this work, adds:—"I now allowed him to depart. Before leaving, he informed me that *he would*

---

[1] See pages 119, 120.   [2] See pages 132-134.

[3] See extract from " Graphic " above.   [4] See pages 137-151, 161.

[5] See pages 59, 60.   [6] See pages 125-135.   [7] See page 154.

invoke the familiar spirits WHO PROTECT MY NATION *(the French)* exactly at the hour of midnight, when the sacred elephants will strike twelve on the brass gongs of the temple of *Shiva* and that *these spirits will manifest their presence to me* in my own bedroom!

"The Indians manifest secret understanding with each other admirably. To guard myself against all trickery, I sent away my two servants to pass the night on board my budgrow. I kept with me, however, my Nubian servant, who had the highest contempt for these evocations and other juggleries of the *fakirs*. His greatest wonder was, and he did not hesitate to tell me so, to see a European uselessly spend his time with such nonsense. He had his own superstitions, it is true, only he felt himself so much above these Indian people that he was ashamed to credit them with any sense or intelligence, or to adopt any of their ideas. I was, therefore, certain that he would not lend himself to the abetment of any trickery whatever.

"*I have, myself, no propensity to believe in the supernatural!* In spite of this, however, I wished, should the phenomena promised come to pass, to be certain that I had not been the dupe of a coarsely-executed trick. I therefore owed it to myself to put every difficulty which lay in my power in the way of the *Sadhu*.

"It was on the seventh story of the palace that the Peishwa had honoured me with an apartment. The furniture in the room was partly eastern and partly European. I could from my rooms enjoy fresh air and the most splendid scenery.

"When it became dark, I minutely visited and searched all the rooms, and assured myself that nobody was hidden in them. I took up the moveable bridge by which my apartments communicated with the other portion of the palace, and rendered access to my rooms absolutely impossible. *At the appointed hour, I heard ten distinct knocks against the walls of my room!* I approached the spot from where the sound appeared to issue, when my steps were suddenly arrested by a knock which proceeded from the glass globe which protected the hanging lamp from the night insects! Some other sounds I heard at irregular intervals from the beams overhead. Then all became still.

"I directed my steps towards the extremity of the terrace. It was one of those clear star-lit nights unknown in our misty northern climes. The sacred river rolled on silently and majestically by Benares, then wrapt in slumber. On the steps of the *ghauts* I plainly saw the dark outlines of a human figure. It was the *Sadhu* of Trevandrum, *praying for the repose of the dead!* This last incident surpassed all that I had seen up to this time, and not finding any possible explanation I was thinking whether I had not been under a hallucination. I spent a part of the night puzzling myself for a solution of this enigma.

"The following day I waited with impatience the arrival of the *Sadhu*.

"It was dark when the *Sadhu* entered, as usual without making the slightest noise, and came out on to the terrace where I was waiting for him.

" ' Well,' said I, as he came forward, ' I heard the knocks you had announced. I must admit that the *Sadhu* is very clever.'

" ' The *Sadhu* is nobody,' replied he, with the utmost coolness. ' He recites the *Mantras, and the spirits lend a favourable ear to them!* THEY WERE THE SPIRITS OF YOUR ANCESTORS (FRANGHYS) *who came to you last night* ' ! !

" ' *Have you also power over* SPIRITS OF OTHER NATIONALITIES ? '

" ' Who can command the spirits ? '

" ' I have not made myself understood. I only meant to enquire how it could be possible *for the spirits of* MY ANCESTORS *to listen favourably to the prayers of* A HINDU? They are not of the same caste.'

" ' There is no caste in the higher spheres ' !

" ' Then they were *my ancestors* who paid me a visit last night ? '

" ' *Yes.'*

" ' Why did they not speak to me ? '

" ' *Did you* QUESTION THEM ? '

" ' No.'

" ' Then you cannot complain. *The spirits only make themselves heard* BY THOSE WHO REQUEST THEM TO THAT EFFECT ' ! !

" ' Can you make them appear ? '

" ' I have already told you, Sahib, the spirits are not under my control.'

" ' Still you can produce apparitions.'

" ' No, the *Sadhu* can produce nothing.'

" ' True, I forget, *you pray to the spirits to manifest themselves* ' ! '

" ' I only recite the *Mantras* WHICH HAVE THE POWER OF MATERIALIZING THEM' ! !

" ' But if, after all, it is optional with the spirits to come or not, *why all these magical conjurations and evocations?* A strong desire to see them should suffice.'

" ' The *Sadhu* recites *Mantras* and the spirits appear if they like.'

" There was no means of bringing him out of this circle. Every time that I spoke to him on this subject, I carefully noted his countenance, in order, if possible, to detect in his glance a covert smile, a something indicative of incredulity. No, he was impenetrable, and appeared to be deliberately convinced of the truth of his assertion " !

Surely, then, such an accumulation of evidence, as these pages afford, of the identity of modern " Spiritualism," *so-called*, with the Demonology and Witchcraft of ancient and modern times, will be sufficient to convince any unprejudiced person of the fact; as well as to warn him that the close of this Dispensation must, therefore, of necessity be now near at hand !

Once more, then, I would repeat the warning words of Scripture, with the added soul-inspiriting promises of our Blessed Lord and Saviour, Jesus Christ, in connection therewith :—

23

" *Ye* therefore beloved" brethren in the Lord, " seeing *ye* know these things before, beware lest *ye* also, being led away with the error of the wicked, fall from your own steadfastness. But grow in grace, and in the knowledge of our Lord and Saviour Jesus Christ. To Him be glory both now and ever. Amen."[1] " Watch *ye* therefore, and pray always, that ye may be accounted worthy to escape all these things that shall come to pass, and to stand before the Son of Man."[2] For Jesus hath said, " Behold, I come *as a thief.* Blessed is he that watcheth, and keepeth his garments, lest he walk naked, and they see his shame."[3] "Behold, *I come quickly :* blessed is he that keepeth the sayings of the prophecy of this book."[4] "He that is unjust, let him be unjust still: and he which is filthy, let him be filthy still: and he that is righteous, let him be righteous still: and he that is holy, let him be holy still. And behold, *I come quickly ;* and My reward is with Me, to give every man according as his work shall be."[5] " He which testifieth these things saith, *Surely I come quickly ;* Amen. *Even so come,* Lord Jesus. The grace of our Lord Jesus Christ be with you all. Amen."[6]

Scarborough, May 23*rd,* 1889.

---

[1] 2 Peter iii. 17, 18.   [2] Luke xxi. 36.   [3] Rev. xvi. 15.
[4] Rev. xxii. 7.   [5] Rev. xxii. 11, 12.   [6] Rev. xxii. 20, 21.

CONTENTS.

CHAPTER III.

From the Flood to the Call of Abraham.

CHAPTER IV.

Touching the Connexion Between the People of Jehovah and the Land of Jehovah.

CHAPTER V.

Jehovah's Dealings with His People Israel.

PAGE

CHAPTER VI.

ISRAEL ENTRUSTED BY JEHOVAH WITH GOVERNMENTAL POWER : THE DISTINCTIVENESS OF HIS DEALINGS WITH THEM.

CHAPTER VII.

THE CONFERRING OF GOVERNMENTAL POWER BY GOD UPON THE GENTILES.

CHAPTER VIII.

THE VISIONS RECORDED IN THE BOOK OF THE PROPHET DANIEL.

CHAPTER IX.

THE CHURCH'S ONE FOUNDATION.

CHAPTER X.

THE INFINITE PERFECTIONS OF EMMANUEL.

OPINIONS OF THE PRESS.

"Under the modest title of ' Outlines of Prophetic Truth,' we
have a considerable volume from the pen of Robert Brown, who is
the author of several other works as well. . . . . We can most
warmly recommend it to the careful perusal of all. The familiarity
with Scripture it displays is marvellous, its evangelical doctrines
are sound, and the tone of feeling is highly spiritual."—*Evangelical Christendom.*

" Outlines of Prophetic Truth, by Robert Brown (*Partridge and Co.*), 12s., is a valuable contribution to literature and prophecy. The whole course of prophetic teaching, 'from Creation to Redemption,' is not only opened out very fully from a doctrinal point of view, but is pressed home to the heart in a practical and experimental way. Mr. Brown is a student of Scripture, whose exposition may well claim attention ; and many will find his volume a *handbook to the study of prophecy*, which will give them a clear and comprehensive view of much that is difficult and obscure. As such, it will prove itself worth many times its cost. The price is large, but so is the book ; and containing nearly eight hundred large pages, it is marvellously cheap."—*Christian Progress.*

" The work of an experienced writer, who thoroughly believes in the verbal inspiration of the Bible, and in Divine guidance in the work before us. The book, in some parts, reads like the standard work of one of the Puritan divines, all the paraphrases and criticisms being obviously connected with the Word of God. There are no startling novelties and perplexing theories, such as we too often meet with, but on the whole, the volume may be said to be accurate in fact, Scriptural in doctrine, and persuasive to practical holiness."—*Clergyman's Magazine.*

" This is a large and comprehensive work, combining the characteristics of what was formerly called, ' a body of divinity,' with those of a commentary. It embraces a vast variety of subjects ; for it may be said to traverse the whole field of Divine revelation, and on every page gives evidence of patient, reverent, and earnest search after the mind of God. The work is manifestly the production of an able and a devout student of Scripture."—*Lobb's Theological Quarterly.*

" Mr. Brown is a ripe Biblical scholar, his acquaintance with, and insight into the Word of God, strike us in every page. He is a firm believer in the plenary inspiration of Scripture, and in the Doctrine of God's sovereignty. No taint of German neology, nor the faintest suggestion of agnosticism is to be found in his pages. The complete fulfilment of prophecy—prophecy not usually recognised as such—prophecy, for example, contained in the names of the Old Testament saints, is traced with skill, and described with power ; and many hitherto unobserved types are also brought to light, and dealt with in a manner which, as a general rule, will commend itself to the reader's judgment. . . . . We must add that much profitable and experimental teaching is interwoven with the main threads of the argument. . . . . As throwing great light on the period professedly dealt with, namely, from Creation to Redemption, we can heartily commend it as being full of instruction and original thought. There is an especially interesting chapter to prove, from the genealogies as given in St. Matthew and St. Luke, that our blessed Lord was the legal representative of David, both as the adopted son of Joseph (adoption in Jewish law giving full legal rights), and also as the actual Son of Mary, and thus that He was really 'born King of the Jews.' . . . . As a general rule, Mr. Brown's scholarship is on a par with his other high qualifications as an interpreter of Scripture."—*The Record.*

" Nearly 800 pages of matter are here devoted, by a well-known champion of the Gospel of the grace of God, to a subject of necessarily profound interest to the Lord's redeemed people. The author of this remarkable treatise distinguishes his method of exposition by constant reference to the infallible Scriptures. Satan's ceaseless conflict with the Divine purposes is traced with a master-hand, and Mr. Brown conducts his readers, step by step, from the hour of the fall to the end of all things, pointing out the *principles* underlying Jehovah's governmental dispensations in our fallen world in their various stages, and claiming, as the glorious issue, a *victory* worthy the wisdom and omnipotence which are inseparable from the Deity of Father, Son, and Holy Ghost. One feature of especial importance to the spiritual mind is the honour done by the writer to the Living Person and to the covenant relations of the Lord Jesus Christ. Mr. Brown is no follower of Pelagius, Arminius, Laud, or of their successors—the modern Pusey-Papists of our corrupted National Church. The *Outlines* are at once critical, prophetic, and expository."—*The British Protestant.*

" This work is the outcome of a whole life's study of the subject by one who is a scholar, a student, and a teacher. The volume covers the whole ground. . . . . Each period is marked off and dealt with efficiently before another is approached, and yet the connecting links which bind all together are clearly expressed ; and then at the close we have a graphic, thoughtful, lucid, and telling survey of the whole. The table of contents contains an analysis of each chapter, which must prove of great service to the student, for it not only shows the details of the work, but reveals also its scope and purport. . . . . The work occupies quite a unique position. It differs in its scope from all the other able books on this recondite subject, but for the general student and popular reader it is, without doubt, the most useful and suggestive of them all. The volume has a substantial and pleasing appearance."—*The Oldham Chronicle.*

" From several previous valuable and important works, Mr. Brown is known as an author sound in the truth, and able both to expound and defend it. . . . In the present work the reader will find a fund of scriptural knowledge. Mr. Brown carefully compares Scripture with Scripture, seeks to give the force of the original Hebrew and Greek, and an interpretation in accordance with the context. In his book not only are the prophecies themselves, but also the prophetic aspects of the types, handled with much ability. The privileges of the believer, his standing in Christ, his call to separation from the world and entire consecration to God, and the increased importance, in these darkening, closing days of the dispensation, of being girded and ready for the Advent of the Lord, are presented with force and clearness. The spirit of the book is everywhere devout ; 'in it the instructed Christian will find little with which he cannot agree, but much to promote his edification."—*The Christian.*

"Mr. Brown's works have been before the Lord's people for some years, bearing on many departments of spiritual truth ; but this large work seems to sum up and embrace the researches of a life spent amid the revelations of God's word. Mr. Brown is one of the few who believe that God means what He says, and that He has a meaning for everything that He says ; and, consequently, he is one of the few whom God honours by unfolding to him the precious treasures of His Word, which, as a wise scribe, Mr. Brown here makes known to all who desire to learn more of God's purposes as revealed in His Word. It is not a book to be read and then laid aside, for, in the first place, it requires more than mere reading. The Scriptures have to be searched—notes have to be made—the heart has to pause and digest the blessed truths as they are set forth, and send up its tribute of wonder and praise to the God of all grace and the Spirit of all wisdom. Instead of being called *Outlines* it ought to be called a *Treasury* of Prophetic Truth. All Teachers and Ministers should possess it, and there are few, if any, who would not be able to learn much from such a student and such a teacher. Mr. Brown seems to have brought together and embodied the researches of his life; and in all kinds of unexpected places the reader will find some beautiful expositions of a certain passage, or some valuable notes opening out a particular line of teaching, or some wonderful suggestions as to the elucidation of difficult passages."—*The Life of Faith.*

In demy 8vo.   Price 10s. 6d., with Coloured Frontispiece.

THE HIDDEN MYSTERY; OR, THE REVELATIONS OF THE WORD.

(Rom. xvi. 25, 26 ; 1 Cor. ii. 7 ; Eph. iii. 2—11 ; Col. i. 25—27 ; ii. 2, 3.)

BEING THOUGHTS, SUGGESTIVE AND PRACTICAL UPON PSALM xix. 1—6.

LONDON : JAMES NISBET & Co., BERNERS STREET.

Opinions of the Press.

"Mr. Brown's publications have long marked him out to us as an earnest, able, and above all, spiritually-minded writer . . . The author proceeds on the principle, that under the most obvious meaning of those parts of Scripture that primarily refer to natural events and things, there lies a hidden spiritual meaning, of which the natural things and events were designed by God to be the illustrations . . . . Fanciful though this method may appear to be, the work is characterised by its scrupulous abstinence from fanciful teaching; every doctrine and lesson are proved from other Scriptures where they are plainly taught; the copiousness of the scriptural quotations forming indeed one of the most marked features of the volume, and one on which the author rightly expects a special divine blessing to rest. There are touching illustrative anecdotes from the writer's own knowledge, interesting prose quotations from other writers, and a number of fine poetical quotations, which add to the pleasing character of the volume. We think it likely to interest that large class of minds that loves to learn through types and symbols, and not only to interest, but to be very profitable."—*The British Messenger.*

" The author, while firmly holding the verbal inspiration of Scripture and maintaining that it should be construed primarily according to the literal grammatical construction of the words, yet holds that it has a second or hidden spiritual meaning . . . . We may say for him that he displays considerable sobriety of judgment in his endeavours to educe this hidden spiritual sense, and that there is much throughout the volume which will be found edifying. Upon the Stones in the Breastplate of the High Priest he dilates at considerable length. He expatiates on this subject as on a favourite field, and although at times what is fanciful is suggested, yet it is a portion of the work which will be read with much interest. The book is evidently the production of a devout mind, and will, we think, meet with much favourable acceptance from those who are of a kindred spirit. Its aim is to bring the believer very near to the comforts and consolations which are contained in the Word of God, and to roll away the stone which may sometimes seem to cover the mouth of the well in which they are concealed."—*The Record.*

" The title of the book may suggest the idea that this work treats Scriptural matter in a fanciful or mystical style, but a perusal of the volume shows that it is not so; indeed, we are struck with the sound and simple manner in which the grand truths of the Bible are elucidated from the analogies of the works of creation. Whilst the author firmly holds the doctrine of the verbal inspiration of all Scripture, and that its primary meaning is that given by the literal construction of the words, he yet believes that there lies beneath a second or hidden spiritual meaning, which he seeks to elucidate, proving everything which he advances by the plain statements of other Scriptures; indeed, one chief feature of the book is its copious quotation of Scripture. To many Biblical students, and those who delight in the teaching of types and symbols, the work will be of the highest value.

ix.

The believer will find the comforts and joys of the Word unfolded, while the unsaved will find a clear exposition of the Gospel of the grace of God."—*Word and Work.*

"It is not often that a scientific mind is employed about spiritual subjects; but when it is so, the researches of such a mind are well worthy of our attention, and will always repay our careful study. We have great pleasure in recommending to our readers the volume before us, which is full of profitable instruction and great interest. The author's aim throughout the book is evidently to show forth the glory of God and to edify his people; and having a good knowledge of the discoveries of science, together with keen insight and close observation of objects around him, and these gifts being sanctified by the anointing of the Holy Spirit, he has been enabled to unfold and exhibit to our view many of the glorious beauties which are concealed from the eyes of the careless and unobservant among the children of God .... The introductory chapters are followed by a deeply experimental one on the Sun of Righteousness. The author then proceeds to treat of Light and Darkness, colour, the Stones in the High Priest's Breastplate, the Precious Corner-Stone, Life and Heat, with the spiritual meanings to be drawn out from these .... The chapters on Light and Colour are rich in spiritual instruction .... We especially commend to our readers the whole of the chapter on the Great Sacrifice."—*Gospel Truths or Old Paths.*

Foolscap 8vo, 3s. 6d., cloth.

AN EXPOSITION, EXPLANATORY AND PRACTICAL, OF THE PARABLE OF THE SOWER.

London: JAMES NISBET & Co., Berners Street.

"Mr. Brown has here given us a most solemn and faithful word, much suited for the present time."—*Quarterly Journal of Prophecy.*

"His exposition is earnest, scriptural, and devout. Many will, we question not, peruse it with profit."—*Church of England Magazine.*

"It is a good, practical, and thoroughly scriptural work. We wish it may have many readers, and prove very useful, by the blessing of our God."—*British Messenger.*

"Truly valuable and excellent, full of Evangelical truth, applied to the conscience of saint and sinner with much power."—*The Bible Reader's Journal.*

"The work is well done. The development is comprehensive; penetrating, and judicious; and the tone which pervades the book is eminently devout."—*British Standard.*

"The account may be useful to those who have such difficult cases to deal with."—*Gospel Magazine.*

"The well-told narrative of a young girl's conversion. The two aspects of her case—the one having reference to the teacher, the other to the taught—are skilfully set before the reader."—*Sunday Teacher's Treasury.*

"An interesting narrative related with simplicity. The Lord's gracious dealings prominently exhibited. The instrumentality by which He works simply unfolded. We have perused the work with pleasure, and heartily commend it to the notice of our readers."—*Gilead.*

"A record of skilful dealing with an individual soul. Mr. Brown is evidently deeply taught by the Spirit of God. The narrative abounds with illustrations of scriptural truth, and is calculated to guide all who wish their pastoral work to be thorough and successful."—*Church Association Monthly Intelligencer.*

Price 6d.

SPIRITUAL BLESSING:

"A LITTLE HELP TO BELIEVERS TOWARDS THE ATTAINMENT OF THIS BLESSED END; WITH SELECTIONS FROM ARCHBISHOP LEIGHTON'S 'RULES AND INSTRUCTIONS FOR A HOLY LIFE'"

LONDON: THE BOOK SOCIETY, 28, PATERNOSTER ROW.

"One of the most admirable arrangements we have have ever met with. Their very collocation and their headings are suggestive of new and spiritual thoughts. The quotations from Archbishop Leighton are fragrant with the savour of holiness."—*Church Association Monthly Intelligencer.*

"It consists of heads of petitions for private prayer, with large selections of scriptural texts in full. The selection, both of subjects and texts, indicates a spiritual mind, in which the word of Christ dwells richly; therefore, we think it well fitted for its intended purpose."—*British Messenger.*

Upon the first part of it, *The Christian* says :—"This is a large number of heads of petitions for private and united prayer. They are divided into two series, and to each petition are attached Scriptures indicating God's mind and will in reference to the special subject. It will doubtless be useful to some souls seeking more nearness to God in prayer."

Upon the whole book *The Earthern Vessel* says :—"The line of Biblical and Puritanical course of walking with God is, in this book,

distinctly marked out, and where the true believer honestly seeketh
after communion with God through Christ, by the Spirit, he will
realize a holy peace which mere pretenders never can know. We
believe in the advantageous results of a violent wrestling with the
Lord for His blessing. All who sympathise with us will esteem this
' Little Help to Believers,' by R. Brown."

Price 6d.

BABYLONIANISM;
OR, THE DEVIL'S TRAVESTY OF THE KINGDOM OF THE SON.
London : MORGAN & SCOTT, Paternoster Buildings.

" Anything from the pen of so clear and learned a writer is worth
reading, but the lecture before us has peculiar merits. It is not new
to the Christian world that Romanism is the structure of Babylonianism upon the religion of Christ, but it is deeply interesting and
important to know in detail how this has been imperceptibly effected.
Such lectures at the present day are of the greatest necessity, to open
the eyes of many to our danger as a Protestant nation, and to lay
bare the wily efforts and aims of the Church of Rome. We heartily
commend this remarkable and able lecture to the Christian public."—
The Church Record.

" A most admirable treatise on the subject, showing that the system
of Rome is but the renewal of the idolatries and iniquities of Babylon."
—*Gilead.*

" Our readers will do well to procure the book for themselves.
There they will find good proof that not only the worship of the
Virgin, but that nearly all the doctrines of Rome, were known to the
old Babylonian worshippers."—*Wiltshire Protestant Beacon.*

" An able and timely exhibition of the impious abominations of
Rome."—*Christian Miscellany.*

" This excellent little work."—*Quarterly Journal of Prophecy.*

" We would commend it as worthy of all attention at the present
time."—*The Londonderry Guardian.*

Price 1s.

JESUITISM;
OR, THE DEVIL'S TRAVESTY OF THE SON OF THE KINGDOM.
London : MORGAN & SCOTT, Paternoster Buildings.

"Mr. Brown is doing right good service to the churches and the
country by his faithful exposure of the awful atrocities of Popery.

Any one who wishes to know what the Jesuits really are, should procure this pamphlet.   We hope it will be circulated by thousands, and may be blessed by God to the dissipating of this portentous blindness, or indifference, of statesmen, politicians, leaders of thought—and through their influence, of the public generally—to the deadly advances of that most subtle and remorseless enemy of Christ's Gospel, and of all precious human interests—the Papacy."—*The Christian Miscellany.*

" One of the best synopses of the Romish controversy. It is short, and of authority ; its terrible statements are beyond question, except in as far as Jesuits have always at hand an arsenal of vilest abuse, and absolute denial of the most palpable facts, when by no other means they can get out of truths and authorities that are fatal to them. . . . . There is as much sound teaching in the space of 90 pages as might have been diffused over 190 pages. We strongly recommend it to the careful reading of, and to zealous distribution by, our readers."—*The Press and St. James's Chronicle.*

"To those who are anxious to study the real principles and workings of Jesuitism, we commend these stirring pages. The men who sneer at the notion of the presence of Jesuits in our English universities should read the extracts here given from the *Monita Secreta* of the Jesuits, which provides for the proselytising of the rich, the clever, and high-born."—*The Rock.*

"Contains many telling points. Some of the extracts given— painful revelations—are absolutely necessary to show people what an unnatural and thoroughly unchristian system Jesuitism is."—*The Record.*

" The object of this little work is to show how gradual and stealthy the progress of the Jesuits has been in this country since the year 1795, when they gained a footing at Stonyhurst, in Lancashire, under the guise of some '*poor* gentleman from Liege.' . . . . . .

" We have not space to notice the awful instances of immorality which Mr. Brown brings forward upon the unimpeachable testimony of Roman Catholic witnesses. . . . . But Mr. Brown deserves great credit for bringing together in so small a compass such overwhelming testimony from their own mouths of the crimes which the Jesuits are ready to commit, and are prepared to justify for the cause they have at heart."—*Church Association Monthly Intelligencer.*

"One of the most startling stirring works that it has been our lot for some time to read. Mr. Brown writes with a master-hand. In the treatise now before us he most thoroughly exposes ' Jesuitism,' showing that it is a caricature of the work of the Holy Ghost in the heart of the saved sinner. And lest any should imagine that such a diabolical system is a thing of the past, he adds: ' Never were the Jesuits more powerful in Great Britain and its dependencies than they are at present, and never had we greater reason to fear them than now.' If our readers desire to read something upon this subject which is clear, authentic, and a thorough *exposé* of the system, we know of nothing more worthy of their careful study than Mr. Brown's '.Jesuitism.'"—*Gilead.*

" We have never read a book on the subject which contained so much in so small a compass. It is just the book for the times. For general readers it is a complete picture of these ' workers of iniquity.' If it could be put into the hands of every Englishman and English-woman, there would be no fear for the future. Jesuitism only requires to be known, and then it will be *hated* and expelled. Prussia has done wisely. England! go thou and do likewise. Reader! buy the book and read it."—*The Voice of Warning.*

Further notices on the two foregoing treatises.

"Since then [the reading of Hislop's 'Two Babylons] we have read no books (and we have looked over many) upon the Popish controversy so deeply interesting as these.

" In two pamphlets of a hundred and forty pages, are given the very quint-essence of Hislop's valuable researches, supplemented by important exposures, from Babylonish Rome's own teachings, of her blasphemous travesties of the Prince of Peace and the Kingdom of Righteousness.

" To those who have not time to read larger works, and to those who have, but would be thankful for a deeply-studied epitome, we commend these books. We think that the ' travesty ' view of Popery is very comprehensive and most expressive."—*The Protestant Layman.*

" The author has long estimated the real nature and danger of a system which has justly been called ' Satan's masterpiece.' In his ' Babylonianism,' he proves that Popery is the true mystic Babylon of Scripture, with all its idolatries, impurities, and cruelties repro-duced; whilst in his ' Jesuitism,' he illustrates the unscrupulous and satanic craft by which the Romish system seeks to wheedle and force its way to universal supremacy. . . . We cordially welcome the vigorous exposures of Mr. Brown, and we earnestly trust his power-ful treatises may meet the wide circulation which they deserve."—*The Bulwark, or Reformation Journal.*

Price 6d.

THE PREACHING OF THE GOSPEL:
HINDRANCES TO ITS SUCCESS;
HOW CAN THEY *BEST* BE OVERCOME.

London: MORGAN & SCOTT, 12, Paternoster Buildings.

" The value of this little tractate consists in its honest and candid exposure of some of the faults of our clerical brethren in setting forth the whole truth of the Gospel."—*The Rock.*

" That which gives the pamphlet its chief merit is the wonderfully clear knowledge of the Gospel economy possessed by its author, and for this we heartily commend its perusal."—*The Rainbow*.

" It is a strong witness for God's holy truth, while it consistently exposes the mistakes and errors of multitudes who are in the ministry. Every honest and enlightened Christian will read Mr. Brown's pamphlet with a firm conviction of its truthful and wholesome character."—*The Earthen Vessel*.

Price 1s.

RITUALISM AT BARTON-ON-HUMBER:
WHEREIN THE SUBJECT IS CONSIDERED THEOLOGICALLY, LEGALLY, AND MORALLY.

London: MARLBOROUGH & Co., The Old Bailey.

" This valuable and interesting pamphlet contains an account of the faithful efforts of its author to check Romish teaching in his parish church. We approve of the position taken up by Mr. Brown, and admire the skill and moderation with which that position is defended."—*The Protest*.

" An excellent and vigorous pamphlet against ritualistic innovations, fitted, we think, to do good."—*The British Messenger*.

" Excellent! Mr. Brown is too many for his clerical correspondents. The pamphlet is well timed. Those who wish to see how an able man deals with ritualistic folly should study its pages."—*Rainbow*.

" Specially deserving of notice on account of its sterling merit."—*The Rock*.

" Very valuable."—*British Herald*.

" The writer has torn off the ritualistic mask in a noble and discriminating spirit."—*The Earthen Vessel*.

" This is the result of a correspondence between the author and the Bishop of Lincoln, relative to the prevalence of ritualism. Mr. Brown stands on firm ground, and fights well; he stands on the Word of the ' Rock of Ages.' . . . . Mr. Brown has written well, and the book ought to be read by all who realise the duty of this ' perilous hour.' We heartily commend it. The ' layman ' is more than a match for ' lawn sleeves.' "—*The Voice of Warning*.

" If every Churchman dealt as faithfully with Jesuitical priests, and exposed their practices as the author of this tract has done, it would be happy for England. But we see false charity instead of faithfulness. . . . . These mask-wearing men, who lie in wait to deceive, have been spoken of and handled too gently. They are wolves in sheep's clothing, and men who, like Mr. Brown, tear off the mask and expose the hypocrite, who rip the sheepskin and show the wolf, are men who command our esteem.

" Mr. Brown, to our mind, defeated in argument both priest and bishop; and, further, has the answer, of a good conscience in having spoken the truth boldly, without the fear of man. His remarks are clear and scriptural. We heartily recommend the book to our readers."—*Gospel Truths, or Old Paths.*

Also lately Published, price 4d.

THE AWAKENING SOUL'S COMPLAINT;

WITH CHRIST'S LOVING ANSWER; AND THE SOUL'S SURRENDER.

LONDON: THE BOOK SOCIETY, 28, PATERNOSTER ROW.

" I have enjoyed, very much, reading ' THE AWAKENING SOUL'S COMPLAINT, WITH CHRIST'S LOVING ANSWER, AND THE SOUL'S SURRENDER.' It always brings rest and quiet to my spirit. I earnestly pray that your own soul may prosper: for the many ways you have been made a blessing to mine is wonderful."—*From a Poor Widow in Lincolnshire.*

" Perhaps as useful a thing as you have written for the Master. Will be a ' word in season' to many, I doubt not."—*From the Editor of the " Sabbath Hour."*

" The poem is simply beautiful! May the dear Lord abundantly bless it to every reader."—*From a Lady in London.*

" What charmed me most was your ' AWAKENING SOUL'S COMPLAINT,' etc. I think it is beautiful. If I had told you the story of my conversion, I should have thought you had been writing of me, the two cases so closely resemble one another."—*From a Lady in America.*

" Your ' AWAKENING SOUL'S COMPLAINT,' etc., with which we are much charmed. May the Lord Himself make the little book a channel of much blessing."—*From the Secretary of the Colportage Association for England.*

JOHN BALE AND SONS, Steam Printers, 87-89, Great Titchfield Street, W.

Also lately Published by the same Author, in Crown 8vo, 4s.

THE PERSONALITY AND HISTORY OF SATAN.
LONDON: S. W. PARTRIDGE & Co.

CONTENTS.

CHAPTER I.
THE PERSONALITY OF SATAN.

CHAPTER II.
THE PERSONALITY OF SATAN (*Continued.*).

CHAPTER III.
THE HISTORY OF SATAN.

CHAPTER IV.
THE HISTORY OF SATAN (*Continued*).

CHAPTER V.
THE HISTORY OF SATAN (*Continued*).

CHAPTER VI.
THE HISTORY OF SATAN (*Concluded*).

OPINIONS OF THE PRESS.

" The author of this scholarly and striking treatise is well known as an earnest and trusted expositor of the Word of God. The volume, which is neatly got up, consists of six ' Bible Readings ' in chapters, and each chapter is obviously the outcome of deep and anxious thought. They are studies of a high order, and are meant for the perusal of both clergymen and laymen. They throw quite a flood of light on a subject of undying interest and great mystery. Students of the Bible of all denominations are sure to prize them highly."—*The Oldham Chronicle.*

" Mr. Brown is known to many as a careful student and able expositor of Holy Scripture. By his former books he has rendered valuable service to the cause of truth; and by the present carefully written work of two hundred and sixteen pages he supplies the antidote for a pernicious and growing error. No believer in Holy Scripture, open to convincing argument, can read Mr. Brown's book without seeing both the personality of Satan and his fearful subtlety and power. But the book possesses the great advantage of showing us our refuge, as well as our danger, together with the object of God in permitting Satan and his demons to be the tempters of His people. Of the book of Job itself, we have not seen a better analysis than that given by Mr. Brown. We may remark that Mr. Brown is a student of the Scriptures in their original tongues."—*The Christian.*

" A most valuable book, especially suited for our own times, when amongst all classes there are those who doubt or disbelieve the existence of Satan. Mr. Brown is deeply versed in Scripture, and this, like his other works, is thoroughly spiritual. He deals with his subject throughout in a masterly manner, and this is especially noticed in the description of God permitting Satan to deal with His servant Job, and again in the account of Peter's sifting by Satan. Many who take up the book will be loth to put it down before it is finished, and having read it once will turn to it again. The author in this, as in others of his publications, proves himself to be a valiant opponent of the Roman Apostacy, and skilfully wields the weapons found in the Armory of ' What saith the Scripture.' "—*English Churchman.*

" The history of the Evil One is traced, in reference to the purpose of God, in the final achievement of good. The aim of the author is evidently to do good, and to present the Gospel plan of salvation constantly and clearly. He takes a glance at the grand scope of God's purpose in redemption, and the final conquest of evil, while he endeavours to unfold the mysterious history of Satan. The work is enriched with apt and copious quotations from Holy

Writ; and there is an abundance of exegesis which will bear the test of ripe scholarship. The Devil's three travesties are according to the writer (1) Babylonianism or Romanism, (2) Jesuitism, (3) the final personal Antichrist. There is a very good *exposé* of the casuistry of Jesuitism under head 2. Indeed, the passages quoted are likely to make our whole moral nature rise in revolt against the unblushing contempt of the law of the Almighty which interprets the Commandments to mean the opposite of their plain grammatical meaning. The book is sound, scholarly, instructive, and spiritual."
—*The Rock*.

"This pretty volume of 223 pages is a lucid and able exhibition of the announcements of Scripture respecting the existence and empire of the Prince of Darkness. The author, a distinguished solicitor, has brought to the dicussion of so vital a theme an acute mind, habituated to logical and legal culture. His conclusions are the result of a careful examination of Scripture. His positions are not the asseverations of a merely professional theologian, but those of an impartial and learned Christian layman. We cordially recommend this able work to our readers, and hope it will secure a circulation commensurate to its worth."—*Irish Baptist Magazine*.

"A most thorough investigation of a subject which is of the deepest importance. The reality of Satan is very much lost sight of, and too little definitely believed. The perusal of this book will do much to correct the mistake, and to present the work of Satan in its most real and solemn light. It is a book much to be commended, and we hope that it will be largely read."—*Christian Progress*.

"The author endeavours to expose the subtle workings of Satan, the powers he has, and that none but Christ can overcome him; and shows that although the Church of God in her fallen state is no better than those who are lost, yet God will not allow one of His children to perish in their sins; but will deliver them from all the works and craft of Satan, and make His own wondrous works of grace, redemption, and His resurrection power to shine forth like a morning without cloud. . . . The writer of the book is a stranger to us, but he brings out a good deal of truth very clearly, and sets it forth to advantage."—*Gospel Standard*.

"In common with Mr. Brown's other works, this timely treatise on the too commonly avoided subject of diabolism is remarkable for close adherence to the inspired Scriptures, for logical clearness, and for a tenderness of spirit when dealing with the experience of God's Satan-tempted people. We cordially recommend this most important and very able volume."—*British Protestant*.

"A very remarkable work on a very deep and important subject. To the author's credit, it must be said that he studiously endeavours to keep close to the testimony of Scripture, and not to strain that testimony by fanciful interpretations. His evident excellent knowledge and judicious use of the Greek language will also be found to throw much light on certain passages, which in our excellent version do not afford that clear view of the meaning of the original, which is so needful on the subject of Satan. Occasionally, as might be supposed, we find an idea colliding with what are now fully established views with us; but we feel no desire to resent the same by any unkind or hypercritical observations." [This refers to the reviewer's disbelief in the coming of a future personal Antichrist.]—*Gospel Advocate.*

Also lately published by the same Author, in crown 8vo, 4s.

GLEANINGS FROM THE BOOK OF RUTH;

OR,

The Book of Ruth opened out by Comparison with other Parts of Scripture.

CONTENTS.

CHAPTER I.

OPINIONS OF THE PRESS.

"This volume of 260 pages, beautifully bound, is a summary of Bible Readings delivered in London and the provinces. A high-toned spirituality pervades the entire work. The learned author views the Book of Ruth as an inspired narrative of facts, allegorically designed to exhibit the nuptial relation between Christ and His redeemed Church; and also as a vivid illustration of the calling, the conversion, establishing, and settling of the individual believer in Christ Himself. Mr. Brown's style is clear, his arguments cogent, and his numerous illustrations glowing with spiritual attractiveness and freshness. We have found the perusal of this volume stimulating, and wish it a place in every Christian home."—*Irish Baptist Magazine.*

"This is an interesting and remarkable work. It differs from an allegory proper in being a true history allegorised after the manner of Gal. iv. 21-31. The Goel, that is, kinsman and redeemer, in Israel, was a type of Christ; and as kinsman and redeemer, Boaz comes before us in the sacred narrative. The reader keeping this in memory cannot fail to be struck with Mr. Brown's analogies. He does not expect all his readers to agree with him in every detail of interpretation. But what is of the highest importance is, that here every believer will find established his 'standing,' or perfect acceptance in Christ, and the connection of that standing, when fully apprehended by faith, with that plenitude of the Spirit which is the power of an overcoming life and qualification for efficient service. While this book gives us sound doctrine, and generally in the words of inspiration, after the manner of inspiration it gives a doctrine to us also in that concrete form which most affects and impresses us."—*The Christian.*

"Mr. Brown has quite a genius for comparing Scripture with Scripture, so as to give us the 'analogy of the faith'—the general drift of the teaching of the whole Word of God on the particular subject in hand. On this principle he beautifully expounds that Hebrew idyll; for the book of Ruth is no less. In Mr. Brown's hands its hidden meanings, its wealth of devout teaching, its message to the men and women of to-day, are all indicated, expounded, and enforced in a tone and temper sweet as the inspired record itself. Mr. Brown not only thinks Scriptural thoughts, but he expresses these in Scriptural terms; hence his volume is in the deepest and best sense Scriptural. Devout Christians will read it with grateful delight, and with a relish. It is truly profitable reading."—*The Oldham Chronicle.*

"The saying that 'the Bible is its own best commentary' receives very apt illustration in this little volume. . . . Under Mr. Brown's skilful and reverent treatment the narrative becomes a vivid illustration of how a child of God typified by Ruth, is first 'called,' and then successively 'stablished, strengthened, and settled' in Christ, each of these stages being dealt with in a separate chapter. At the outset the principle is rightly insisted upon that 'no one has any right to put any construction or interpretation upon the Word other than that which the Holy Ghost has Himself given us of it in the Divine Word itself.' As good specimens of the spiritual 'beating out of that which is gleaned' we may note the remarks on chap. ii. v. 17, and the *discursus* on chap. ii. v. 20, touching Christ as the kinsman-Redeemer. . . . But in every portion of the book, Mr. Brown shows that valuable spiritual lessons lie hidden; he throws the strong clear light of innumerable other Scriptures upon the passage under treatment, and sometimes enforces his meaning by instances culled from his own experiences with seekers after God, and souls 'in a spiritual bog.' These passages display a very extensive familiarity with Holy Scripture, and they are 'begun, continued and ended' in the Bible. . . . Mr Brown is evidently a firm believer in the plenary verbal inspiration which so many now-a-days are throwing overboard, and he declines to abandon as exploded, any of the old Evangelical truths, or to be entangled in the 'new theology.'"—*The English Churchman.*

"The author has produced in many respects a choice and interesting work. His design was to open it out 'by comparison with other parts of Scripture,' and he has, on the whole, succeeded admirably. While there was so much in the well-known narrative that found a beaten track among preachers and writers, Mr. Brown has entered into many fresh features of the bearings of the history, and, at the same time, has produced a Christ-exalting and sinner-abasing work. Much in this book may more properly go under the term adaptation than interpretation; yet it is so abundantly laden with Scripture quotations and profitable hints from the original, as to make a very valuable contribution to sound, if not intensely strong, doctrinal literature."—*Gospel Advocate.*

"Here is a fund of knowledge and a store of savoury food for meditative and spiritual minds."—*Protestant Echo.*

"A clear, choice, and sound little volume, full of spiritual and suggestive teaching. We have seldom read a book which more commends itself to our mind. It is just the book for those who desire to be taught."—*Silver Morn.*

www.ingramcontent.com/pod-product-compliance
Lightning Source LLC
Chambersburg PA
CBHW032014120726
47902CB00013B/776